AF595570

LAWLESS FRONTIER

CRIME, JUSTICE, AND THE DEPUTY MARSHALS OF JUDGE ISAAC PARKER'S COURT

VELDA BROTHERTON

FOREWORD BY NEW YORK TIMES BESTSELLING AUTHOR MARC CAMERON

also by

VELDA BROTHERTON

Nonfiction

The Boston Mountains: Lost in the Ozarks

Images of America: Washington County, Arkansas

Springdale: The Courage of Shiloh

Wandering in the Shadows of Time

Novels

Beyond the Moon • *Remembrance*

A Savage Grace • *Once There Were Sad Songs*

Stone Heart's Woman • *Wolf Song*

Images in Scarlet • *Angels's Gold*

The Twist of Poe Mysteries

The Purloined Skull • *The Tell-Tale Stone*

The Pit & the Penance • *Masque of the Rising Moon*

The Fall of Hermitage House • *Quote the Endling*

The Victorians Series

Tyra's Gambler • *Rowena's Hellion*

Wilda's Outlaw

The Montana Series

Montana Promises • *Montana Treasures*

Montana Dreams • *Montana Fire*

Montana Destiny • *Montana Legacy*

With Dusty Richards

Blue Roan Colt

Texas Lightning • *Texas Fury* • *Texas Wildling*

LAWLESS FRONTIER

CRIME, JUSTICE, AND THE DEPUTY MARSHALS OF JUDGE ISAAC PARKER'S COURT

VELDA BROTHERTON

FOREWORD BY NEW YORK TIMES BESTSELLING AUTHOR MARC CAMERON

an imprint of
Roan & Weatherford Publishing Associates, LLC
Bentonville, Arkansas • Heber City, Utah
www.roanweatherford.com

Library of Congress Cataloging-in-Publication Data
Names: Brotherton, Velda
Title: Lawless Frontier: Crime, Justice, and the Deputy Marshals of Judge Isaac Parker's Court
Brotherton, Velda, Author
Description: First Edition. | Bentonville: Otterford, 2026.
Identifiers: LCCN: 2026935993 | ISBN: ISBN: 979-8-89299-130-8 (hardcover) |
ISBN: 979-8-89299-131-5 (trade paperback) | ISBN: 979-8-89299-132-2 (eBook)
Subjects: HISTORY/United States/19th Century | TRUE CRIME/Historical |
BIOGRAPHY & AUTOBIOGRAPHY/Law Enforcement
LC record available at: https://lccn.loc.gov/2026935993

Otterford hardcover edition July 2026

Jacket Design & Interior Design by Casey W. Cowan
Jacket Art by C. Michael Dudash, *On the Outlaw Trail*
Editing by J.B. Hogan, Don Money, Amy Cowan & Casey W. Cowan

Thanks to my best pal, Dusty Richards,
for teaching me all I needed to know about the American West.
It was a true pleasure spending 30 years writing alongside him.
He sits there still.

Enter the Lawman
Painting by Edmund F. Ward, 1924.

TABLE OF CONTENTS

PUBLISHER'S NOTE

HISTORY DESERVES TO be read. That may sound obvious. These days, though, it's anything but.

Traditional nonfiction, carefully researched, rigorously documented, and written in the familiar academic cadence, is essential. But we are living in a time when fewer people are picking up those books, especially younger people. Attention is fragmented. Screens dominate. If history is going to compete, it cannot simply inform. It must also *engage.*

Lawless Frontier: Crime, Justice, and the Deputy Marshals of Judge Isaac Parker's Court does exactly that.

This is *not* a conventional history text. Velda Brotherton chose to tell these stories through narrative vignettes, placing the reader inside the lived experience of Judge Isaac Parker and the deputy marshals who served the United States in one of the most dangerous jurisdictions in American history. Each chapter adopts a close, character-driven point of view, allowing the men and women portrayed—as well as the era they lived in—to breathe. The result is creative nonfiction that entertains while remaining rooted in careful research.

Some readers may initially be surprised by the format. That is intentional. Velda believed—and, as her publisher, I agree—that story is one of the most powerful vehicles for truth.

I am more than simply a publisher, however. This particular career came about purely by accident. By education, I'm a military historian. My path toward that goal began the day I picked up Michael Shaara's Pulitzer Prize-winning novel, *The Killer Angels,* at the age of eighteen. As the son of an avowed history nut, I had already understood the broad outlines of the Battle of Gettysburg. What I had not yet grasped was the human weight of it. Stepping inside the minds of men like Robert E. Lee, James Longstreet, and Joshua Lawrence Chamberlain during those three days in July 1863 transformed the battle from a sequence of maneuvers into a study in decision-making and humanity under pressure. It deepened my understanding of just why it was such a watershed moment in world history. How? By revealing the simple truth that isn't being taught in schools—history is not merely dates and dispatches, names and places. History—*real* history—is about people, flawed, feeling, and forced to act with incomplete information, unaware of how their choices will echo beyond their own lifetimes. When readers step inside a moment—ride the trail, stand in the courtroom, face down an outlaw—they do more than absorb facts.

They *remember.*

This is not to say that every moment portrayed in this book occurred exactly as written. Story can illuminate history, but it also requires interpretation. To ensure clarity between dramatization and documentation, most chapters conclude with "Beyond the Badge," Velda's historical and authorial notes. In these brief asides, she discusses the sources behind the narrative, the historical aftermath of the events portrayed, and the choices she made in shaping each vignette. The goal is transparency. The hope is to spark curiosity, encouraging readers to explore further the remarkable history of Judge Isaac Parker's court and the deputy marshals who enforced federal law in the Indian Territory.

Fortunately, there is no shortage of resources for readers who wish to go deeper. Numerous excellent books and documentaries examine this turbulent period of frontier justice. Visitors can also experience the history firsthand at the Fort Smith National Historic Site, where much of the site is devoted to the story of Judge Parker's court, including reconstructions of his 1880s courtroom and gallows and the infamous "Hell on the Border" jail. Just down the street stands the United States Marshals Museum, a stunningly beautiful facility on the banks of the Arkansas River which is home to one of the finest collections of artifacts and exhibits tracing the history of the U.S. Marshals Service from its founding to the present day.

This book also serves another purpose. It honors the United States Marshals Service—the nation's oldest federal law enforcement agency—and the generations of deputies who have served, often quietly and at great personal risk. The stories of Judge Parker's deputies are not relics of a distant frontier; they are part of a living legacy that continues today. For that reason, this volume includes a foreword by retired Deputy U.S. Marshal and *New York Times* bestselling author Marc Cameron, along with endorsements from others who have worn the Marshals badge. The men and women who rode for Judge Parker helped establish a tradition of federal law enforcement that endures to this day in the Marshals who hunt fugitives, protect the courts, and carry the same badge into dangerous places in service to the nation.

As a publisher, I have long been committed to preserving Western and American history in ways that resonate with modern readers. Popular history can—and should—be both compelling *and* responsible. Younger readers, in particular, deserve an entry point into the past that feels immediate, human, and approachable. If this book inspires someone to learn more about Judge Parker, the U.S. Marshals Service, and the broader story of the American frontier, then we've done our job.

On a personal note, this book carries weight for me beyond its subject. Velda Brotherton was my close friend, mentor, teacher, and, in many ways, a surrogate mother. She passed away in early 2023, leaving a void in both my personal and professional life that I still feel on a daily basis. I miss her wisdom, her humor, and her steady encouragement more than I can adequately express here. Everything I do as a publisher is informed by what Velda and her longtime writing partner, legendary Western author Dusty Richards, taught me during our all-too-brief years as friends and colleagues. They believed very deeply in the power of the written word and in honoring the West without mythologizing it. They also believed writers should respect their readers enough to tell the truth, and tell it well. This book reflects those principles. Velda set out to honor the men and women who carried a badge into dangerous country, bringing their world to life for a new generation. I believe she accomplished that.

I hope you agree.

—Casey W. Cowan
President & Creative Director
Roan & Weatherford Publishing Associates
Bentonville, Arkansas

FOREWORD

WHEN I WAS growing up, perhaps the highest compliment a cowboy—or deputy U.S. marshal—could give was to say you were someone to "ride the river with." Rivers are often wide, of uncertain depth, and filled with unseen dangers. As one of my old partners said, "I don't want to go after a fugitive with somebody who might pee down their leg and run off screaming at the first hint of trouble." The message was clear. If you're going to ride the river with someone, they'd best be trustworthy—steady in all weathers.

Lawless Frontier tells the story of just such steadiness—and I count myself extremely lucky to have met men and women who are cut from that same cloth.

Not long after my fifteenth birthday, I watched a tall man with a gun and silver badge on his hip step out of a pickup on the courthouse square in my hometown. He wore creased jeans, a starched white shirt with long sleeves, and a well-shined pair of cowboy boots—the uniform of the day for most cattlemen and bankers in Parker County, Texas. The man snugged down a silverbelly felt hat and then, instead of depositing quarters, he threw a canvas bag with a locking metal collar over the parking meter. The bag read—*OFFICIAL BUSINESS: US MARSHAL.* I'd watched plenty of lawmen in the movies and on TV, but as far as I know, this was the first time I'd ever seen a deputy U.S. marshal in the flesh. Then and there, I made a decision that would affect the trajectory of my life. I had to get me one of those canvas parking meter bags.

Some fourteen years later, that same deputy I'd seen on the courthouse square happened to be the one to conduct my background investigation when I joined the United States Marshals Service.

I never had the pleasure of meeting Velda Brotherton, but reading her marvelous book, I can tell she knew her subject. *Lawless Frontier* focuses on the work of deputy U.S. marshals in the Indian Territory, a violent no-man's land presided over by Judge Isaac Parker. Ms. Brotherton has done her research and then some, drilling down to the nitty gritty of what it was like to bring justice to what was then the largest and most dangerous judicial district in the United States.

First appointed by George Washington, U.S. Marshals have been around since 1789. From Census takers to strike breakers to fugitive hunters, deputy U.S. marshals have historically done it all—and in many respects they still do.

Though deputy U.S. marshals fall under the Executive Branch of government, reporting through chain of command to the Attorney General, we often say we "ride" for the judge or judges in the district where we're assigned. Our executive bosses dictate policy and procedure—"how" we do our job. But now as then, it is the federal judge in the district who generates the paperwork that sends us forth with a court order to arrest that person, seize that cash, or quell that riot. The deputy U.S. marshals who enforced the law in the wilds of the Indian Territory rode for Judge Issac Parker. When I began my Marshals Service career in the two-person suboffice in Sherman, Texas, just south of the Red River and what was once same territory, we rode for District Judge Paul Brown.

Late one evening way back in the 1900s when I was a freshly minted deputy U.S. marshal, my partner and I found ourselves in a quiet Paris, Texas, café seated at the table with Judge Brown. Our office and the judge's chambers were in Sherman, sixty-one miles to the west, but the judge held court in Paris every few months—much like the circuit-riding judges I'd watched on Gunsmoke as a boy. My partner and I considered Judge Brown our judge. We had keys to his judicial chambers, answered the duress alarms if a visitor got rowdy, and intercepted mail with threats or suspicious white powder before it ever got near him. The outlaws we captured stood before his bench. The warrants, summonses, and writs we served bore his signature.

His courtroom held the solemn reverence of a church. If court began at nine, we would sit in the gallery flanking our prisoners and watch the second hand sweep the clock. The moment the hand touched twelve, three precisely timed knocks shook the courtroom. On the heels of the final knock, a heavy oak door swung open, and a slight man in a flowing black robe strode in. A bailiff, chosen for his booming voice and impeccable timing, opened court as the judge made his way to the raised oak bench. Even now, when I'm falling asleep, the words sometimes echo in my head: *"All Rise! O Yea! O Yea! O Yea! The United States District Court for the Eastern District of Texas is now in session. The honorable Paul Brown presiding."* By this point, the judge had reached the bench and stood solemnly in front of his big tufted leather chair. The bailiff continued, *"God save the United States and this honorable court."* Judge Brown closed his eyes for the prayer, along with everyone else in the courtroom—except the deputy marshals.

Paul Brown was in his early seventies by the time I came on board. He was slightly built with thinning gray hair and a tremor in his hands. But there was never any doubt that he was in charge. If a witness or juror didn't show up for court, he sent us to get them. If someone caused trouble during a hearing—including attorneys—he'd catch our eye and bark—"Marshal, sit that man down!" or, if he deemed the situation rowdy enough, "Marshal, place that man in custody!" When there was no court, my partner and I hunted fugitives. When Judge Brown traveled, we traveled with him, producing the prisoners who would appear in his court and offering protection from the long list of enemies he'd earned over a career of sending people to prison. That's how my partner and I found ourselves at that little café in Paris, Texas.

Normally, we sat at a nearby table and observed, but the law clerk retired early that night, and the judge invited us to keep him company. He knew I was a budding writer, so he asked me about that—which was at once cool and embarrassing because I'd yet to get anything published. The conversation moved on to him quizzing us good naturedly about the law, gauging our understanding of the Constitution in particular. I'd been in the district long enough to know that he often referenced "The Framers" in his rulings from the bench. He seemed satisfied enough with our answers, and the conversation became more and more familiar as the evening drew on. Eventually, my partner—a former Texas Highway Patrolman and ten years my senior—in a fit of the philosophical, asked Judge Brown where he got his judicial power. The judge paused for a long moment, as the best lawyers always do, and then quoted the Judiciary Act of 1789 and several sections of U.S. Code chapter and verse.

"Due respect, Your Honor," my partner said. "That's your authority. I'm talking about your power."

"Very well," the judge said. "Enlighten me. Where does my judicial power come from?"

My partner opened his suit coat to reveal the circle-star badge and handgun on his belt.

Judge Brown appeared to chew on the notion for a while and then said, "Just as The Framers intended."

There are gobs of stories about law enforcement in the Old West, but very few look at both the marshals and the judges who sent them out to do their jobs. Lawless Frontier does an amazing job at showcasing the relationship that is unlike any other in federal law enforcement. For many readers, Ms. Brotherton will pull back the curtain for a look behind the scenes. For me, she brought back memories of the incredible men and women I was fortunate enough to ride the river with.

—Marc Cameron
Chief Deputy U.S. Marshal (Retired)
Anchorage, Alaska

PREFACE

IN MAY 1875, cleanup of the un-tamed, 74,000 square miles, declared as the United States Western District of Arkansas, would begin in earnest. Isaac Parker, at thirty-six, the youngest judge ever appointed in America, was handed the job of District Judge. Life would soon change on the abandoned frontier, much of which was known as Indian Territory.

Perched above the joining of the Poteau and Arkansas Rivers overlooking the Wilderness Territory, Fort Smith, Arkansas, recently deserted by the U.S. Army, had grown into the most lawless settlement in the southwest. The sometimes dusty, often muddy, saloon-lined streets of this noisy town snuggled against Indian Territory soon flourished knee-deep in outlaws of all varieties.

Perhaps because, in those days, many measurements were taken with the hide of a cow or a reasonable facsimile, historians do not agree on the precise measurements of this enormous land area.

Let's try to picture it. Begin with seventeen counties in the western portion of Arkansas. Add a fifty-mile-wide section of southern Kansas and what today is Oklahoma, then mostly known as Indian Territory. Some of Oklahoma was not Indian Territory. All this belonged, under federal law enforcement, to the United States District Court of Western District, the largest in America. Our minds can scarcely envision the size. For an idea of that much land, ride to the caprock of Texas, and standing in your stirrups, look west. On a clear day, with binoculars, it's worth the ride, believe me.

Imagine how difficult it must've been to bring law to such a massive chunk of wilderness. Especially since nearly every thieving, murdering, and raping outlaw between the Mississippi River and the western border of Oklahoma Territory did business there much of the time. That numbers up into the thousands of wild owl hoots afraid of no one.

Outlaws by the thousands made the mistake of trying out their chicanery riding hell-bent for leather across those unending plains. After all, there was no one to stop them. None realized or could imagine how things were about to change with the arrival of young, tough, and honest Judge Isaac Parker and his army of untrained, determined men. Men qualified if they had a weapon, they could shoot, and a horse they could ride.

Those men are who you will read about on these pages. Young and old, determined and untrained, strong and frail, they rode and fought under the title of Deputy U.S. Marshals. Few were recognized nor received medals, yet we celebrate them here not the outlaws.

Prior to the Civil War settlers avoided the huge area because of their fear of a Native American attack. After the Civil War, the Native American problem settled, the westward movement was crowded with those searching for a better life. The presence of so many hard riding law breakers hiding in the territory made times difficult for those headed west. Because of the dangers posed by such troublemakers, many families avoided the district like the plague. But times they were fixing to change.

Prior to the appointment of the new judge, the Western District was mishandled by Judge William Story, a dishonest, corrupt man obviously no better than the worst lawbreaker brought before him.

A big reason for President Grant's choice of Parker was the man's youth and reputation for a renowned honesty. Because of his impressive background in the law Parker was hired to take on the job of taming the Territory. He inherited a tremendous and difficult task.

When his boots hit the ground, Parker went right to work. Within eight days of his arrival, he had opened the Civil Service court, hired a new court clerk, a new marshal, and signed up two hundred deputy marshals who went to work ordering witnesses to testify and reopening cases of unsolved murders. Though his courthouse was located in Fort Smith, Arkansas, most of Parker's work load originated from Indian Territory.

In his first term, eight men were found guilty of murder and on September 3, 1875, six of them were hanged in public from gallows at the same time. It was the largest show ever put on in front of the courthouse, where thousands of witnesses watched. Of the two spared the noose, one was killed during an escape attempt and the other was commuted to life in prison due to his youth.

Today, because of movies, television, and pulp fiction, the men who took on the dangerous job of cleaning up this territory are often referred to as U.S. Marshals, their stories romanticized and exaggerated. Only seven men carried that title during Parker's years as judge. All the thousands of men who served bravely and honorably under them were Deputy U.S. Marshals. Men came from around the world to join the famous lawmen. Either Judge Parker or one of the U.S. Marshals appointed them. All carried the oldest continuing law enforcement badge in the United States today, a five pointed star within a circle. Occasionally the badge is seen with six points but five is correct.

While the Texas Rangers were founded much earlier, they were disbanded a couple of times losing that title forever.

During the years 1875 through 1896, Parker, his marshals, and their deputies carried out what most folks thought would be an impossible task. They put an end to the worst cases of law-breaking known in the Western District. Out west in the territory, every outlaw thought he was entitled to take whatever he wanted. After all, there was no one to stop him. At least not until the arrival of Judge Isaac Parker and those tough, hard-riding lawmen serving under him.

Unfortunately, no records were kept of many of the deputies who rode hard and often died harder or simply moved on once their jobs were done. Just as many of their brave deeds were not recorded, you may be sure carrying out the impossible task was more difficult than we can imagine.

In telling the stories based on history, I have done my best to authenticate each one as far as actual names, dates, locales, and occurrences are concerned.

These unbelievable tales are based on the lives these tough men faced while attempting to enforce laws difficult, if not impossible, to enforce in this the largest U.S. District Court in America. During those exciting and dangerous years of our country's westward movement, lawmen expected to confront the wildest challenges. The stories you'll find here are based on true events of those long-ago days, which I hope you'll enjoy. We'll begin with the early years of Judge Isaac Parker, who faced down the worst of the worst and created the largest and harshest law enforcement district known round the world.

—Velda Brotherton

LAWLESS FRONTIER

CRIME, JUSTICE, AND THE DEPUTY MARSHALS OF JUDGE ISAAC PARKER'S COURT

Judge Isaac C. Parker, c. 1860–1865. Appointed federal judge for the Western District of Arkansas in 1875, he later became known as the "Hanging Judge."

HERE COMES THE JUDGE: ISAAC PARKER

DURING ISAAC'S GROWING-up years his pa repeated many times what their neighbor, Maddie, had said the night he was born. Pushing open the squeaking screen she emerged from her midwife duties in the cabin onto the porch where his anxious pa waited.

"Listen to that squalling. You have yourself a boy, and you can bet he'll always get his way what with that loud complaint."

As if he overheard her every word, that's what Isaac did. He made his thoughts known, sometimes to his detriment. One thing he kept quiet about were his feelings concerning farming. He hated everything to do with working the land, but when his father set a task, he was too proud to fail the man he adored, so he went to work and got the job done, much as he disliked it. On the other hand, he enjoyed school.

One evening, when he was thirteen, he sat at the kitchen table, a serious frown wrinkling his face. With a hesitant tone, he finally spoke up. "Pa, we need to talk."

The weak glow from the lamp in the center of the table cast dark shadows across Pa's stoic expression. Ma must've guessed something was up 'cause she hurried to finish the dishes and hustled from the room before Pa could respond.

Joseph glanced through his heavy brows and nodded toward his son, then went back to cleaning his pipe and filling it with tobacco. A signal for Isaac to begin.

Not sure how or where to start, Isaac drew invisible pictures on the oilcloth table with his thumbnail. One thing he hated was to disagree with Pa, but this had to be settled. While Pa showed his age, his thick hair and eyebrows turning white, Isaac was almost a man and needed to have his own way about the life he had planned.

Waiting for him to speak, Joseph took his first puff on the pipe, then urged him on. "You got something to say, get it out, boy."

"Uhm, yes, sir, I certainly do. Next year they tell me I can teach classes at Breeze Hill Primary, and I'd like to do that if it pleases you."

Pa studied him somberly. "You feel you can handle such a task? And of course keep up your farm work? Some of the students will be older than you, bigger too. It's quite a large job to take on. Teaching all day and completing your chores into the night."

"Miz Riley says I'm smart enough." He paused, studied his nails for a moment. "And as for the chores, I'm strong enough." He waited, gaining courage when Pa didn't shut him down. "I want to go on to Barnesville Classical Institute, and she told me it would help me learn more if I teach for a year first. Do you think we can afford me going on to school, Pa? I want to apprentice to a lawyer here in Barnesville later, so I need the education. I'm sorry, I know teaching in the primary school to pay for my education won't cost you nothing but...."

"...but the loss of a blamed good farm hand." Pa's scowl upset Isaac in a way that surprised him. It was heart breaking to disappoint Pa, yet he could not live a life that would make him miserable, and in his heart he hoped Pa did not want that for him.

The elderly man opened his arms in an unexpected hug, enclosing Isaac tight. Whispered in his ear as if embarrassed to speak aloud. "I'm so proud of you, son. You stick to your hopes."

Before Isaac could respond in kind, Pa turned away. Raised his voice. "Ma, didn't I smell a blackberry pie earlier? I sure could use a bowl. And pour some of that thick cream on it, would you?"

She hustled into the kitchen, removed the pie from the oven warmer, filled bowls, and drowned them in yellow cream. It was the best pie Isaac had ever eaten.

OUTSIDE THE WINDOW of Isaac's classroom the arrival of spring painted the rolling hills of Ohio in shades of green. It was time at last to begin what he'd planned when he left that farm house for a richer life. At seventeen, he had finished teaching and graduated at the top of his classes at Breeze Hill. A prominent Barnesville attorney accepted him to read the law. And his uncle, who had a successful law firm in St. Joseph, Missouri, promised him a place at his side when he finished his studies. His dreams were coming true.

That afternoon, after classes, his best friend, Eric, rapped on the door and stepped inside the room where Isaac sprawled on the bed amidst open law books.

"Listen, Isaac, I've got this invitation to an evening gathering. I think you should come along. You just plain work too much. You're going to freeze your brain."

"Aw, Eric, you know how I am with a room filled with strangers. Besides, I need to get this done."

"Tomorrow, man. It's spring break. Besides, this time you'll be sorry the rest of your life if you don't come along. I promise you." He reached down and grabbed Isaac's arm, eyes flashing with delight. "There's this girl you need to meet. She's gorgeous, smart, funny. Believe me, you'll kill yourself if you miss this."

"Sounds like she's just for you, friend. I've got too many plans to let any girl interfere. You know my life is all worked out. Besides, I forgot to make room in it for a girl. If she's so great, you go ahead. Take her."

"Aw, come on. You'll never forgive yourself. I'm telling you, she's just the one to go through that life with you. Besides, I've already met my forever one and there's nothing like it. I promise you."

Unable to escape his friend or avoid the invitation, Isaac gave in. "But just for a little while. One drink and the introduction. And then I'm out of there." He could escape and hurry right back.

Outside, still talking, Eric walked backward along the pathway. "You won't be sorry. Her name's Mary. Meet me at the Lion's Head, and we'll go from there. It's at Gwenn's place just off campus. We can walk over. Save your fare."

A bit later Gwenn opened the door to them. Eric's date turned out to be a wholesome country girl, and Isaac expected the same when his friend motioned for him to meet Mary. Not someone to take into a life of politics and law. Oh well, he'd stay a while, have a good time, then go on back to his rooms and pack up his law books to take with him when school let out.

A hand on his arm felt like someone had lit a fire under him. His eyes met hers. He'd never believed in love at first sight. He still didn't think it could be true. This sweet, gorgeous creature would take one look at him and trounce away. She would break his heart if he didn't run like fury. Yet, the dread of watching her walk away surrounded him with a darkness like clouds on a sunny day.

Eric grinned like a possum. "Mary, Isaac is my best friend, and you'd better be nice to him. He's going to be president someday."

She gazed up into his eyes. "I don't doubt that one bit." The words were like music. Good God, he was smitten and speechless.

All he could do was give her the silliest smile he'd ever managed, but she didn't seem to mind. She gathered him next to her. "Well, then we'd better get busy. We'll have plenty of plans to make."

Giddy with those plans that included months studying the law they married in a simple ceremony at the farm to make sure Pa and Ma were included. A week later they moved to St. Joseph, Missouri. Settled there in a law practice their life became an exciting whirl of politics. Isaac served as city attorney, and meanwhile, Mary presented him with a son while managing to carry out her wifely duties. True to his hopes, he moved up to become a prosecuting attorney. The birth of a second son didn't slow Mary down a bit. Nor did the Civil War stop Isaac's progress. He joined the Missouri State Guard early in the war, but took little part in it.

A staunch Democrat, he immersed himself in the cause of the Republican party along with the Douglas Democrats of Missouri and other States. For a while it looked as if he might be headed for the presidency. In 1864, he was a presidential elector and assisted in casting the electoral vote of Missouri for Abraham Lincoln. With Mary, an excited partner at his side, making acquaintanceships with important men and women around them, he was appointed judge of the Twelfth Judicial Circuit of Missouri.

One evening he came home with the best news he'd expected to ever tell his wife. Seeing the excitement on his face she grabbed his hands in hers. "You're going to run for President."

Laughing, he kissed her knuckles. "You've never forgotten Eric saying that, have you? Well, it's not true, but I suppose it could still be a possibility. I'm going to resign the judgeship and run for Congress."

"Oh, Isaac, you know what that means. It's only a matter of time till I'm first lady."

He held her so close she trembled.

Though he served with distinction during his congressional career and was reelected to Congress in 1872, he envisioned other plans. His life was missing something. One of the committees on which he served was the Committee on Territories. It would appear he briefly came closer to his wife's dreams. James Garfield, a president, and William Wheeler, a vice-president, graduated from the committee he served on.

To Mary's chagrin, Isaac's career took a quick turn in 1875 when General Grant appointed him Chief Justice of Utah. Before she could recover sufficiently, Grant withdrew the appointment and appointed him to a position he was to hold to the admiration and disbelief of most of the entire world for the remainder of his life. At thirty-six, he became the youngest judge appointed to the federal bench, and set out to follow what he had begun as a young man. The enforcement of the law. And he began it in the largest U.S. District Court in America. Also, the largest criminal enforcement district in the world.

And he and his wife and two sons embarked on a trip that took them to the most lawless area they could have possibly imagined.

Mary probably never recovered from her first look at the muddy, noisy, stinking streets of Fort Smith, Arkansas.

MAY 2, 1875, the Parkers carried their two boys onto the dock from a boat rocking on the busy Arkansas River. Isaac turned to help Mary pick her way through stacked bales of cotton piled shoulder high to her. A rather disreputable looking man kept one eye on Parker while assisting her. Of everyone embarking from the flatboat on the Arkansas River, the Parkers appeared the most respectable. A man who had come onboard leading a goat followed Mary, who carried James.

Parker held Charles, who was now five-years-old. The child pointed at the animal and laughed. "Papa, see the doggie."

Mary revealed a shocked expression and clung to the smaller child as if he might be spirited away.

"It's a goat, Charles." Parker frowned and stepped aside just as a man in ragged shirt and pants tossed huge bales of cotton onto the scow headed upriver.

Mary tugged at his shirt sleeve. "There must be some mistake, dear. This can't be where we get off. Is this Fort Smith?"

"It appears to be. Don't worry, it will look better away from the docks."

A black man stepped off the boat hauling their bags over his back and in both hands. He let them slide clumsily to the wooden boards that formed a wide walkway between the river and what looked like a mud hole. Several buggies waited there, horses stomping dirty water. Parker set the boy down beside his mother and waded toward the larger of the two buggies. It better be something sent to carry them to their home, though he had no idea what sort of arrangements had been made. Muddy water oozed into his boots, soaking his stockings and feet. Mary grimaced and lifted her stained skirts.

Thank God he understood they at least had a house to live in.

"Excuse me, sir." He touched the shoulder of the driver who stood beside the nearest buggy. "May I hire this conveyance for my wife and family? We'd like to go to Fort Smith."

"Ye be the new judge? I'm here to fetch him."

Parker chuckled. "How fortuitous. I am the new judge, and I could use some help getting all our bags off the dock and into the buggy."

"I don't carry bags, sir. Ye need to find yourself a colored to do that for ye."

Parker resisted shouting at the man. But it just might not be a good way to begin his relationship with the powers that be. He'd never met any of them with the exception of President Grant who sent him here with well wishes. Easy to see why. He cleared his throat to swallow a remark.

"I wonder if you might find someone to do that for me? I would be happy to pay you for the service. My wife and children and I are exhausted from our trip."

The driver spit in the mud and held out a hand. "Four bits would cover it."

Parker dug the coins from his pocket. The man scooped them into his hand and turned to collect the bags.

A well-dressed gentleman hurried their way. "Judge Parker? Sir, I'm sorry to be late, but I have a conveyance just there for you." He pointed toward the end of the line of buggies to a nice surrey with a roof. "My name is Smith, sir. I'm a city councilor, and I'll take you and your things to the house that's been prepared for you. We are very happy to have you here. Come with me. I'll accompany you and your family and see to your luggage."

The man cast a sour look at the other driver.

They were soon loaded in the comfortable surrey, the boys staring out the side windows at the people wandering or riding around town.

"What is this place?"

"Ah, sir, this is Fort Smith."

"It's quite primitive. I count six saloons so far."

The councilor laughed. "There are a few more than that, sir."

"And women of pleasure, I presume."

Mary nudged his shoulder. "Isaac, dear."

Before Parker could warn Smith, he babbled on, as if proud of the facts he shared. "Belle Starr owns the largest of those, toward the other side of town."

Parker's eyes bulged. "The outlaw? Why is that allowed?" Surely there was some mistake for this was nothing short of unbelievable. Perhaps the President had no idea of the conditions here or how could he have thought it could possibly be cleaned up? "Is there more to it, downtown? Where might we find the Indian Territory?"

"This is downtown. Won't surprise me if you turn right around and leave, and I wouldn't blame you either. Most everything here is allowed by law."

For a moment, he stared at the buildings, clearly some were what remained of the old log fort. Most were little more than tossed together slat shacks with various signs announcing the availability of everything from evening doves to harsh drink and poker games. The few businesses failed to stand out as if hidden in shame to be found in such company.

He would wait to ask about the territory. The surrey hauled up when the driver yelled whoa. Parker peered out to see they had gone down a narrow street to a brick building. I think you'll find this comfortable, sir. It's close to the court house, as you can see." He swung an arm toward a rock structure not too far distant. Paused a moment as if for a reply, then went on. "If it is not suitable, your wife can look around and find something else."

Isaac bit his tongue to keep from saying he wouldn't let Mary go alone anywhere in this town for anything, no matter the circumstances.

One thing for damned sure. This job was cut out for him.

He surveyed the surroundings. Granted there were a few trees as if someone had attempted to make it look like a park. Otherwise the air stank of the heavy horse traffic. From the dock came the shouts of workers. An occasional gunshot sliced through the evening sunset. No one paid much attention.

Something would have to be done. And obviously he was the someone to do it. What had he agreed to? Pah, as if he'd had a choice once he accepted the president's appointment. Couldn't there be a more civilized place to settle a court established to… well, hell, to civilize half the damned west? Quite a job set out for him. Chuckling bitterly, he gathered himself and stepped into the muck of the road, glanced up at his wife and children staring down at him as if the world had gone berserk.

A large tree shaded the walkway to the entrance of the plain brick house. He stopped to mop his sweating brow and clean the mud from his boots before heading there. Hard to believe this was the largest federal district in the land, the only court with jurisdiction over all of the enormous Indian Territory. Jurisdiction didn't end there, but covered some fourteen counties in western Arkansas and a wide strip of southern Kansas. From what he'd heard this place was riddled with corruption and ineffectiveness. He'd soon take care of that. He would not tolerate such nonsense and laziness of any sort.

He glanced up at his nervous wife. "Stay there, my dear. I'll make sure we are at the correct address. I shall be right back. Don't worry, now." The last words he threw over his shoulder to keep from looking at her shock-stricken expression.

To his surprise a man in a blue uniform came out of the brick building to greet him when he was halfway to the door.

Hand out, he introduced himself as a Major Breckenshire. "I've been charged to meet you and get your family settled. A residence has been prepared on the ground floor. I'm sure it will suit you temporarily until your home is ready."

Reluctant to say much till he saw the residence, or rather till Mary approved, he followed the major inside and down a hallway to double doors on the left that opened to a well-lit room furnished tastefully. He let out a breath of relief. Boxes were stacked neatly around the walls leaving room for a scattering of furniture.

The major indicated the room. "These cartons arrived yesterday by train, and we took the liberty of moving them in. The furnishings are a part of the housing, but I understand they can be removed if you prefer your own."

He nodded. "It's fine for now. We've had a very long trip and my wife is weary. I'll fetch her and after we've had a few days of rest, who shall we contact if she wishes to make other arrangements?"

The young officer looked around as if puzzled, cleared his throat, and smiled. "As far as I know, sir, you will take up residence and be... well, in charge of the entire district, so final arrangements will be entirely up to you and your wife."

"Then if you would assist me in unloading my family and our luggage, I would appreciate it. And if you would then take me over to the court house, I'd like to see the facilities."

The major snapped to attention as if Parker were a general. "I am at your disposal, sir. Anything you wish, just ask."

"I presume you have notified every one of my arrival. I wish to meet them all by the beginning of next week. Otherwise I shall be looking over the holding jail and in and out of the courthouse. Are you to remain my liaison, or will that be a civilian?" Without waiting for a reply, he continued. "In any case, I shall begin to hire deputy marshals and appoint a circuit clerk next week as well. Oh, and I understand George Maledon is my executioner. If you would, ask him to call on me first thing next week please. Now, let's get Missus Parker and the children unloaded and settled."

Parker led the Major to the surrey with a slight smile. For once in his political life he felt in charge of something that would be important for many years. For a whole hell of a lot of years.

Within three days of his arrival, he had notified newspapers of some of his plans. The front page of one such paper in Fort Smith, when announcing Parker's arrival, referred to the problem in Indian Territory as caused by the "rendezvous of the vile and wicked from everywhere."

He did not succeed in hiding it from Mary, and when he returned from the courthouse one day, she held the folded paper up in front of him.

"Were you aware of this, husband? The vile and wicked?"

He tried to escape by changing the subject, calling it the usual reporter riff-raff, but she was having none of it. "That's not all either. I heard one of the soldiers talking, and he referred to Fort Smith as Hell on the Border. What kind of place have you brought our children to? I'm half a mind to catch a train and head for home."

"Now, Mary, I would never place any of you in danger. The Army is here and soon we'll be well guarded by two hundred deputy marshals. Besides, you know how newspapers exaggerate everything."

The way she narrowed her blue eyes at him, he wasn't sure he had convinced her, but he escaped by assuring her he was going right then to begin to hire those lawmen who would soon tame not only Fort Smith but Indian Territory.

Before she could reply, the children raced into the room, Charles chasing the crawling squealing James. Taking advantage of the interruption Parker hurried directly to the train depot and sent out word by telegraph wire of the expected hiring of at least 200 deputies. He then opened the courtroom and hired a new court clerk, then began interviewing deputies from the crowd of men waiting to apply for the job. Surprising how many descended on the town eager to serve. How long some of them might last he had no notion. The marshal serving under the previous judge was nowhere to be found.

The applicants were small and large, young and not-so-young, hairy and bald, noisy and quiet. Some so bow-legged they'd obviously lived astride a horse, others hugged weapons that ranged from muskets from the Civil War to newer Remingtons and side arms of all makes and models. From the lot, and by listening to their bragging, he doubted he could find very many qualified to be set loose with the badge of a Deputy U.S. Marshal. But there had to be at least 200 ready to swarm into the midst of the cruelest of men on this earth and drag them kicking and screaming into his courtroom.

President Grant would appoint the first marshal to step in and assist Parker in the huge job. Up to now there was no law in the territory save what the Native Americans invoked, and that was spotty and not applicable to the white man. So the barren 74,000 square miles offered never-ending hideouts for an unbelievable flood of outlaws who did not hesitate to commit any of the most vicious and cruel crimes imaginable. It looked like there would be plenty of men ready to step in and give the new judge a hand. An ever-moving line continued to form where he'd tacked up a sign and placed his clerk, a man by the name of Ramey Jones, behind a table.

Isaac stood by and listened for a while to make sure Jones had everything straight. The man had carefully taken down notes, but he had to make sure no false promises were made.

After laying out his register book, two pens, and a bottle of ink, Ramey greeted the first man.

He began with his rehearsed greeting, speaking loud enough that those close by could hear. No sense in repeating himself any more than was necessary. Many might walk away with the first information spoken, Parker had told him.

"The job of Deputy U.S. Marshal pays no salary as such, each man draws six cents per mile whether you're tracking a wanted fugitive or bringing him in. However you receive two dollars each upon delivery of a summons or for each time you deliver a warranted prisoner to the courthouse here in Fort Smith, Arkansas. You carry in a prisoner, then the court pays the cost, which usually means that of a cook, chuck wagon, prison wagon, and extra mules and horses. So, you'll bring back the criminals, obtain witnesses and evidence of the crime, then you have to produce this evidence in court for a jury to pass judgment of guilt or innocence of whomever has been charged with the crimes. Oft times you'll be off yonder in Indian Territory for weeks or more, it's a big district.

"You'll furnish your own arms and ammunition and horse. Be somewhat careful, for if you kill a prisoner, you'll pay for his burial." Ramey glanced up at the men, then cornered a look at Judge Parker, leaning against a pillar near the courthouse keeping an eye on him. "This ain't no job for sissies. That there is Judge Parker, and you'll report to him for now, until a marshal gets hired. But he's still your boss. Now, who wants to put down their name and go to work?"

A few of the men gathered, grumbled among themselves and drifted away, shaking their heads, some laughing and making crude remarks.

To Parker's amazement, considering the low scale of salary, many of them hung around in groups till they could take their turn with pen and ink. Some could write, others printed clumsily, a few made their mark and Ramey wrote in their name after it. The enrollment of Deputy Marshals went on for close to a week, the last day or so seeing only a few stragglers.

When it seemed no more would appear, Parker strolled outside, and he and Ramey went through the register book together, Ramey counting aloud as each page was turned to the next. "A hundred and eighty-eight," the man said in a low voice.

Parker urged him. "Let's take this all inside, leave the sign outside the courthouse on the door. There's bound to be some stragglers, but this isn't a bad start. You did tell everyone who signed up that they're to show up this Sunday afternoon here on the lawn where I'll hold a swearing in and make a little speech. They can invite any one of their friends and family who might want to show up."

Ramey nodded. "Yes, sir. Some wanted to know about badges, so I took to explaining that for now they could make their own, and you'd show the design when you swore them in."

Parker slapped Ramey on the shoulder. "Good man. You handled that all very well. I'd appreciate it if you'd take the job on permanently of doing work for me on a daily basis."

"How much per mile will you pay for that, sir?" Ramey squinted at him with a glimmer in his eyes.

Parker laughed. He liked a man with a sense of humor.

By Sunday, twelve more men had signed up inside the courthouse and Parker had his goal of two-hundred deputies. A few men had talked to him about the job of U.S. Marshal, but none had seemed particularly suited. The President would make the choice and appoint his man, but Parker had hoped to find someone qualified he could recommend.

The President notified him that it would be a while before he appointed a U.S. Marshal, but he could go ahead and put the men to work. They could report to the previous Marshal Fagan who currently served under Judge Story until July 2, 1875, or to Judge Parker to help handle that many deputies once they started to do their jobs. The first job was to identify and bring in witnesses to testify in cases of unsolved murders Parker had reopened.

After studying the files Jones had delivered to him, Parker chose to open two unsolved murder cases. Sunday at the swearing-in he handed out the names of witnesses to the killings.

He assigned other jobs. Most of the workload was from the Indian Territory where there was virtually no law enforcement. Two main cases were of Whites violating Native American sovereignty by grazing their cattle or living illegally in Indian Territory and illegal liquor brought into the Indian Territory.

Basic court procedures proved to be surprisingly simple, and he was pleased not to complicate them. He assigned officers to remain in the courthouse, explaining that a crime might be reported to one of them or to a deputy in the field. A deputy could also come across evidence or witness a crime, then ask for a writ and make an arrest. However, a person could be arrested with or without a writ. The suspect would then be brought to Fort Smith before the U.S. Commissioner to plead guilty or innocent and also to determine if the case went before a grand jury. Sometimes during these proceedings the charges would be dropped. Bail will be set or denied. If denied, the suspect was placed in jail. If the grand jury determined there was enough evidence, an indictment was issued and the case went to trial. The district judge presided over the trial and the case was decided by a trial jury. Defendants were entitled to a defense attorney. The plaintiff in the cases was the United States, represented by the District Attorney or one of his assistants. The judge would hand down a sentence when the jury returned a guilty verdict. The death penalty was given to those convicted of murder or rape. Other crimes carried a sentence that varied from monetary fines to jail time. Those sentenced to more than a year in prison were transported to facilities in other places: Little Rock, Detroit, Illinois, New York.

When at last all questions were asked and answered and the crowd drifted away, Parker remained at the courthouse in the stillness of late afternoon. Down the street, gunfire broke the silence. Men yahooed, a crew from a nearby ranch rode through town at a gallop, reined in at the Elk Horn Tavern and disappeared inside with much ado. The echo of piano notes hung over the town.

Shaking his head, the new judge arose from the bench against the front wall and headed home. He sometimes walked the blocks to the house he could not yet think of as his home.

A PRESIDENTIAL APPOINTMENT: JACOB YOES

LET'S GET ACQUAINTED with a U.S. Marshal, one who hailed from Washington County, Arkansas and was well known there for his business reputation. Yoes was the fifth U.S. Marshal appointed to serve under Judge Isaac Parker during his stay at Fort Smith. President Harrison chose him January 29, 1889. His life story is a fine example of the quality of men who served as U.S. Marshals in the Western District. All were upstanding, honest, and honorable. They came from all parts of the country to serve and help Judge Parker carry out the cleanup of Indian Territory for the twenty-one years his work continued.

"GET THAT BOY up out of the dirt and off Joey 'fore he kills him." Hands planted on her ample hips, Mama faced Papa with a look that stopped him cold in his footsteps. "I'd swear if the good Lord might forgive me. Jake is just about as tough as a knot on an oak tree."

Which Jake wished he was, but when Mama spoke a rule, he turned all gooey like the sap from a tree.

"Now, now, dear. You don't want a sissy pants, do you? Let the boys work it out. They generally do." Jake darted a glance between his parents to gauge who would win out. He was about ready to pop Joey one, but Ma might give him the same. So he held back.

Mama's nod came fast and firm. "Yes, but with Joey taking a beating. I want you to talk to Jake about his behavior before he gets turned out of school. Both boys need an education if they're to make anything of themselves."

With a weary nod, as if he'd heard all he could take, Papa stomped down off the porch where his parents discussed this latest problem, yanked Jake and Joey apart by the nape of their shirt collars. "Now that's enough, let's call this settled before your ma gets in on it. Both of you have extra chores the remainder of the week. If you don't stop your fighting, there'll be he-heck to pay."

Jake suppressed a snicker at Papa's almost saying the hell word aloud and offered his well-worn excuse. "Joey started it, Papa."

"Oh, I'm sure he did. Just to see you get your bottom tanned." Smiling, Papa dusted Jake's britches off with a flat palm and took a swipe at Joey's sending dust flying. He always tried to make it look like he was disciplining equally, but he never did truly punish. He left that to Mama, a tall thin woman who definitely ruled the hearth and home.

Jake was nearly six years old before he learned that Mama was boss around the house. To raise her ire was a mistake. Mama declared that to spare the rod spoiled the child. Papa, on the other hand, was a soft spoken man who'd rather stay out of squabbles.

Going back into the house Mama scolded whoever was listening. That'd be Jake, who was careful to hear what she said. "I swear that boy'd rather fight than eat."

Papa chuckled. "The boy will do fine learning to stand up for himself."

Jake only had to go to work with Papa once to find out he was admired by all who dealt with him. He was the boss there, that was for sure. He was boss at plenty of businesses in town. Must be that's why he let Mama run the house. He had lots to keep him busy. That was okay. Didn't everyone say they were a happy family?

First time he heard someone call Papa Coonrod, he laughed. Asked what it meant.

"Oh, it's my nickname. Guess I've had it since I was your age."

"But what does it mean, Papa? Something a coon does?"

"I reckon, son. People who can cross water by tossing down a tree limb and walking across it are said to have cooned a stream. Since I was little I hated to wade water, so that's what I did. And my name being Conrad, everyone just gave me that nickname."

"Could I have a nickname?"

Papa laughed. "I reckon as soon as you do something strange or weird you will."

Jake worshiped his Papa. One day at school he beat up Herman Manly when he called Papa henpecked. Even though he wasn't sure what that meant it didn't sound like his Papa.

He loved Ma, but it was different from the way he felt about Papa. The babe born to Ma last winter was number nine, and she kept peace in the household with a firm grip on a tree limb which she hung above the back door but seldom used. Like all his brothers and sisters, he feared she might one day so the household was more or less peaceful.

Four of the older boys were already bigger than Papa, two of 'em tall as Ma, which probably explained her taking up a weapon of sorts. He had to be tough, having such big older brothers.

Finished with the discipline, Papa leaned close. "Don't worry son, you'll get your growth soon. Stop trying to prove you're the toughest. Time will come you will be. I can see it in your eyes."

He sure hoped Papa was right, but while it seemed okay for the older boys to be bigger and tougher, he wasn't sure it was fair that only the young ones were smaller than him. So he had to work harder, and he meant to. How could he become a tough sheriff when he grew up if he never really grew up?

FIVE YEARS LATER he left home at the age of thirteen, having gotten his growth he'd so long wished for. He was bigger than all but the oldest of his brothers. He carried with him two dollars in the pocket of his only britches and one piece of advice from Papa. "Pay all your debts, be truthful, be honest." He had a job over in Granby, Missouri in the lead mines. Tough work, but it would make him stronger. Papa carried home good money, but he believed in the boys making their own way.

Sharing a room with two other workers meant he had a bed and a hook on the wall to hang his pair of britches. The three of them played cards on Saturday night and Jake went to church on Sunday morning. Otherwise, he had few contacts. He missed his large family and the farm on Signal Mountain where they'd moved from West Fork before he left home. So after working long enough to put away some cash, he headed back. His dream of being a sheriff fading fast.

Walking up the lane, and avoiding muddy ruts beaten in the ground by wagons and dozens of horse's hooves, he could scarcely wait to see everyone. The walk had been a long one, and he was plumb wore out by the time he came in sight of the sprawling log house. Coming home brought a lump to his throat, though he didn't plan to stay long.

Winter in the Boston Mountains of the Ozarks was fast coming on, the air filled with a chill that spoke of ice frosting the trees with a shimmering glitter. He'd be happy to sit beside the heating stove with Papa and his brothers and warm his bones. Almost three years away from home and nothing had changed much around the place. He stomped up onto the porch and the door swung open.

His sister Maggie burst out and almost ran him down. "Oh, my gracious. Who are you?"

"Get a good look, Maggie. I'm your brother, Jake."

Her squeal brought some of the kids running. Jake grinned and pounded on their backs in a family hug.

"Well land sakes, look who's here." Mama came rushing through the parlor wiping her hands on the ever-present apron tied around her middle. "Never reckoned to see you again."

He took her in his arms, gave her a big hug while the smallest sister hung onto his legs and others crowded to hit him on the arm with a fist. Everyone laughed and chattered till no one could make out a thing of what was being said. He'd forgotten what it was like to be with his large family.

Mama interfered. "Okay, now children. Let him get his breath." She took his arm. "Come on in and set a spell. Tell us what you've been up to all this time."

"Yeah, Jake. Did you see lots of places?" A little one, maybe three, stared up at him from the crowd.

"I sure did. And who is this?"

"You been gone a long time. That's Cynthy. We got us some more little 'uns since you left." One of the boys laughed at Jake's confusion. Another boy who shared looks with the first one, the dark hair and round face, punched the first one on the arm causing a brief wrestling match that ended when Mama thumped them both on the head with a middle finger.

She turned back to Jake. "Your pa will be so happy to see you. Last we heard was your letter... when was that... a few months ago? You was still working in the lead mines. Such a dreadful job, mining. So happy you're home.

"Me too, Ma. Don't think I'll take up mining for a living. There's better ways to make pocket change."

"Hope you're gonna stay here with us for a while. Papa could well put you to work."

"I think you got enough living here, Ma. Two more since I left. I'm thinking of building me a house here on the place if you and Pa don't mind. I'm ready to settle down for a while."

Jacob "Blake Jake" Yoes (1839–1906), a soldier, entrepreneur, and politician, served as a prominent Deputy U.S. Marshal under Judge Parker.

Less than a year later he met Mary Ann Reed at a church picnic. She and her folks lived over the hill down in the holler, and it was accidental she came to the picnic with a cousin who belonged to their church, otherwise he might never have met her. Men here tended to marry the girl next door or a church member.

On her first visit to the Yoes home on Signal Hill, Mary Ann underwent all the questions natural in such a case. Ma sat beside her in a rocking chair. "Which Reeds are you related to, child? Some are our second cousins." The point of her needle continued to stitch a quilt block as she spoke.

"Reuben and Rachel. They're from down in Chester. No relation to the Reeds up here."

Satisfied, Ma nodded. "A sin for cousins to marry, you see."

Mary Ann glanced at Jake. "We just met. It's only one picnic."

He might've objected too, but he'd set his mind on Mary Ann Reed the first time he laid eyes on her. She was a beauty, nice and quiet with a fine sense of humor which a woman would need to put up with him. He was well aware of that. And other things too. He had no notion of staying put on the farm much longer. His dreams were much loftier than that, and he needed a woman ready to climb to the top with him.

It didn't take long for Mary Ann to convince Jake she was his one and only. She always claimed he lured her into his arms. Either way they were married the day after Christmas in 1858. With his dreams tucked away in the darkness of a country caught up in turbulence, Jake remained on the farm while his father tended to his various businesses.

By 1862, with the country sunk deep in a destructive Civil War, things changed for the worse. Arkansas had split on secession but finally broke away from the Union.

Hearing that dreadful news Jake paced the floor, his boots thunking on the hardwood. "I tell you, Papa, this war will destroy the country. Hard to sit by and do nothing. Hate to take the Federal's side, but it's how I believe. It's hardest though to leave Mary and the children."

"I'll see to them, son, if this is what you have to do. Wish you didn't though. When this war is over, it'll go hard on them that betrayed their raising. Folks around here are pretty much against secession, but at the same time they feel obliged to fight for their freedom. This is our land, our home."

Jake stared out the window across the farmland spread over the top of Signal Mountain. Some of the boys worked the crops while others tended to various family businesses. Papa's success as a man involved in a collection of businesses kept the family well enough off, but Jake feared what would happen to them what with the dark clouds of war looming. Southerners who were well off would suffer the most, though Pa had never owned or used a slave to gain his wealth.

As if reading his son's mind, Papa shook his head in anger. "Never had a slave, never thought it right to hold a man in bondage. But there's a lot more for the south to this war than that. It's our living, cotton and labor and the economy. The country has no right to interfere. I don't blame those for seceding, but still we have to keep this country together. I see a great future for us if we can. But it's going to be hard, blamed hard to get through this. Before it's over I fear we'll wade knee deep in bloody fields."

In June of 1862, Jake enlisted in Company D, First Arkansas Cavalry of the U.S. Army. He rode away from home down the very lane he'd returned from the mines on years earlier. Over his shoulder he watched Mary and the babes as long as he could see them, tears on his cheeks like heavy dew.

He fought at the battle of Prairie Grove, but for the most part was on detached duty. Constantly on the run from bushwhackers, he was shot in the right hip, in the left hip, and in the left leg by a posse of Confederates. Though he hid out and escaped capture, he later was caught and taken to Van Buren to the Confederate prison camp. He was exchanged in 1863 and in 1864 refused a First Lieutenant commission offered by the Army because he'd killed at least fifty bushwhackers. An accomplishment of which he was not proud.

He stood before his captain who made the commissioning offer, eyed him with a long silence. "Well, sir, I reckon I'll just take my discharge and get on with my life. There's plenty of living out there for a man like me."

"A man like you is what this Army is looking for. With your record of kills, men like you will be needed to protect those who will pour into the west once we take care of those pesky red men standing in the way."

Jake came to attention as much more as his aching hips would allow. "Precisely why I'm wanting out of this man's army. I intend to be a big part of what's coming. On my own. Not by killing Native Americans or Whites."

The officer chuckled. "And just how much you got jingling in your pocket right now, boy?"

"You mean Army pay?" Doubling a fist Jake stared beyond the man's shoulder and through the window. "I'm done with killing." All he wanted was to get on home where his sweet wife awaited. But he had big plans.

It was already 1864, time was chasing him fast. He'd survived the war. Sooner he could leave the cavalry behind, happier he'd be. By God, he had plans, big plans. Three young'uns waited at home with his sweet wife. He had no notion of spending his sweat and tears plowing and scraping a crop out of the rocky land and seeing them in rags and hungry.

Papa had taught him young how to make a living without coaxing it out of rocky soil. He was meant for a more important life. The south was ripped apart. He knew how to help put it back together.

The sweating horse between Jake's legs chafed the bullet wounds he carried from the war. With a grunt he shifted and pushed on till he could take the pain no longer. It was still a long way home. Sure wouldn't do to arrive at Signal Hill after these years of absence and be unable to march right into his house and hug Mary Ann. Shade trees along the banks of a creek cooled the hot August air. Bade him rest a while. Without a command, his mount drew up, blew air through his nose, and cricked his head as if to protest. Enough. This was enough. For both of them.

With a painful chuckle, Jake slipped from the saddle, leaned forward to steady himself against the horse, then limped into knee-high grass and sank to his sore butt.

"Go on, you old bone head, get yourself a drink. You've earned it." The reins slid from his palm. "I have too."

"Tongue's dry as a boll of cotton." Calling on the last of his strength, he crawled to the creek bank, swept off his hat, and sprawled on his stomach to slake his thirst. The water, cold as a winter's snow, hurt his teeth, sent shudders through his mouth that rushed clean to his belly. Caused his forehead to tingle and hammer. He finally came up for air and swiped an arm across his wet lips.

Damn me if that Ozark spring water ain't the best of anything in life right this minute. Refreshed and cooled, he dunked his head, held it there till he came up sucking air. Black hair lay heavy and wet around his shoulders. While imprisoned at Confederate prison in Van Buren there'd been no way to saw it off or cut the scraggly beard that shadowed his jaws. He sure didn't resemble the man who'd left Arkansas to fight on the side of the Yankees. No doubt his body was eat up with lice. He felt a desperate need to scratch the itch.

Good Lord Almighty, he must look like some wild man. If Mary Ann didn't shoot him before she figured out who he was, she'd rid him of the vermin, then come at him with a pair of shears, laughing and snipping away. He ached for the sound of her voice, the feel of her fingers in his hair.

Arms hugging away the damp, chilly air he wished for a tent, but there hadn't been time to waste chasing down supplies in a devastated south. Best to hurry home. A tad over two years he'd spent in the U.S. Army. His wife bearing their third child while he'd been gone. But he enlisted, by God. Done a man's duty. And he was sure as hell done with that.

Laying out under the stars, embracing a breeze dancing its way across the singing water, he mulled over plans made in that filthy Confederate prison. At times he'd sure wished he'd supported secession. If he had, he could be in a Yankee prison instead of starving along with the Rebs who didn't even have food for themselves.

It was all over though. He was free, the war and everything about it left behind, he would go after what he wanted. First thing, he'd find work while he read the law. And then nothing would stop him. Lord, what if his folks had been burned out? He had no way of knowing.

The next morning, as the sun splintered the pale sky with gold, Jake washed up in the cold water and was on his way. He'd make home today if nothing untoward happened. No more than two hours later he came to a trading post on the banks of the stream known as Frog Bayou. A trading post slouched behind a short boardwalk with a sign that read Wright's Trading. Out back sat a log cabin. Family wash hung draped across thick shrubbery. Good signs the area had survived being burned out. There was time to buy something to eat with the scant salary Company D had paid him for offering up his life.

A man in overhauls pushed out the door just ahead of Jake, raised a hand, and nodded a howdy.

"Good morning, sir." Jake grinned and made to enter the store.

"Say, you look familiar, but you ain't from around here, are you?" The man smiled to reveal tobacco colored teeth.

Seemed friendly enough, so Jake responded. "Not from far though. Up on yonder mountain. Me and my folks got a farm on Signal Hill."

"You must be one of Coonrod's boys then."

Wonderful to hear his Papa's nickname used with admiration.

The man didn't wait for a reply. "Reckon you're coming back from the war? Heard you was in a Reb's prison camp down there. Uncle Jeb reported on it when he come home. Welcome back. Good to see you made it. Name's Chester Wright. Sorry to know you fought for the Yanks, but 'spect it's time to let all that go."

Jake stared off toward the mountain where his family waited. "I'm a bit proud of making it myself. What's done is done, I'd say. Hope folks around here can let it go. Forget about our differences. Happen you hear how mine made out?" If he never heard another word about those fifty bushwhackers he'd killed, Jake would be a happy man. It wasn't nothing to brag about. Far as he was concerned he'd go to his grave with his mouth closed on that one.

"Done okay. Your pa was able to keep business working for his family and some of us others. I 'spect if you don't start nothing, no one else will."

Jake nodded curtly. "You can count on me. Reckon I'll go in and grab a bit of breakfast before I head on home. My stomach thinks my throat's been cut."

"Any of your folks know you're back?"

"Nope, and I'd appreciate it if no one told them. I want to surprise everyone."

"Good luck to you, then. I'll not tell the old woman, for she'll have it all over the place in a whip stitch." Wright laughed heartily and walked away, shaking his head.

A fading sun lay a golden glow across the tree covered Boston Mountains. Halfway up the steep incline Jake reined in to enjoy the welcome scene of green peaks. He needed to let his horse rest anyway. Odd how he wanted to hurry and see the look on Mary Ann's face, but at the same time he held back.

Maybe she wouldn't even recognize him. What would she say when he announced himself? Would the same crooked grin greet him, or would her forehead crease with a frown like she wasn't sure who this bedraggled stranger might be, riding onto her place with dark fast falling? She might even take a shot at him. No reason for her to know he'd survived. And what of the babes? None of them would remember him, two young, one not yet here when he left. Boy nor girl, he had no idea.

Night shadows crawled along the ground and the flame of daylight slowly faded. He rode on, eyes searching the hillside for signs of lamps in the windows of his home. Ma ought to have hers lit in the house nearby his sweet Mary's. Dear God, had something happened to them? Why was it dark all the way to the top, outlined by a silvery evening sky?

With a nervous touch of his heels to the horse's flanks he headed along the path, worn there by wagon and animal passage over the years since the Yoes settled on Signal Mountain. A breeze picked up, whispered loud through a grove of oak trees hanging thick with leaves. The rattle spooked his mount into crow-hopping and kicking fist-sized rocks that tumbled noisily in the silent air.

Knee-hugging settled the dun and Jake patted his neck. "Whoa there, boy. You'll wake the dead. It's nothing but shadows."

After nights spent on the battlefield he wasn't immune to being spooked himself. A barking dog stiffened his backbone. Time he arrived at the big house, thank God it remained standing, Pa would be on the porch, rifle tucked loosely under his arm. Just in case. Surely Wright would've known of destruction, would've told him. Finally, the dark shadow of a house stood against the woods.

He cupped a hand around his mouth. "Hello, the house. It's me, Jake. I'm home." He swung to the ground and dropped the reins. Before he could go to meet Papa, the old man shouted a greeting.

Conrad Yoes had been known as Coonrod as long as Jake could remember. Many were the tales told of his young high-jinks. Gave Jake the feeling that he and Papa were way more alike than it seemed. The idea surprised him, for he'd never felt that way till this very moment. The war had done things to him he hadn't expected. Papa's following words interrupted his thoughts.

"Let me light this lantern, boy. I been waiting for you out here the last few nights."

Just like the old man to know he was coming. Some said he had second sight. On the porch a match flared, a lantern glowed to life and Papa came off the porch as agile as his son. "Aw, son. Aw. We were beginning to think you might be dead, till just a few days ago I knew you were on the way. Your ma will be so happy, as will your dear wife and children."

Voice breaking he wrapped an arm around Jake's neck. Never an outwardly emotional man, Papa went silent and cupped the back of his son's neck with a broad palm. "How are you? Have you been well? When did you take leave of the army? Go on to the house, I'll put away your horse." The old man talked to himself while he headed for the barn leading Jake's dun.

Tears clogging his own throat, Jake hesitated for a long moment before turning toward the little house. Mama rushed out the door of the big cabin and caught him in her arms. Her tears ran hot against his neck. After hugging her and his older sisters, he turned, more anxious to go out back to the smaller house.

"We'll be right on over, Mama, I need to see my Mary Ann."

"You go on. I'll fix you some supper. Bring them all over with you."

Before he could cross the porch toward his door, Mary Ann rushed out and threw her arms around his neck. He held her so tight he liked to bent her in half. And he couldn't let go either. No matter how much went on after that, he had hold of the woman he loved. His sister Margarette had fetched his little ones, the eldest one a boy, who hung back behind Mary Ann's skirts, the babe in arms crying when he gave him a kiss. Everyone laughed and Jake hung on to his wife through it all.

After a while Mama jostled him. "I swear if you squeeze that girl any tighter, you'll split her right in two in the middle. Come on, there's food on the table aplenty. You don't look like they fed you too good in that dreadful army."

The celebrating went on into the night, him telling stories of his adventures.

"I was put out to wander most of the time. It was a strange arrangement. Called detached duty."

He didn't mention being shot three times while pursuing Rebel bushwhackers, nor did he mention he'd brought down fifty of them. Maybe he'd never have to bring that up again in his lifetime.

Everyone finally got to bed, and he held on to Mary Ann all night like maybe she might disappear if he didn't. The little ones piled in the bed first thing the next morning, and he tickled and played games with them while his wife fixed breakfast. In his arms, the youngest tried to pull out his beard, to the delight of everyone.

He was home, finally home, and he couldn't wait to get started on the plans he'd made for his life. For his family's life. All the while sitting in the prison camp, it went through his mind what he'd do if he made it home. Now it was time to get started. Right after, he finished tucking away ham and eggs, biscuits and gravy, and at least a gallon of coffee.

Only a few days later a rested Jake announced his plans at the supper table. "I'm hoping to read for the law, maybe get elected as sheriff of Washington County soon."

No one could've been more surprised than Mary Ann. "I always knew you wouldn't be content to be a farmer, but sheriff?"

He lifted his cup of coffee and watched her with shining eyes. "That's only the beginning. The fastest and best way to get noticed and go places in the county and state. I've got big plans, and it's going to take some time, but I'll get it all done."

"What exactly does read for the law mean? What you have to do to be sheriff?"

"No, not exactly. But it helps to learn law from a lawyer, be elected sheriff, then maybe go on to serve in the government."

Eyes glistening in his direction, Mary Ann laid a hand on his shoulder. "Oh, I have no doubt you will, I just didn't expect you to be in such a hurry."

"Life don't leave us be, my dear. It just don't. That war stole time from me, and I need to make it up."

He worked for his pa and made plans with the earnings he saved over the next six years.

DESPITE HIS PLANS he had a strange feeling something was about to happen even before a rider approached while the coffee was still steaming hot. Carrying the cup he stepped out on the porch to see who this might be who couldn't possibly know he was home. Surely Mary Ann hadn't given up on him and took to courting someone else. He'd wanted to talk to Papa about how he knew he was coming home. He peered at the rider. Who could this be? Hair bristled on the back of his neck. What if his fears were true? He studied Mary Ann's curious face. Naw, he was being hang-down dumb.

It was James Martin Smith, a member of the city council. He rushed to meet Jake on the porch steps and shook his hand. "So it's true. We heard you were home from Mister Wright, and I for one couldn't wait to get over here and talk to you."

Jake leaned through the front door. "Mary Ann, could you bring James a cup of coffee?" Relief filled him to be found welcome here after fighting for the Yanks. Some had gotten shot for such. But the war was over, the heated anger cooling like blacksmith coals under a bucket of water.

When the coffee came, the two men sat on the top step and were silent while they took a couple of sips.

"And what's your big hurry, James? Other than you couldn't wait to visit with an old friend?"

"It's as if it were fated. The county badly needs a sheriff, in fact, funny as it is, we already took a vote to see if folks would want you to fill that spot, and you were voted in before we even heard you were home."

Jake stared at him. "I can't imagine how you knew I was coming home. Papa knew it too."

"Oh, you 'member that fella Archie Crewson, went off about the same time you did?"

Jake nodded, mystified where this conversation might be going.

"Well, he come home couple weeks ago. Seems he was in the same division or whatever that you was, and he told around that you had been discharged and would be home soon. Filled me up with tales of your war years. So we decided to go ahead and hold an election since everyone on the council figured what a good sheriff you'd make."

Jake rubbed his bearded jaw. Blamed Papa anyway, letting him believe that tale about him having second sight. He chuckled. "And here you are, not even waiting for me to get a shave and fixing to be on his way to see about that very thing. Being sheriff. Funny, I wouldn't think you'd want someone who fought for the Feds."

"As many of us voted against secession as did to secede, so it's of little difference now. The war is over, and it taught many men to fight. We're ready to sign you to keep the county safe. Right now if you're willing."

"I'll have to think about it. I need to read for the law to make a good sheriff."

"You're young. You can read for the law while you serve."

"Wait, what about the election?"

"That'll come, that'll come. I 'spect it won't take folks long to see how good you are at it."

"Let's not rush this. I need to prepare myself for something like this. Tell them folks on the board that I'll be down first thing next week to discuss this with them, see if they're still sure it's what they want." Dang if he wanted to act too eager. It wasn't fitting.

"Oh, it will be, Jake. No doubt about that at all. You're an upstanding citizen. Just like your Pa." James rose, fitted the hat on his head and shook hands. "See you first thing next week and let us know what you've decided."

It was his dream come true, riding out across the mountains keeping the law, but somehow Jake had this feeling he ought to do things in a better order. He was young and as such might not be as smart as the folks of Washington County judged him to be.

But oddly enough Papa changed his mind without even setting out to do so when he told him that it wouldn't be long before a railroad come through from up North in Missouri.

"Think of what land around here will be worth when that gets out. If I wasn't getting so old, I'd invest in some myself. There'll be a crying need for businesses along the line and these small towns will grow like mushrooms under an ash tree."

As a result the following week Jake told the board he'd take the job as Washington County Sheriff. "I've got me some business to do, but I'll need that job."

When he laid out his plans to the city council, they agreed he could pin on the badge while he looked around the county for opportunities to invest in. Long as he kept the law and was available when needed.

Smith swore him in at a special meeting the next evening. Half the town of Fayetteville crowded into the city hall built to replace the one burnt during the war.

It was 1870, and the South badly needed to return to her former glory, and he knew how to do that. The next week he pinned on his shiny new badge, kissed Mary Ann and the children good day and rode down into Winslow. A fellow down there had come home from the war all tore up and could no longer run his small store. Jake tied his horse outside where the man sat on a bench in front of a partially burnt log building visiting with an older fellow.

He climbed down, removed his hat, and remained in the dirt street. The two men stopped talking and eyed him.

"Mister Vaught?" Jake waited, giving them both time to size him up.

Finally, the younger one who only had one leg nodded. "That's me, sir. Can I help you?"

"Names Yoes, sir. I'd like to make you an offer. You owned this trading post before the war?"

Vaught nodded. "Still do, I reckon, for all the good it does me. Don't know what you could offer me, though. It's partly gone"—he stuck out his empty britches leg—"as am I."

"I'm looking to open a store here, and I'd be obliged if we could make a deal."

"Ain't much to—"

Jake held up a hand. "Begging your pardon, but I'd be pleased to take the place off your hands if we could arrange a monthly stipend once I get it up and running. I'll stand the cost of rebuilding and at the end of a year if I've paid you enough which we can settle on, I would take ownership."

The older fellow rose, held out his hand. "Name's Sam Meaders. Sounds like it might be too good to be true."

Jake smiled. "Hopefully for the both of us. You're welcome to see a lawyer, sir, if you'd like to consider the offer."

"Costs money."

"There's one in Fayetteville, I could have him come see you."

"Friend of yours, I reckon." Meaders again. Not too trusting a fellow, but then with all the carpetbaggers and the like flooding over the south to cheat folks out of what little they had left, it wasn't surprising.

Vaught interrupted. "You say your name is Yoes. Any kin to Coonrod?"

"My dad, sir, and of a fine reputation."

Vaught chuckled. "Indeed he is. Fact being he set me up in this here place back before the war. Loaned me enough to buy it, and I paid it back with little interest."

"Usury." Meaders grumbled. He slitted a look at Yoes. "Heard you fought on the side of the damned Yanks."

Vaught evidently had enough of Meaders interruptions. "Sounds like a fine offer, Mister Yoes. But you get your lawyer down here to explain and make sure it's legal for the both of us. I trust anyone with the name of Yoes. I ain't fit to be running no store."

"Oh, you misunderstand. I'll pay you a wage to run the place for me. No reason you can't do that, ain't they a young'un in town you could get to do the lifting maybe for groceries for the family once a week? I got me a job and running this county will keep me busy.

Jake whistled Pretty Mary all the way home. He had good reason to. He'd struck his first deal.

There was plenty of time to fulfill his dream of reading the law. Of wearing a badge and keeping the law. He could and would do it all, for wasn't he Coonrod Yoes son?

WHAT CAN ALWAYS be said about dreams is that if they are well buried within the abilities of the dreamer, then they will reach fruition. And so did Jake Yoes's dreams, for the next morning he rose from his bed. After downing a large breakfast of bacon, eggs, and fried taters smothered in gravy, he rode into Fayetteville where he began inquiries into available land along the obvious routes where growth would inevitably find possibilities. And he made his plans. Papa had taught him well. He understood business and how it worked, what it took to be a success. And while Judge Parker went about his search for his first lawmen down in Fort Smith, U.S. Marshals who would help enforce the laws, Jacob Yoes enforced the law in Washington County while he bought and improved land along the railroad route through the Boston Mountains into Fort Smith.

Black Jake Yoes was one of the most popular sheriffs of the era for the way he kept the county cleaned up of outlaws. It's a bit puzzling, even to Jake where the nickname Black Jake came from, but from then on he was known as Black Jake. Some believe it had to do with the color of his thick mane of hair. Otherwise it's never been explained.

Black Jake Yoes became known as the merchant prince with stores along the Frisco in West Fork, Woolsey, Winslow, Chester (Porter), Walker Switch (Armada), Mountainburg and Graphic. There is a town south of Alma still known today as Yoestown where Jake owned a cotton gin. When his father Conrad passed away in 1891, Jake inherited $33 from him.

Having had all these successes, Black Jake then turned back to his first love, the law, which had served him so well in earlier years. He was appointed U.S. Marshal of the Western District of Arkansas, Judge Parker's Court, in May of 1889. There were two hundred deputy marshals under his command, including two of his own sons, George Allen and John Wesley. Jake was directly involved in the capture of members of the Dalton Gang after they robbed the Coffeyville bank.

As with all great men who are obsessed by such ambition, Jake had a secret side to his life. And in this day, when like secrets are being revealed about our great presidents, Jake probably wouldn't mind if his too came to light. There was a mysterious woman in Jake's life, a woman by the name of Emaline Winn. She was born into slavery and was freed by her master prior to the Civil War. She chose to remain with the Winns, however, but Jake lured the lovely, erotic Emaline away from the only family she had ever known. She moved to the huge brick hotel in Chester where it is widely accepted that she bore Jake a child. The child soon died and is buried at the Chester cemetery, the stone marked only with an "A x B." Emaline later went to live with Abigail Yoes (Jake & Mary Ann's second child) who cared for her until her death.

Jake's son John helped compile material for the book Hell on the Border, said to be the one upon which True Grit was based. Jacob did not want his name connected with the book, but early editions had his picture in the front. It was removed from later editions because he insisted.

He died February 6, 1906, and is buried in the National Cemetery at Fort Smith. Black Jake Yoes was truly one of the first Arkansas folk heroes, and he left a legacy still visible today in the historic buildings alongside the railroad lines from Missouri south into Van Buren. And if history serves him truly, he followed his father's advice to the very end. "Pay all your debts, be truthful, be honest."

BEYOND THE BADGE

Thus began the story of the man who would soon earn the title of Arkansas's merchant prince. One day he would also play a huge part in what was about to turn the Western District of Arkansas into one of the most outstanding stories of law enforcement in America's history. But that's a story that needs to be told through the eyes, ears, and fighting guns of the men who accomplished it.

Not only was Yoes one of the seven U.S. Marshals appointed by Judge Isaac Parker during his reign, his service while a U.S. Marshal is just one of the amazing, unbelievable yarns to be linked with that of the sort of men standing ready to rescue Fort Smith from the worst of the west's outlaws.

While Jake quickly cleaned up Washington County, and invested in his state's growth, some forty miles to the south in the Arkansas River Valley, the small settlement of Fort Smith, originally built in 1817 to hold back and defend the rest of the state from attack by the Native Americans out West, struggled to outgrow its bad reputation.

Unidentified Deputy U.S. Marshals of the Western District of Arkansas, ca. 1880. Each is armed with a Model 1874 Winchester rifle.

RIDING FOR THE JUDGE: THE DEPUTY'S DUTY

BEFORE THE STORIES of the Deputies are told, you must understand what was expected of these tough men brave enough to take on the job and how little coin they received.

Deputies could arrest for any crime committed in the 74,000 square miles of the federal court's jurisdiction. A set of instructions issued by the U.S. Marshal's office in Fort Smith gave an idea of the crimes and problems involved:

"Deputy U.S. Marshals for the Western District of Arkansas may make arrest for: murder, manslaughter, assault with intent to kill or to maim, attempt to murder, arson, robbery, rape, bribery, burglary, larceny, incest, adultery. These arrests may be made with or without warrant first issued and in the hand of the Deputy or the Chief Marshal."

One would think the financial reward for putting one's life in danger would be substantial, but most deputies did not earn more than $500 per year. This was due to the fee system that would not be reformed until 1898. A deputy received two dollars for making an arrest and could receive six cents per mile for going to the place of arrest and ten cents per mile for himself and a prisoner returning to court.

If a deputy failed to make an arrest, he received no payment. If he killed a suspect while attempting an arrest, the deputy had to bury the dead man at his own expense unless he was fortunate enough to find relatives to claim the body. In that case, the deputy could collect one dollar for the time and money he would be out in making that arrest.

Serving subpoenas, finding witnesses, and other routine court business earned fifty cents per service. A deputy could receive six cents per mile for going to the place of service, but nothing for the return trip. After totaling the fees for a trip, the U.S. Marshal deducted his twenty-five percent before the deputy received payment.

Despite the risks and uncertainties of the job, conscientious Deputy Marshals did much to curb the disorder rampant in the Indian Territory. These men enforced the law and established the idea of justice in the region. Judge Parker said that without the brave men who rode for the U.S. Marshals Service, he could not have done his job. Their history remains one of the most colorful chapters of America's story.

There were nearly 1,600 Deputy U.S. Marshals who served this Western District. Some were appointed for only one period of time, while others, like Bass Reeves, served for decades. Coming from British Royalty in the House of Kent in Gloucestershire, James Wilkinson served forty-two years, possibly the longest single term ever served.

A total of 171 Marshals Service employees, or closely related, are buried in the Fort Smith area. Of that total, 4 Marshals, 2 Chief Deputy Marshals, 116 Deputy Marshals, and 27 guards, posse, bailiffs, jailers, and related U.S. Court employees have now been identified as buried in Oak Cemetery. The archives in Fort Worth, Texas, provided 1,200 names of those who served the Western District Court.

Ironically, a long list of criminals who were brought in by these heroic men lie in graves at Oak Cemetery. Resting at peace side by side, their differences are long ago forgotten. But what should not be forgotten is the bravery of the men who served in the U.S. Marshals service. Visit the Western District U.S. Marshals Museum in Fort Smith and enjoy the memorabilia on display there.

THE FIRST HANGING: CHARLES VENNOY

VENNOY SHOVED HIS way through the dark saloon, tossed his hat in the general direction of a table, yanked out a chair, and ordered a mug of brew. Damned if he was happy about what was going on with the law lately. Marshals bringing in owl hoots, court turning them loose. He was about to the point of not enjoying being a deputy marshal at all.

If he ever got his hands on that low-down John Childers, he might opt to hang the sumbitch to make sure he paid what was owed the law. He was as mean as any rattlesnake. When a lawman had to be as ornery as the scumbag he hunted down, things were getting bad. The murdering thief had slipped from the law's clutches once again and was on the loose running wild ever way he could. All this after he'd brought the man down yet one more time.

His friend—another deputy—strode into the saloon and joined him at his table.

Vennoy took a deep sip of beer and peered at the younger Peavy. "You look like I feel. Ready to chuck it in?"

"Thinking about it. If this joke of a judge would do something after we drag 'em in, it'd be one thing. But he just slaps that gavel on his desk and says 'next case,' like the one in front of him weren't worth considering. I hear they're fixing to build a gallows over to Fort Smith. Lot of good that'll do. Hell, they ain't no one to hang. I say line 'em all up, clear down the street if necessary, and drop 'em in, dozen at a time till this mess is cleaned up. What are us Deputy Marshals worth if they let 'em go fast as we catch 'em?" Peavy's dark looks reddened.

"I take it you're talking about John Childers. That half Cherokee breed. I heard he got away with it again. He's bragged around about finally getting himself that black horse. Not making any bones about how he stole it and killed the owner in the process."

"Bastard killed that poor old peddler who owned the horse?"

"Seems so. Rayburn Wedding never done anything to anyone. He made his living traveling through Indian Territory trading flour and bacon for hides and farm products. Damned shame."

Vennoy stared across the dimly lit bar for a minute, then turned to his friend. "Let's get the bastard. Let's get him once and for all. I've been after him since he killed that poor feller up in Kansas months ago. No one ever heard tell of his name even. Had to be buried without a marker. No man deserves such an end."

"Do us little good to just haul Childers in now. With no court in session and that Judge Caldwell being set off. Ain't no telling when or if outlaws will ever pay the price again."

Vennoy nodded and finished his beer. Held up the mug to signal the pretty redhead serving the noisy customers.

"Ready for another?" Peavy rose to go fill their mugs, stopping to joke with the busy girl serving drinks. When he returned, he took up where they'd left off. "Bringing in a new federal judge in January. Fella by the name of Story. Building a gallows over to Fort Smith."

Vennoy grinned. "Well, ain't you a fountain of information? Heard about the gallows, did you? Hell, I told you that while ago when you came in. Losin' your memory or what?"

"I clearly am new to Van Buren. Just a stranger passing through. Heard it while waiting for these to be drawn."

"They shutting the Van Buren courthouse down? It was burned end of the war. It's just built brand new. Real purty too. Seems a shame just so they can herd owl hoots in one door and out the other." Vennoy pointed a crooked first finger at the drinks. "Be surprised what you'll hear at a bar."

An hour or so later, feeling no pain, he rose to his feet. "You ready to get going?'

"Where we going?"

"Let's go get a new warrant for that escaped no-good Childers and pair up. This time we'll bring him back and maybe they'll hang him on that new gallows. Or maybe we won't." It made him feel better, having a goal.

"Who's gonna give us a warrant? That crooked Judge Story is gone, the other won't be here till after Christmas."

His pal was sure reluctant to do much but drink.

"Surely there's a Marshal in town in charge of something or other. If not, we're all doomed." Cramming his worn hat down on his head, Vennoy shoved his way through the noisy crowd, not waiting to see if Peavy followed.

He did, muttering all the while. "Reckon we can find one. If not, let's just go get the bastard without a warrant. There's bound to be wanted posters on him since he escaped twice already from custody. He's been running free for months and no one doing much about it. Telling you, what we need here is a judge, but I don't reckon they make good ones anymore. And I'm fed up with it. Besides, it ain't like this was Childers's only crime."

A scantily dressed woman staggered in front of Vennoy, and he pushed her aside. He was just drunk enough to set out with this crazy young deputy who sounded ready to do just about anything. Maybe they'd just hang the son of a bitch, like the kid said. It'd been done in the face of no other choice. Or from simple madness on the part of someone who'd taken all they could from one of these carousing gangs here in the territory.

"We'll head up to Kansas. I'm betting that's where he'll be hunkered down. His old home place. Someone will have seen or heard of him. Let's ride out in the morning. We'll need a pack mule and some supplies."

He squinted toward Peavy who appeared to be thinking over more outrageous suggestions to bring up. Hell, maybe they would hang him, from the highest damned tree. No one was going to put him on that brand-new gallows because there wasn't a judge here with the balls to do it.

Back in camp Vennoy retired on the ground under a tree, and when he awoke wasn't sure what he might have agreed to or suggested with the brash young Deputy Marshal. He was soon to find out. Before he could scrub his hands and face in the nearby stream Peavy rode up leading a small mule. Ready to go.

"Figured we'd go to the mercantile together to pack this little feller up and get to moving. And I ain't forgetting a hangin' rope."

With a frown he shook his head, stretched, and fetched his horse. Looked like they were going after Childers. Tightening the latigo around the animal's belly, he experienced a feeling of exhilaration. First time in a long time he'd been excited about doing his job. Maybe he'd just plain been a marshal too long… or was too old, one or t'other.

Two days later Vennoy led Peavy north through a bitter snowstorm to seek shelter in a barn. Huddled inside with the horses and mule for added warmth, he mumbled his discontent. Hadn't he not wanted to do this in the first place? Should've stayed sober. And now a confound blizzard to freeze their balls off. Or hang around this place stinking of manure and old hay.

Damn-fool Peavy was having a gay old time. Grinning, rubbing his hands together, and peering through the gloom of the barn. "You any idea where we're at? Or would it do any good to know?"

"I have a fair idea. Been in this country once after the good-for-nothing. Best thing is to wait this blizzard out. We ain't going anywhere and neither is Childers."

"You really reckon he's tucked in at his old place?"

"Yeah, just long enough to wait this out fore he does some more killing. We might never catch him. Probably wasting our time, this weather and all." He wanted nothing but to go home. They'd just turn the butcher and his crew loose or he'd escape again. There was no way this man would ever hang. The very devil ran with him, kept him free.

"He has to be stopped. Man doing the evil he is. Raping women, no respect for them or the law. We'll get him or someone will." Peavy was young and determined, but he'd soon learn how justice worked or didn't.

Vennoy was silent for a long while. "I'm beginning to wonder if that's so. Some of these old boys just keep it up till they die."

"If I can have anything to do with it, this one will hang on that new gallows."

"And if he doesn't?" Vennoy glared at his partner.

"Well, then I reckon I can find a handy tree that will accommodate him."

Days passed before the horses could move through the drifted snow. After being confined in the stinking barn, Vennoy was more than ready to head south. He'd had his share of chasing after Childers. Ready to chuck it in for good he saddled up and followed Peavy to the nearest town where he could buy supplies before heading home.

A man wearing a badge stood in the middle of the snow-muddied street. Reining his horse to a halt, Vennoy dismounted, stomped crusted snow off his boots, and squinted at the local law, whose name he didn't even know. "Deputy Marshal Vennoy, sheriff. What in thunder's gone on here? Looks like a tornado hit this town."

"Might as well have been. That wild ass Childers and his bunch tore it up bad, ripped it apart. Everyone was hid out waiting for the storm to subside, but it didn't stop them. They raided several homes, killed whoever got in their way, committed unspeakable acts to some of our women. Stole stuff from the stores, broke windows, and lit out." He scrubbed at his mussed hair, tears shimmering in his eyes.

Vennoy whipped his hat against his thigh. "Bastard. I've done run him all over Kansas once only to have him turned loose again. Makes me want to shoot 'em all down and have done with it. Damnation."

The sheriff stood in the center of the churned-up street, cut by horse's hooves and wagon wheels, breath puffing steam into the cold air. "I got no deputies to go after 'em. Near as we could tell by prints they headed southeast back to Indian Territory. But they hurt this town. The folks in it and all they held dear. You two Marshals needs to go after 'em before locals destroy all the tracks. You may could catch up with 'em or at least go the way they went."

He scratched up under his hat. "I gotta go see to storing the bodies till we can dig in this here frozen ground and bury 'em. Them butchers ought to be hung up by their toes and beat to death, is what I think. You got my best wishes, but I have to stay here and care for my folks."

"Hell, I was ready to head back to God's country, but this sumbitch done it now. He destroyed another town, and I've had it with him. He's gonna keep at it till someone stops him. Reckon it'll have to be the two of us. Makes me madder than a tore-down hornet's nest. Peavy, you ready to go on, I am too. Be danged if I'll see my name put down as the marshal who let this evil Childers and his gang go free. Meaner they are, meaner I git. Let's see what they got left in the mercantile, refill our supplies, and head out. A gang that size won't be hard to follow in this snow once we get clear of town."

Peavy slapped him on the shoulder, sending him stumbling. "I was afraid you was about ready to quit. But if you're up for more of the same, count me in."

The sheriff pointed toward the store front with broken windows. "Take whatever you need from in there, and I wish you the best in running down the most of 'em."

Vennoy nodded. He had never been a coward, not in the war and not now. He'd not ride away from this and shame the family and the badge he wore. "We'll be grateful, and we'll be on our way."

After gathering what few supplies were left in the ruined mercantile, Vennoy followed the new-cut tracks out of town. Without speaking at all, he wrapped a muffler around his nose and mouth and huddled deep into a blanket to escape the ball-freezing temperatures and winds that cut through his coat. Ay God he'd not quit.

Whatever Peavy thought, he kept to himself. Mouths wrapped in mufflers made it hard to share words but surely the man felt the same.

The trail of destruction left by this gang finally led to the river. The ferrymen claimed not to have seen any of 'em. Probably were bribed or threatened, so they went on to Fort Smith.

"We can restock and ride out again if you're up to it."

Peavy agreed. "I ain't stopping now."

Near the court house, the sound of hammers on wood echoed through the afternoon air that had cleared enough to unwrap their ears and faces.

Taking off the muffler, Vennoy stood in his stirrups and peered toward the side yard of the stone building. Removed his battered hat and twirled it in the air with a loud wahoo.

Peavy came up behind him and hollered. "What the hell's got into you?"

"I'll be damned if they ain't actually building the gallows. I'll see that sum bitch Childers sets foot on it if I have to drag him up there step by step. Let's go celebrate and have a brew before we hit the road again."

His companion kept silent for a few minutes, and Vennoy found nothing to say either. At the mercantile, Peavy finally spoke his piece, dismounted, and tied his horse. "Don't see we got much to celebrate. Probably ought to wait till we catch him."

Vennoy slapped him on the shoulder. "We're gonna catch him, and this time they'll hang him."

While they reloaded the pack mule, Peavey gestured toward the Broken Spur. "Before we leave, let's have one last mug of ale. It'll be a long time before we see another watering hole or a red head as purty as the one in there."

Vennoy itched to get underway, but he liked to keep his partner happy, so he agreed. "Okay, a quick one."

Inside, the pretty gal his partner had mentioned brought beer to their table. Peavy wrapped an arm around her waist. Hand going under his coat she kissed him on the forehead. "Is that a badge? You a marshal?"

Peavy glanced around. "Uh, yep. Why?"

"You looking for that Childers?"

Vennoy shot her a sharp glance, lowered his voice. "You know him?"

"You bet I do. He comes in here sometimes."

"I'll be damned. We've run him all over the territory, and he's been here?"

"He's holed up in the territory. Sneaks in after everyone's gone to bed. The whole dang gang comes with him. He wouldn't come in if he knew you two were here. He's real cautious."

Peavey ran a finger over his beer mug. "And why are you telling us this?"

"Cause, he mistreats the girls, and I don't like it. Next time he comes in, I could let you know somehow if you'd promise to put him in jail for good. That's what he needs. Him and that whole bunch."

George Maledon (1830–1911), Judge Parker's hangman, reportedly carried out as many as 81 executions, making him one of the most prolific in 19th-century America.

Peavy glanced at Vennoy. "We could hang around town till he shows up. Keep it quiet. What do you think?"

"Better than running all over the country looking for him." He turned to the girl. "I've got ten green backs right here in my pocket you could have if you'd get us next time he shows up." He didn't dare tell her he couldn't promise keeping the man in jail or hanging him.

Her eyes popped. "Show me."

With a thumb and forefinger, he slipped a corner of the bills out. "Can you do it? I don't want you hurt."

She leaned down to look. "I can indeed. But how do I let you know when he's with me?"

He hitched a thumb toward Peavy. Either him or me will be back yonder in the dark corner from now till you can do it. How often does he usually come in?"

"Ever few nights. Always late. Stays till near dawn. Been a while. Wouldn't surprise me if he don't come in tonight or tomorrow."

"You up for this, Peavy? I'll stand first watch."

"If it'll save us another trail ride, danged right I am."

The girl fixed her gaze upon Vennoy. "Wait, how do I know—"

He slipped a few bills out. "Give you these to get him back there in your arms. You can have the rest of them when we haul him out."

"Sometimes there's rewards for outlaws. I've seen posters." She patted Peavy's cheek and stuffed the money between her breasts.

He exchanged a fast look with Peavy, then nodded. "If there's a reward and you deliver, you'll get it. We deputies don't get the rewards, but I'll see you get it if we haul that sumbitch in."

Hand still patting she looked into Peavy's eyes. "I get him in my crib you'll make sure and see to it too?"

"Course I will." He grinned at Vennoy. "We wouldn't lie to a purty gal like you. Get us a table back in that dark corner right now and let's see if we can get this done and over with. Maybe then you and me could curl up in your crib for true."

"Only if you pay me for it." She laughed and kissed his lips. "I'll signal you."

Soon both men were seated at a table invisible to anyone entering, and she went back to tending to customers.

Sometime later Vennoy immediately recognized Childers, who sneaked in like a rat, some of his gang with him. "Let's git 'em all. You go with the gal when she takes him to her crib. I'll handle the rest of them out here."

"I'll have him and give you a hand to boot." Peavy watched the gal lead his prey into the back and followed.

Vennoy gave them a minute or two, then sidled to the table where the remainder of the pack sat. He pulled his gun and rounded them up. "I'm ready to shoot the first one that makes a wrong move or opens his mouth."

The nearest one, whose back was to him, whirled and raised one hand. Glad for an excuse he shot him, moved to warn the others. "Guns on the table or you're next."

Peavy came through the crowd shoving the cursing outlaw Childers ahead of him. "Took him right out of her arms the minute you fired a shot. Perfect timing."

Vennoy laughed. "It sure as hell was."

BEYOND THE BADGE

Childers had, indeed, been in the arms of that redhead when he was captured. The beginning of the second week of the first term of Federal court ever held in Fort Smith, the grand jury returned eleven true bills of indictment, naming sixteen persons charged with various crimes. John Childers was at the foot of the list. He was arraigned on Thursday, May 18 of 1871. The trial lasted from November 6th until the 18th before he was judged to be guilty of murder. He was kept confined in the garrison dungeon in the shadow of the new gallows until May 19, 1873, when he was sentenced to be hanged. On August 15, the gallows, still smelling of fresh cut lumber, served its first duty and saw Childers hanged from the neck.

It would be two years before Judge Isaac Parker sat on the bench and sentenced the first lawbreakers to hang.

Bass Reeves, the most famous of the Black deputy U.S. marshals who served the federal court of Judge Isaac C. Parker.

PREACHER, SLAVE, DEPUTY: SAMUEL WALTERS

WHO'D EVER THOUGHT walking all the time could make a fellers feet feel like they had a headache? And he was still in the land of his enslavement. It had rained all day but that felt fine since it drove away some of the heat. Darkness cleared the cloudy sky and sparkled with so many stars long fingers of timber reached out to touch them.

It was time to end the day on the bank of the singing water. Settling in the bed of soft sands sheltered beneath spreading trees he knew no enemy nor feared nothing. The river whispered its secrets, and he paused to listen before tamping his long-stemmed pipe with fragrant tobacco. Nearby, a herd of white-tailed deer watered, their soft grunts announcing their presence, sharp hooves clicking in the rocks. The smoke from his pipe drifted into the starlit silence.

Lordy, here he was free and not sure what to do with the feelings. Once he worked in the big house for Mister Jim and slept next to Maisy on a corn shuck mattress. Next he knew, he was kicked out and told he was no longer a slave. The war was over, and he had no place to live. For months he and his people wandered wondering what to do, where to go. He spent some time in the Choctaw Strip where some of his fellow slaves settled with their kin. But he had no kin 'cept Mister Jim Davis. A white man. And Maisy who left with her Choctaw owner.

Where was he to go? One thing for sure. He was tired of wandering. Of looking. Of watching the years move on and nothing to pay for being free. There had to be a place for him. He asked the Lord about it but so far no answer. He'd keep looking. Everyone was created for some reason. Far as he knew, his had been to serve Mister Jim.

While he pondered the answers sleep crept over his slumped shoulders.

The morning sun filtered dancing shadows through overhead leaves to surprise him awake. Without a fire or breakfast, he packed up and headed down toward the river. Off to his left a string of jade mountains rolled away toward the east to frame a wide green valley. Compared to the stark Indian Territory this was lush country.

Here he belonged, here he would remain. He missed the others. Shanda, Marlee, Dellon, all friends, now scattered to the wind. He would likely never see them again. The end of the war brought a new cruelty to the Choctaw Nation whose skins were black and red.

At the edge of the river, ferrymen with small boats carried passengers across the muddy water. The few coins in his pocket should be enough to see him through till he could find work. A big strong man like himself could always be useful to the white people coming here.

The dirt road into Fort Smith opened into a busy, noisy town. Along the docks, Blacks toiled loading bales of cotton onboard flat boats that slithered away to other ports. Red, black, yellow, and white men carried out their jobs, some laborers, others in charge of crews. White families with expressions of despair stepped delicately from boats and looked around as if lost.

Here he could get work. Because Mister Jim had taught him to read and write he would be fine. He was young and strong, and loved the Lord. This would stand him in good stead.

Raising his head, breathing in the odor of water and fish and burning fuel of the boats, he picked up his pace. Ahead a large man with a peg leg helped a youngster load boxes from a huge stack into a wagon. The two sweated and strained to handle the weight.

Sam stopped, set down his small pack, and approached. The man, being white, naturally intimidated him, but his owner had taught him much about dealing with the white man. He removed his hat and held it in both hands over his chest.

"Excuse me, sir. Name's Sam, and I would be pleased to help with that. I am strong and could use some work."

The man stopped, turned, and wiped his forehead with a red bandana. "Got no money to pay you."

The boy stumbled, dropped one side of his load to the dock. Sam bent and picked up a corner and swung it easily onto the wagon. "Got anything to eat?"

The kid tugged on the man's shirt tail. "Ma's making supper."

"Hush, boy. We don't know this man."

Sam picked up another of the boxes and swung it onto the wagon, turned to get one more. "It is fine. Perhaps you could just give me a biscuit or two from supper to carry off with my pack in return for me helping. I am from over in the Choctaw Nation, came looking for work and a place to settle down. I could work cheap, sleep in a barn, and bend my back all day long. You look like you could use someone like me."

"Go on, boy. I said I can't use you. Can't pay no hand. Specially no damned black Indian."

"Pa, please."

The man's big hand struck out, knocking the kid flat. "Shut up, now, and get back to work. And you." He faced down Sam. "Go talk to one of them nigah's yonder. They got work for the likes of you. I ain't got time to mess with you. Got a load to carry to Van Buren before nightfall."

Lordy, if this man didn't need help. Sam dropped to his knees and lifted the crying boy up. "No call for hitting the boy, sir. Hit me if the good Lord declares it necessary. I caused the problem."

The man whirled on the wooden peg, eyes wide with surprise. "Well, listen to that educated speechifying. Where you brought up, boy? Who taught you about my Lord and Savior?"

"Mine too, sir. Mine too. I would reckon you would know that seeing as how you know him."

The man's face crumpled, and he dropped to his seat on the stack of crates. With one big hand, the same one that had toppled the kid, he wiped his face in shame. "Indeed he is. I'm plumb sorry. It's been a long, hot, hard day. I'm not always this ornery. I tell you what. If you'll forgive me my trespass, I'll give you this here job." He smiled again. "Not that I'm doing you a favor, but if you'll give us a hand taking this load over to Van Buren, I'll carry you out to my place for a good meal and a spot to lay your head for the night. That's all I can offer. But you have to promise not to scalp us in our sleep." The man offered a weak grin as if half believing the possibility.

Sam chuckled, knowing a good joke when he heard one. "I believe I can make you that promise. I have not took a scalp in so long I am broke of the habit."

The big man laughed and limped over to the boy, pulling him to his feet. "Sorry, boy. I lose my temper too often here lately. Let's get this done, with Sam here's help it won't take long, then we'll scoot on home so we can partake of some of your Ma's good taters and gravy."

He turned to Sam, held out a hand. "Name's Thomas Smith, and this here's my bo,y Lucas."

Sam took the hand. "Glad to meet you, sir. I thank you for your kindness." He turned to Lucas. "Good to meet you too."

That night, hands and faces scrubbed clean at the yard well, and seated at the table together, Sam offered to say grace for the meal and the new friends.

"Dear Lord, we give our most humble and awesome wonder for your gifts of love. How great thou art. Thank you for new friends. Amen."

For a moment Thomas stared at Sam, making him most nervous. He finally lay down the fork he had picked up after the amen. "Have I offended you, sir?"

Thomas shook his head. "No, of course not. You are truly a man of the Lord, Sam."

"Most humbly so, sir. Are not we all?"

Thomas shook his head. "Not so that every man admits it or acts it. We could use a man like you in our community. Would you consider holding services in the name of our Lord, just to see if we and you are a fit? I believe we would be. We're in sore need."

And they were. It was not something Sam would have expected or believed, but he was soon embraced by the small community on the outskirts of Van Buren, Arkansas. There was a small log church where he could hold services and a somewhat rundown house offered a roof over his head.

One night after he'd been in the community several months a large black man drifted into the church while the group sang hymns. The man slid down the wall to sit cross-legged on the floor and listen until they began to sing Amazing Grace. The visitor raised his head and sang with such gusto in a beautiful tenor voice that the rest of the singers including Sam quieted to listen.

When the song finished, there was a long moment when no one moved or spoke. Finally, Sam rose from where he sat at the front of the room. Did he dare praise the man or thank him? It might embarrass him, but perhaps he could simply invite him to return.

"We have a new visitor this morning. Welcome, sir. Everyone introduce yourselves to our friend with the angel's voice."

Before anyone could approach him the man slipped out the door and was mounting a beautiful white horse before Sam could catch up.

He shouted to halt him. "Sir, if you do not mind, my name is Sam. Who would you be?"

"It's not important. I hope I did not interfere with your services. The songs,

I heard them riding by, and it sounded so wonderful out here in the wilderness to hear such beauty. I must be on my way."

"Could you at least offer your name, sir?"

The big man smiled, reached down with one hand. "Name's Reeves, boy. Bass Reeves. Sorry for being impolite. Thanks for making me welcome."

"You are welcome. Please do come back any time you would like. You have a voice straight from the angels."

The man laughed heartily. "I would wish that to go from your mouth to God's ear, sir. I could use the blessing." With that, he urged the white animal forward and was gone, riding so fast the animal's hooves kicked up clods in his wake.

The following Sunday morning Sam kept an eye out for the return of the big black man who so intrigued him, but he never came. After a few weeks, he lost hope he would ever see him again. He obviously didn't live nearby or he would have run across him in the small town grocery or riding that magnificent white horse along the road or up and down the town street.

It was almost winter when he saw him again, in such an unusual and frightening situation he could scarcely believe he eyes or ears.

Sam rode one of the mules his congregation loaned him when he needed to go to town and happened to be in Fort Smith, not a place he frequented often. He rode past the Federal Building and the big man called Reeves rode by on his white stallion, leading another horse with a man on it. He dismounted almost before the animal drew up, dragged the man off into the dirt in as vicious an act as Sam could imagine. Arms tied behind him, the man was obviously a prisoner and in bad shape. Reeves, who had sung so beautifully in his church, pushed his prisoner stumbling up the walkway and into the door of the jail entrance.

Astounded, Sam dismounted, tied his animal and followed them inside. He'd heard of what went on here, had been curious, but had not the courage to ask more. It was told that to the west, Indian Territory was filled with the wickedest of men performing the cruelest and most vicious acts daily to their fellow humans. Hard for Sam to imagine men so vicious. Yet hadn't he just seen it in Reeves, the man who sang like an angel?

According to talk, a young judge had come to town and hired a bunch of new deputy marshals to put a stop to such actions. Was Reeves like the men hired to handle those who committed such acts? Unbelievable. Yet someone needed to stop what he had heard was happening to people who came up against those brutal monsters.

Inside where Reeves had disappeared with his prisoner fliers hung on the wall, they announced such men as were wanted for cruelty. With pictures and drawings of some of the worst. He took one, not sure why, but the Lord always guided him. He went back outside where a bench sat, settled on it, and read the invitation from Judge Isaac C. Parker to men ready to serve their country by helping cleanup evil in Indian Territory. He had to talk to this fellow who must be involved in this effort. It was time he did more than preaching to a small roomful of people. Reeves looked like a man who could fill him in on the real story, make sure he knew what was truly going on. But did he really want to wander into such a dreadful world?

His people were often told one thing while the truth was another. This judge was supposed to take law into the Territory with his Marshals and Deputies. A frightening excitement built in him as he considered being a part of such an effort. He could speak Native American dialects so perhaps he could help settle disputes in peaceful ways. Being black would not hinder him since Reeves was black. It was time he did something for mankind.

BEYOND THE BADGE

After the Civil War, Sam married Lucinda Quesenbery from Missouri and had a family in Van Buren, Arkansas. Being able to read and write, Walters became known in the Crawford County community and emerged as a leader, serving as a Minister of the Gospel in his NW Arkansas home. He frequented the Choctaw Nation, however, a land to which he had become accustomed.

By the late 1870s, he was one of several Blacks hired to work out of Judge Isaac C. Parker's court. He was bilingual and served both the Choctaw and Chickasaw Nations. More than once he helped settle disputes between the Native Americans and the Whites in peaceful ways.

In the early 1880s, Samuel Walters had his own personal case that was heard in the Fort Smith court. He was bringing a criminal from the State of Texas who had several warrants for his arrest. He stopped along his route back to Fort Smith, at the Little River courthouse and jail. The prisoner, James Campbell, was housed in the Little River, Arkansas, jail and managed somehow to escape. Samuel Walters was accused of having accepted a bribery allowing the prisoner to escape. Walters fought this case vehemently. For the next two-to-three years, he spent time defending his case held at the Fort Smith court. The final outcome is still being researched.

One of his defenders referred to Samuel as having been an honest man, and an extremely professional Deputy U.S. Marshal of high integrity and honesty.

THE TRAGIC TENDERFOOT: JOSEPH WILSON

AT JUST TWENTY-FOUR, Joseph Wilson served under Marshal Thomas B. Needles, U.S. Marshal for Indian Territory in Muscogee, Oklahoma.

Riding along the pleasant trail out of Tahlequah was enjoyable enough to make Joseph forget his job now and again. But not for long. His warrant called for hauling in a young Cherokee, name of Sam Hickory, who'd been on the run for three months. It was high time he was drug before Judge Parker and made to pay for his crimes. Conveying whiskey into Indian Territory wasn't a hanging offense, but it was serious, and it was breaking the law.

Joe Wilson did not abide seeing the law broken.

His favorite pastime anytime was running down lawbreakers. He was made for it and proud of it.

Today he searched for a place belonging to Big Alek Stop, an uncle of his fugitive. There he might find Sam Hickory. The man had been wanted for a while, and it was time Joseph laid hands on him. It was a beautiful day for doing just that. In fact, leaning back in the saddle he was downright pleased to ride loose and carefree. If he had his way, he'd do this the rest of his life. Nothing like being a lawman and disposing of killers and thieves.

Sam Hickory lived off and on with Big Alek Stop. Their farm was supposed to be about ten miles out of town on Fourteen Mile Creek, but for some reason he continued to either miss the turn or the place itself. Probably well hid. These sort seldom hung their names out for all to see.

John Carey's place was right ahead, so he rode up there first to see if he could direct him.

John was chopping wood and stood to watch him approach. A short-legged man with the stout build of a Cherokee, he was friendly with the deputies in the area, as were most of the Cherokee in the territory. Unless they were outlaws, of course. And that was a different matter. Most of these no-account, dirty outlaws were white men, but not Hickory, the one he pursued today.

The man he approached this moment welcomed him with a grin. "Get down. I'll fetch us some iced tea. Who you chasing this morning on such a pretty day? Or are you just out for a ride?"

"I thank you, but I'd better be on my way. I've spent half a day searching for this fella and hoped you could show or tell me how to get to his place. I'll not say you did."

Carey brushed at his sandy hair. "Ah, whose been up to no good lately?"

"You know Sam Hickory?"

John hauled off and buried the axe deep into a chunk of wood with a popping noise that made Joseph jump. "Damn right I know him. He's not a good Cherokee or a good man."

Joseph chuckled. "He's not a good *anything* I expect, and I'm planning on taking him in today, one way or another."

"Well I'd advise you to take care. He's meaner than a bear with a toothache. And he lives here and there but stays with his uncle. I can show you the way, but I am not going near that sumbitch. He is a mean fella."

"No need, just direct me to his place. I'll do the rest. I'm not much afraid of any sort of sumbitch, mean or otherwise."

"Then you'd best watch him close. He's liable to fool you with his tricks. Hope you are taking him off to visit Judge Parker. What's he been up to now?"

It was best not to jaw too much about lawbreakers so Joseph shrugged.

"Aw, just this and that. Enough to see him get some time behind bars. I've got a warrant for his arrest. He's been on the run for six months. Time someone took him in. So, if you could just point me the way, soon as I have him, I'll fire one shot in the air, and you'll know it's safe. That he's tied up good. Just direct me, and stay away. I'm not afraid of dangerous fellas or any other kind. He'll come with me or be left on the ground in a pool of his own blood. I don't tolerate any foolishness."

"I'd give a greenback dollar to see that, and believe I will soon as you fire that shot. Now I mean it, he's a bad one. He may be a kid, but danger rides with that boy."

Joseph smiled. "I'm a bad one too, John. That's for sure."

"I aim to follow you and keep watch from a distance. If he kills you, the other marshals will want to know." John fetched his horse, saddled him, and rode out slowly. He reined in after traveling up the creek bank less than a mile and pointed at Joseph's destination.

"His place is just yonder, through those alders. You'll be right up on it fore it's visible. He keeps a good hideout. This is far enough for me. I don't want to get mixed up with this fool. Heard he peeled a fella's scalp off for back talking him once."

"He ain't getting that close to me. Never fear that. You wait here." Joseph slipped his six shooter from its holster. "When I have this yahoo, I'll fire into the air, and you can come on out. If he's not there, I'll check with his neighbor on the other side, see if he knows where he is."

John leaned across the gap between horses. "I will come when you fire your gun or if time passes and you don't. And Joseph, please be careful."

"This is my job, John. Stay back. When it's over, meet me at Brown Prairie, and you'll see him hogtied."

John waved and chuckled bitterly. "I'll do that for sure I want to see this one bound and gagged."

Passing a growth of trees, Joseph rode into the open and into view of a man plowing behind a team of horses. No place in sight. This must be Hickory—or his uncle. Without hesitation Joseph rode out across the field, jumped from the saddle, and faced the man, gun drawn.

The man dropped the leather reins and made to pull a six-shooter strapped to his waist.

"Do it, and you're dead, Hickory. Deputy U.S. Marshal and I'll shoot you where you stand you draw that gun. Pull it easy and toss it down in the dirt. Do it now. You're under arrest."

"Okay, okay. I ain't shooting at no marshal. But you're mistaken, I ain't the Hickory you want. Name's Big Aleck." He slid the gun from its holster and dropped it on the ground.

"Unhitch those horses and let's go get one saddled. Less you can direct me to that no good nephew of yours I'm taking you in."

"Fer what, dadblame it? I'm just plowing my field, not doing nothing."

"If you don't tell me where Sam is, then you're breaking the law."

The old man went to work unhitching the mule, grumbling loud enough for Joseph to hear him. But he made no move to fight.

All remained peaceful most of the way to the house that came in view beyond a thick growth of trees and beneath a decline. The man was old, stumbling down old, and he tripped on the bottom step of the porch. Joseph lurched forward to catch him and his gun went off. Fool that he was, he'd thumbed back the hammer for good measure. Someone inside the cabin fired back. Rifle at the ready, John rode down the hill at the same time a woman burst out the door screaming. He fired, the woman knocked the old man aside, then shoved Joseph away. Pushed into a stumble, Joseph hesitated before he was able to fire again. A gun battle ensued, and he ducked his way through the door where another bullet slammed through his middle, sucking the life right out of him.

He clawed air and the light spilled away from him in great, sharp flashes. John shouted his name once like an echo in a deep, dark cave.

BEYOND THE BADGE

Hickory was able to dispose of the deputy's body with the help of a neighbor, but it was found under a steep bluff by a searching party three days later. John fled, and later told people he heard gunfire but, fearing Hickory, had stayed away. He never came forward to testify. After three trials, Hickory was found guilty of manslaughter, claiming the Deputy Marshal had fired on him first. After serving five years in the jail at Fort Smith, he was sentenced to five more in the penitentiary in Columbus, Ohio. This case is one of many that proves Judge Isaac Parker did not always hang defendants, even when they were guilty of murder.

THE LADIES: S.M. BURCHE & MAMIE FOSSETT

1898

FROM THE TIME she could read, Sara preferred being called S.M., and let it be known often. Her brothers quickly shortened it to Sam and there it remained.

Though she secretly liked the nickname, the choice annoyed Ma to no end. "You should hang on to the name I give you, girl." S.M. just grinned, like she did a lot around Ma, for who would want to start a fight with the woman who birthed you? Keeping important thoughts to herself was most important to her. But there came a day when her own ideas took over.

Sitting at the kitchen window, legs hugging the buttermilk jar, the churn became her mount and Sam hunched astride her brother August's fine green broke stud bucking about in the corral. She ought to just jump up, butter be damned, and run out the door to freedom. It was again time for fall roundup, once more a time for her to be left behind while the boys brought the cattle herd to home pastures for the winter.

Washing clothes and hanging them outside, she watched the crew brand the spring and summer calves and break the mustangs yet one more time. Without her. Being a girl was like eating clay. And she would wait no longer to declare her freedom. Desperate she appealed to her youngest brother for help.

Out of sight of the house August taught her how to break a green mustang, and her heart embraced every moment. Approaching the jumpy young horse. Touching the soft nose. Speaking in an undertone that reassured the nervous wildness that connected to her own. And finally, when day after day of reassurance passed, they were one and the same, her easing onto the trembling back. Riding high in the air, all but tossed clear of earth's bonds. To land with a jar, to climb back on and do it again. Outdoor freedom was the life she deserved above all else. And eventually she would get away from Ma's apron strings and be on her own. And when she did, better watch out.

One day her younger brother Nate and older brother August returned from a Saturday trip to town with Ma and Pa, where she had helped Ma search for embroidery thread till the world looked like rainbows. Pink was pink and blue was blue, but not when it came to finding threads for Ma's sewing projects. Oh, and all those needles, some too small, medium, or large, none quite suitable. At home, evening after evening, pricking her fingers to help decorate more pillow cases. The rest of her life headed in the same direction.

On the way out of the mercantile, she'd grabbed a paper off a table that told about homesteading down in Oklahoma. All the way home, bouncing along in the wagon, she read how couples could claim so much land and prove it up. Riding along, the Kansas wind all but sweeping her from the wagon and out across the prairie, she steadied the jittering page. Nowhere did it say couples had to be married, or even had to be a man and a woman. Why couldn't two women do the same?

This was what she wanted. A place of her own. And she'd need herself a partner. To do something like that alone wasn't practical. Two could help each other. But a man? She shook her head in thought. Men expected the woman to obey their commands, to cook and sew and clean and have babies. Nope. A woman? Perhaps, but did she know one looking for the same life? Too many were little weaklings. Both had to be tough. Had to free themselves from the traditional woman's role. She already fit that bill, but did she know another woman who did?

At home, late that night, tucked in bed under the rafters of their bedroom, she told her younger brother of her secret wish.

"I'd be your partner." Nate's eyes glimmered in moonlight coming through the peak window.

"Oh, that's sweet, but Pa needs you here. He's getting old, and you and August will take over the ranch. Together you can own half of Kansas the way things are going with the cattle trade."

"Why can't you do it with us? You're family." His voice broke from high to low. At fourteen, he would soon be a man, and Ma and Pa would be so happy to see him step into partnership with them and August. If only she weren't a girl, her life would be the same. But she was, and it wouldn't. Curse whoever wrote such stupid rules. She would have to carve out her own space. It would mean leaving home and Ma and Pa. That would be hard but not so hard as the alternative. She had graduated eighth grade two years ago. Time to move on.

It wasn't fair being born to wear dresses in a life that carried so many dumb rules. Every fall it was the same. For the past two years, she begged to go on the cattle drive for months before it began. The answer was always no. Ma said it wasn't proper for a young lady to sit around a campfire in the dark with young men and then sleep out in the open with them every night.

"You just never know what they'd be thinking of you."

No more. Enough was enough. Ma already spent time every Sunday at church checking out the boys grown into men she'd watched since they were small. Looking for a husband for her only daughter. And her only sixteen. Frantic, Sam shared her feelings with her best friend, Mamie, in hoarse whispers while they sat in pews in the back of the holy gathering place.

"I can't figure why my youngest brother, just turned fourteen, gets to go along on the cattle drive and I, who am a whole two years older than him, have to stay home. Ma claims it's not my age but that I'm a girl. And that reminded her it was time I looked to charming me a young man."

Mamie admitted to having problems too. "It's worse at my house. Ma does nothing but urge me to start walking out with that goofy Martin Groomsby, all but has us jumping the pole."

Sam gazed at her friend. "I thought you were happy to marry Martin. He's going on the Oklahoma Land Rush, I hear."

"Starting from scratch. Living in a soddie. I'm not crazy about the idea one little bit. If I'm not careful, it'll be his and Ma's eighteenth birthday present to me. I'm sick of it."

Sam giggled. "Why didn't you tell me this? If we're old enough to marry or worry about that sex stuff we're not even allowed to talk about, we ought to be able to decide what we want to do with our lives."

Mamie dug an elbow in her friend's ribs. "And marrying some man ain't it."

Sam tried to hide her laughter with a loud hiccup. "That's the truth. You see in the paper at the mercantile yesterday how they're urging men to homestead land in western Oklahoma? I don't see why women can't do the same. We could go together, get our own place so we can do what we please.

Mamie stared at Sam. "Pa mentioned it. But just women? What a great idea." She grabbed Sam's arm, shook it. "Let's do it. Together, just you and me."

Too bad it wasn't as easy for Sam to make such a decision. Oh, how bad she wanted to do just that. But actually plan it? Go through with it? Face Ma and Pa with it? Speechless she watched women parade down the aisle while church broke up. Some of them cast dirty glances at her and Mamie. No doubt their discussion had disrupted the prayers and singing.

"But wouldn't it take lots of money?" Sam smiled at Ma who frowned and tromped on down the aisle. Dang, she was in for it when they got home. Whispering in church was forbidden.

"Naw, Pa said the land is free. He's talking about sending August and Uncle Jim down to claim some. Said you just have to prove up, whatever that means." Mamie rose, took Sam's hand, and pulled her through the throng of gossiping women to sit under a nearby shade tree. "Where is Oklahoma, anyway?"

"You're serious. Aren't you?" Her insides trembled with excitement. Homesteading sounded exciting to Sam, especially with Mamie, who seemed ready to get moving.

Sam could hardly sit still. "Let's figure out how far it is over there to Oklahoma, what we need to take, and plan on heading out come spring. I swear I can't needlepoint for another year." Could she do it? Would she really have the courage to leave home?

"I'm going to enter it in my diary, and we can start working on it." Mamie squeezed her hand so hard her fingers popped. Could this really happen?

THE FOLLOWING SPRING, Mamie, sitting high in a beat up farm wagon with canvas covering, and Sam, riding a green-broke mustang August had given her, rode out with all they owned stacked in the back. A cow and calf from Pa tread along behind. The wagon carried each item as listed in Mamie's diary.

Two large trunks held their clothes, most sewn that winter from flour sacks, plus each had borrowed a pair of britches and man's shirt and long handles from their brothers for the outdoor work they would have to do. Besides handmade quilts, they had horse blankets, tinware they'd traded off a peddler riding through town, a ham from Mamie's family's smokehouse and potatoes from Mamie's folks' garden, and a cage with four chickens and a rooster inside. Mamie's dead grandmother's rocking chair was roped inside the bed.

Sam's younger brother, Nate, gave her his jack knife. "For cleaning rabbits on the trail," he told her. Swore to Pa he lost his and got a new one for Christmas that year. Mamie's eldest brother gave her a shiny sharpened axe. "To cut wood for your fires." He grinned. "Ought to get practicing on that."

Guns had been a bit harder to come by. But Mamie laughed and said there was a boy named Martin who was missing an old single-shot Winchester he'd given her for promises made that surely wouldn't be kept. Sam did a bit better with arms. Her grandpa had been in the Army and let her have his Navy Colt. Hadn't been shot since the war, but he'd cleaned it every month, and it was fit to use.

"But don't you go and shoot no one with it, or I'll come back to haunt you." The kind old man grinned and ruffled her hair, for all he'd wanted to do with guns when he got home from the Civil War was absolutely nothing.

The girls left behind sobbing Maws, four sisters, five brothers, and one Paw shaking his head, the other out back of the barn drinking corn liquor and muttering. "They'll be back, you wait and see."

By the time winter's snow melted across the Kansas prairie the young women entered Oklahoma in search of the homesteads being offered and shown on the map they carried. They were out of supplies and low on money, living on rabbits and squirrels they shot and cooked over a campfire. Neither of them minded one bit. In fact, they were as happy as the wild things running on the plains.

"We're going to have to get jobs for a while. It's bound to cost something first beginning our homestead." Sam, as usual, was the practical one.

"Fine, but I'd rather help build fence as to take on washing some cowboy's dirty sox."

"Look, ahead. Is that Guthrie?"

"Awful big building. Sure sticks up in the air, don't it? Windows all up and down. Nothing like that in Kansas. Oh, it's the county courthouse so maybe that explains the size. Looks sort of strange poking up out here in the middle of nowhere though, don't it?"

"No other town around on the map. Has to be Guthrie. Let's make camp yonder under those trees and ride in to see what's what."

"Good idea, my butt is hurting from the bounce of this blamed farm wagon. Next time you drive and I'll ride."

It sure enough was Guthrie and the courthouse was huge, built of brick with tons of windows. A sign in one of them on the ground floor told of homestead registering. Sam reined up out front. "Let's check on this right now." Without waiting for a reply from her friend she swung down, tied the weary mount and climbed onto the boardwalk. The sign told to go inside for homestead information. Another poster, a bit more ragged like it'd been there a while, said Deputy Marshals wanted. Sign up inside.

Grinning and pointing at each one, she reached for the heavy door. Jerked once, twice. It didn't budge. "Dang, reckon it's closed. Must be getting late. Let's go on down to that saloon. It'll be a good place to find out more about this than if we wait for morning to go in there."

Mamie laughed. "Imagine them seeing us two stride in there like we belong?"

"Too bad, cause we do belong, I don't care what they think. You see that sign about Deputy Marshals wanted?"

"Sure did. You're not thinking --?"

"Nah. Just found it interesting, that's all." Sam led her into the first smoky, noisy saloon they came to. In their brother's britches they mostly got away with looking like men, even if young ones. An old bearded fellow made room for them at the bar.

Sipping their sarsaparilla it was Mamie who came right out and asked about Deputy Marshals. Sort of surprised Sam. Soon they had plenty of information to feed their wild imaginations.

Mamie grabbed her arm. "Let's go to work as deputies and earn some money before we look for homesteads. It'll be loads of fun riding around looking for outlaws. And we'll have some money to do that proving up thing."

Sam stared at her friend in disbelief. "All this time planning to homestead, and you want to change our minds? Maybe we'll need some training or something. Women probably not even allowed. It's got to be dangerous."

"Course it could. Where's the fun if it ain't? The man inside there said just had to have a horse, a gun, and lots of gumption. That's what he said. I'm excited about this. Let's give it a try."

Sam allowed they both had plenty of gumption, so the next morning they waited outside the courthouse all set to sign up for Deputy Marshals. She'd give Mamie the satisfaction that they'd tried, then they could settle on finding a homestead. No one would hire girls to go running about chasing outlaws. No more than they'd let them break horses. Only a scrappy boy leading a dog on a leash joined the line.

"You here to sign up for Deputy Marshal? How old are you, anyway?"

Spraddle-legged. the boy faced them. "Old enough. Why you care?"

Sam dug her elbow in Mamie's ribs. "Why else would he be standing here?"

"Well, he don't exactly look like a lawman, now does he?"

The boy regarded them with a sneer. "You two the ones what doesn't look like lawmen. You'uns don't even look like men, if you'll beg my pardon."

"If you're any example of a lawman, why then, excuse me, but I reckon we're in the wrong line." Mamie was bound to keep up an argument any time she could.

"I'll get on fore the two of you do, just watch." The boy moved away from them.

After a while, a neatly dressed young man strolled from the brick building and came to stand beside the sign advertising for U.S. Marshals. He nodded at them and smiled, but said nothing.

Maybe he wasn't taking names.

After waiting a while, Mamie cleared her throat. "'Scuse me, sir. You one of these U.S. Marshals?"

He nodded in what was almost a bow. "I'm a deputy, ma'am." He went back to looking up and down the street.

"Well, when does who is doing the hiring arrive, then?"

"Didn't get that?" He leaned down as if hard of hearing.

"Why? Is the sign incorrect? We're here to hire on as deputies."

He covered his mouth with a fist.

"You're laughing. What's so funny?" Sam was quickly coming to a breaking point.

"Well, ma'am, to tell the truth, it's been a while since we had anyone of your—uh sex?—apply to be a deputy. Where did you find out we was hiring women?"

The boy and his dog got in on the discussion. "I was here first, if you're ready to hire deputies. Since I ain't neither one, what's the problem?" The dog barked and jumped about.

Mamie muttered where only Sam could hear. "Probably be hiring that noisy mutt rather than us." The deputy stared from one to the other. His question appeared to carry a threat for whoever had been telling that falsehood, but Mamie raised herself in height by an inch or two and glared up at him.

Sam quickly took her friend's arm. It wasn't a good idea to get on the bad side of Mamie. She hated to see her take this man down in the street. It wouldn't bode good for their new plan to be deputies instead of homesteaders. She had no doubt Mamie could whip this guy. She'd seen her take on two of her near-grown brothers and keep them on the ground.

Her friend struggled against her. "Could you get that mutt to shut up?"

"Shh, Mamie, they won't hire us if you whip one of their deputies in public right in front of the courthouse. It'd just be way too embarrassing for them."

The man cleared his throat. "Excuse me, you discussing her taking me on?"

Before Sam could answer, the boy stood high on his toes and stared her in the face. "He ain't a mutt." By now the dog was ready to join the fight, his four feet kicking up dust in the street.

Sure as the world Mamie could take that little snot nosed brat. And she looked about ready to wade in on him. She adjusted her wide brimmed hat, gazed at the man for a moment, then settled a glare on the boy. "He don't shut up that mutt I'm gonna shoot the both of them."

The kid's eyes bugged. Easy to see he was making up his mind whether to lay into Mamie or not. Eying her doubled fists he reconsidered and ran off down the street dragging his poor dog, who sent back noisy barks. His retreat startled a couple of horses who danced about under their riders. In turn, a wagon team decided to tangle their traces causing more disturbance in the busy street.

Sam sighed. The both of them were gonna end up in jail, sure as shooting.

Unable to contain himself, the deputy laughed. "You're the first who've wanted a job then nearly started a danged stampede. I'll go in and fetch Marshal Thompson. He'll have to come to a decision on this one. I'm standing back. He took a humorous measure of the two of them, then turned and hurried back inside.

Sam settled her friend down a bit before the marshal opened the door, a curious expression on his face. He wasn't as big as the deputy who had deserted them, but there was no doubt he could whip them both if he took a notion. He looked the two of them over with a steady harsh gaze that forced even Mamie to let out a long breath of defeat.

He stuck out a large hand. "Marshal Thompson. What might I do for you?"

Lord, she hoped they hadn't lost the job. Standing straight as she could, she stuck out her hand. "Good to meet you, sir. I'm S.M. Burche, this here's my partner Mamie Fossett. We'd like to sign up for jobs as deputy marshals."

On the last word she swallowed her fear till it almost choked her.

"And we apologize for any trouble we might've caused." Mamie's usual loud voice pronounced the words like a lady.

By the time they'd finished, Thompson was actually smiling, his bright eyes revealing humor.

He stepped out of the doorway and gestured them in. "Well, you're first in line, so step on in, and we'll talk about this."

He seated them in two chairs facing a desk. He settled on its corner, arms crossed over his chest. He had asked them in, but to Sam that didn't look too good. When Pa considered something he was going to forbid, first thing he did was hug himself sort of like that.

"We both ride and shoot and fight tough as men."

Sam wanted to smack Mamie for blurting that out.

"Oh, is that right? Where'd you two youngsters learn to do that?"

"Our brothers were mean... *are* mean, I mean, and we had to survive. And we aren't youngsters."

He nodded, smiled. "Ready to kill you, were they? Or maybe you tried to kill them first?"

"Course not, it's just that it made us tough is all."

Sam rose. Mamie was ruining everything. She was always so sure of herself, never stopped to think.

"Come on, Mamie. He's just making fun of us. They don't want to hire no women to do this job. Probably afraid we'll outdo them, is all. Come on."

The marshal rose. "Back in ninety-one, I hired a young woman feisty as the two of you. She worked with me for several years, right here. Served writs, did whatever I requested. That's what working with me requires. Man or woman, you do whatever is asked, no question." He scratched his chin. "Name of Deputy U.S. Marshal F.M. Miller. She was the first to serve in Indian Territory out of Texas if memory serves me. Did a damned fine job.

"Tell you what. You ladies look fit, and we do need deputies. Have to warn you, we've lost over a hundred men out here in the territory. It's dangerous work, but long as you understand what you're in for." He came to his feet, standing straight as an arrow. "We're going out back of this building where there's a field and some targets the fellas practice on. This'll be your first test. See if you can shoot. Fetch your guns."

THAT EVENING WHILE camped outside Guthrie, Sam relaxed next to Mamie. A fresh-killed rabbit sizzled over the fire. Sure smelled good, mingling with the aroma of burning hickory wood. Her insides clenched with excitement. Marshal Thompson's words spoke while he signed them up echoed in her ears. He presented them each with a silver badge that read Deputy U.S. Marshal inside a circle surrounded by six points.

"You will both follow my directions. When I ask you to work in the office, you will do so without complaint. When I send you out after some evil son of a bitch, you will bring him back."

He fingered the brim of his hat and tilted his head. "As you have promised, you will work in the field together, each protecting the other. Is that clear? Like I said we've lost over a hundred deputies out here in the wilds. You have to know what you're getting into." She nodded stiffly, glancing at her friend to see her doing the same.

Marshal Thompson told them their first work would be carried out in connection with an Indian Territory murder case. They were to go to the country of the Sac and Fox tribes, deep in the wilderness of the territory and bring in some unruly witnesses—an extremely difficult and dangerous task. He gave them a crude map to follow.

He helped them make arrangements for boarding their wagon and storing their other things till they might sell or settle, whichever they decided. "Y'all might need a place to live in between assignments. We can help you see to that as well."

Later in the peaceful darkness of night camp Sam hugged herself against a momentary fear. "What's the difference? Losing men or losing women? Dying is dying, no matter which we are." She drew a circle in the dust near the fire.

Mamie was silent for a while. "Well, we ain't gonna die. My goodness, we're Deputy U.S. Marshals with our first assignment. Ain't that exciting?"

Mamie lifted the stick, placed the sizzling meat on a rock between them. "You know something? I'd rather be out here doing this anytime than housekeeping. I hope we do a good job." She gazed upward. "Look at the stars. Ain't they pretty? Sure named 'em right. Stars. Such a pretty name."

"They sure are. And we will do the best job in the world. The very best." Sam held up a piece of steaming rabbit. "Are you afraid at all?"

"Of getting killed? Nope. Course not."

"That's good." Mamie appeared a bit shaky but Sam said nothing. "Tomorrow we pick up a writ for witnesses and there's no backing out. We're in this, up deep to our necks. A writ to bring in three witnesses to murder. Wild Native American witnesses who have run off and hid to keep from coming in. They're gonna be ornery and fit to be tied." Sam laughed and studied her friend's face reflected in the firelight.

Mamie groaned at the pun. "And we're just the ones to tie them."

Both laughed, for the moment feeling like schoolgirls. Off in the distance an owl hooted as if in reply. This brought on more giggles.

"The marshal said we'll be riding through some of the toughest territory anywhere in this country. The toughest. My goodness, can you believe we're getting to do this?"

"I know, it's like a dream, isn't it? Like a dream."

"But it ain't, and we can't for one second believe it is. This is real and will be hard and dangerous... and I can't wait to leave out tomorrow."

FOR NEARLY A week they kept a wide distance from residents of each village of bark houses. They didn't dare go knocking on doors and get caught by the suspicious Native Americans. Still they spotted no real suspects. Time to worry. Perhaps the men had moved on. This was one of the most dangerous areas of Indian Territory, for not only was it full of outlaws, the Sac and Fox who lived here were not fond of white men and made no bones about what they would do to anyone who bothered them. In the late 1800s, what was left of their tribe was moved into Indian Territory. The address they'd been given for those men on the writ was a joke of sorts. No one put up addresses in this wilderness. Blood ran thick on sand and trails. Every settlement meant hide and watch.

Exhausted and grimy, Sam led Mamie through another long day's pursuit crouched behind a brushy rise. She had stopped stepping forward as the natural leader, and the two traded off. The search ended at a vague gathering of bark houses deep in the wilderness territory called Blue Sauk Springs. The name was listed on one of the wanted posters. They were getting closer. Inside any of the dwellings could lurk their prey. The only way they would make sure and never be spotted was remain as still as bushes.

Near their dry camp a small gathering settled into noisy merrymaking around a huge bonfire. Raising their spears into the night sky they shouted words neither of the deputies understood. Sam pointed out symbols that made it easy to read veiled threats against an enemy. That enemy being any white man. Or woman

The long trip had finally paid off. Sure enough, their three wanted witnesses were here. There was no denying the identity of those who matched the descriptions and never seemed to alter their clothing.

Badges hidden in case they were seen or caught, Sam and Mamie appeared like anyone but women, or deputies, or even white men, their clothing and skin muddied and torn. Sooner or later they would find a way to sneak up on the three witnesses and take them down.

A weary, hungry Sam settled against the bank and muttered to her companion. "Listen, Mamie. It sounds like they're celebrating something. Maybe they'll get drunk. We ought to try to take them tonight if that's the case."

"Agreed. The three we're after are gathered yonder. See, the fire lights them up." Both studied those whose descriptions and names they had memorized from posters.

Sam pointed out Henry Breech Cloud, who wore a distinctive fur hat with a spray of stiff feathers on top and a long eagle feather to one side. His leather breeches had bead ties around the legs just below the knees.

Mamie gestured with no words, at his brothers Yellow Bird and White Peace Pipe each shaved around the ears and to the tops of their heads where blue paint adorned a brush of hair. Huge bibs of colorful beads hung around their necks and fastened at the waists. All three were easily picked out of the dozen or so celebrating in the firelight. They appeared to be drinking something that was affecting their dancing and singing.

Worrying about them wasn't as bad as was keeping an eye on a large half-naked man leaned up against a nearby tree watching and not drinking or dancing. An obvious guard. And dangerous.

"We have to take him down fast. Let's hope they're making so much noise they'll not hear us coming." Sam pointed at the giant. "The rest are going to pass out soon."

The women of the tribe had retired inside the houses. No doubt to avoid watching the men make asses of themselves. "We have to be far away by morning when they wake up sober. They'll be after us then, and they'll track fast."

"We'll get their horses first and tie 'em with ours. Scatter the rest."

Crouched on the ground making their plans, Mamie took up a stick and drew a squiggly line in a partial circle. "Member this place? We passed through it back a ways? Had to leave the trail and go higher and far out around the scattering of rocks and scrub?"

Sam nodded. Let Mamie have the lead. She was a good planner.

"I'm thinking if we let 'em trail us below that, one of us will stay back while the other hustles the three captives on through and out the other side. Up to that point they'll be hours behind us after sleeping off their drunk. Once they come to we'll be easy tracking cause of our prints in the soft ground. Can't be helped. But once we're in there we can lose 'em in the rocks."

"But they'll know we have to come out the other side. They'll just run us down."

"Not if we nab 'em first. You go on with the three prisoners, I'll ride high behind the rocks. As they follow your obvious tracks into the swale I'll pick them off from above. I'm a good shot, you know I am" With dirt on her face, Mamie looked fierce.

Sam worried some about the idea. "If it backfires, if they guess what we're up to, then we're divided, and they can easily pick us off and take back our prisoners. You'd have to make sure they didn't figure out where you were while you hit eight or nine."

Mamie shrugged. "I can do it—you know I can. But if you can come up with something better.... Why you always argue with me, Sam? We're outnumbered.

We can't just walk in and draw down on them before they react. Even drunk, three or four will get us."

Resting without a fire, they lay their heads close to discuss their plan. "I'm worried about so much shooting on the rise. It'll attract too much attention. Maybe some others are close."

Mamie sighed. "Dang, Sam. Saw no one around there for miles except this bunch. No smoke, no fires. Far as I see, they're all we have to worry about if we get to it now. Other side of the flint hills, we'll meet and head south on the Chisholm trail into Oklahoma. If there's any of them left, we can lose them there."

Sam nodded. Mamie's plan was good, and she didn't have a better one. All she hated was separating. Marshal Thompson said to take care of each other. Still it'd take them both coming at it from two ways. She finally agreed.

They lay in silence holding hands while the celebration quieted and the flare of the fire grew smaller, less bright.

"Shh, listen. They're settling down. Time to put up or shut up. Time to shoot us some Indians."

"Okay, Mamie. Time to do our best with your plan. Ready?"

They rose, crept on foot to the Native American's horses, hipshot and sleeping. Sam had ropes tied in bits on two when she spotted a guard half-asleep against a nearby tree. Unable to warn Mamie, she ducked down and guided the animals slowly away just as her friend came in sight. The guard saw her. Poised against his leaning post he raised a spear above his head. Sam dropped her rope, launched herself at his back and brought him down with a grunt. They rolled around on the ground beneath some dancing hooves. One of the horses neighed and Mamie came from out of the dust to belt the guard on the head with a chunk of wood. Scrambling beneath shifting animals, they rope-tied one more, released the rest and scattered them as best they could. Creeping in silence they hurried toward where they'd left their own mounts. If anyone heard, they made no sound.

Spitting dust and sweating, Sam touched Mamie on the arm. "Okay?"

"Yep, course. All ready to grab 'em and go?"

"Let's hunker down for a second, give the horses time to settle and go quiet. That ugly fella we want is sleeping on the edge of the campfire. The other two are drunk as can be in a pile near the woods."

Mamie nodded. "I'll get him first. You get them, and we'll take them together."

Sam wished Mamie would let her handle that big one, but there was no time to argue. Besides he wasn't much bigger than Mamie's brother, who she could put down in two fast moves. Good to hope for the best at this point.

Only vaguely conscious of the scuffling and a muffled grunt from Mamie in the background, she came upon the other two guards. Wadded bandanas kept their mouths muffled and after some struggle she took a moccasined foot to the mouth. Tasting blood she shook her head, grabbed up a rock and knocked him silly. Twisted and rolled around a bit with the other one, so drunk he could scarcely make a sound or fight back. Arms and legs tangled, her knee connected with his jaw. It popped, and he yelped like a puppy. Good thing they were drunk or she'd not have taken them both.

Sudden silence. What had happened to Mamie? What if she hadn't handled the big one?

Don't worry, do your job, let her do hers. In not too long she had their wrists bound. Still no sound. She tasted dirt and spit more blood while dragging the first one, then the other, to where they'd left the horses.

Panting she leaned against a tree till she could stop gasping for air, then turned to go in search of Mamie. What if they'd somehow caught her? But there in the brush Sam found Mamie struggling to drag the big one from the camp. Dead weight, he was more than she could handle. One of his arms flopped around and kept hanging up on twigs. Sam bent, pulled it loose, and together they dragged him the rest of the way, put their shoulders to his butt and heaved him up onto the third horse's back. All were finally roped wrists to ankles belly down.

After securing them tightly, Sam first, then Mamie, scrambled out from under the restless mounts and walked the horses along the path to where theirs waited. Both were soon underway, riding into the darkness.

"That worked pretty well. Next time we remember what a good idea it is to get 'em drunk before starting to fight 'em." Sam covered her mouth to muffle the nervous laughter that boiled from her throat.

"Yeah, good thing they thought of it, huh? Let's get away from here, one of 'em yonder is sure to wake up and rouse the camp."

"Nah, they're so drunk, it's gonna be late morning before they figure out what day it is, never mind what happened. Still, let's go slow and easy till we get out of hearing." Sam rubbed her mouth. "That damned sumbitch kicked my tooth loose."

"Why Sam, I don't believe I ever heard you use such language before."

"You should've heard me when I wrestled ole Yellow Bird down. He had a distinct odor nearly made me puke."

The all-night ride out of the rolling hills of northern Indian Territory took them into a deep crevice below a half circle natural formation of the southern Kansas hills that rose against the sky. As Sam remembered from the trip up, the lower side of the trail led steeply downward through brush, a tumble of rounded boulders and scrub oak to a wide pond. Above that a neat row of all sizes of white stones were lined up on the ground as if put there by some ancient farmer to mark his pasture. The hills, like other formations in Kansas and Oklahoma, appeared in flat country as a surprise and disappeared the same way. Small water holes or ponds dotted the lower portion, so the lowest trail was in constant mud to make tracking difficult if not impossible. For a few minutes they rested the horses and sat on a boulder above the steep decline. The sun greeted them brightly over the rise.

"They may be waking up soon. We'd better be getting out of sight. What do you think?" Mamie rubbed sweat off her face with a dusty bandana.

"That all you did was smear mud over your nose and mouth." Sam laughed, and Mamie cleaned some more. "If you can get all the way through this cut before dark tonight, I need to be up yonder picking off any followers who might be trying to track you."

"Reckon they're after us yet?"

"Oh, I'm sure they are. Okay then by you if I take the high road?"

"Yep. You need to ride on up there with your granddaddy's rifle. I saw what you did when we shot for Marshal Thompson. You go on and get settled where you've got yourself a good spot. I'll manage to lead these three through that rock and water down there. Even good trackers get lost on such trails."

Both were quiet for a while. "The marshal told us to partner up." Sam couldn't help but murmur.

"That's what we're doing. We let 'em ride hellbent for leather after us we won't make it back. You know that. About now they're coming out of their drunken stupor and realizing what has happened. We need to get on the other side of this gulley and on our way out of Sac country before they can figure it out."

Sam stared off into the shimmery distance. "Mamie, if one of us don't make it, well, then I want you to know this has been the best few weeks of my life."

"Mine too, Sam. Mine too." She rose and slapped her thighs, sending a cloud of dust flying. "But we will. We both will. You get through down there, and I'll cut those sumbitches down and meet you where the trail heads south out of Kansas. We'll ride in to Guthrie together, by God. Together. We'll show those hotshot male deputies a thing or two."

The last Sam saw of her friend was the back-lit haunch of her mount climbing the steep incline. Then she was out of sight behind a rise. Catching up the ropes of the three horses carrying the Fox witnesses, she led them down the rugged trail. It was slow going, their hooves kicking rocks that tumbled between them and made the horses nervous. Once something far above rattled, disrupted the peace, but when she stopped to study the landscape, there was nothing but morning sunlight. The trail grew steeper, the horses stumbled and snorted. They were wearing out and so was she. Did she dare stop and rest them for a while? Only a little ways to flatten out.

Surely she'd come to more water, had been hearing its flow louder and louder. Still nothing. Exhausted, she drew up in the shade of a gathering of cottonwood to take a sip from her canteen. Her eyes fluttered, and she jumped awake.

How long had she been asleep? She gazed around. The horses stood, heads hung low, sweat white from under their saddles. She had to rest them. How far had she come? How long ago had Mamie left? She shaded her eyes and peered upward at the distant circular hill. Tried to imagine Mamie up there taking down the trackers. The sun hung higher in the sky, but no one was up there. Not firing a rifle, anyway.

No one. Nothing. Of course not. Mamie would not be seen. If they were lucky, they'd be long gone before the Fox even got on their trail. They wouldn't dare follow them into Oklahoma, would they? Surely not, what with many more deputies on patrol there and now allowed to stop Native Americans on the attack.

Deep in thought, too late she heard the scatter of rocks underfoot. Her horse jerked sideways and dodged a body that flew through the air. The mustang she rode had saved them both. Still being wild and jumpy he spooked and screamed so that the Native American who leaped at her missed his target. Beneath her, the horse rose high into the air, first with a stiff four-legged buck, then reared with clawing front hoofs. She all but came off. Weight in the stirrups, knees hugged to heaving sides, she rode him through a sideways trail slide that nearly lost both of them. She hung on till he landed on stiff legs and gave up his part of the battle.

The leaping Native American tumbled aside and crunched head-first to stillness against a boulder. The other three animals took off awkwardly with their passengers bouncing about. Having no choice, she drew her Colt, shot the man, and took off to capture the in-flight prisoners. She couldn't shoot them or they wouldn't make very good witnesses, so she ran them down. The animals were so exhausted and the trail so narrow it didn't take long.

Even as all the horses drew up, snorting and stomping, a glimmer of sunlight caught her eye. Water had pooled just ahead. It was all she could do to keep the thirsty animals from stampeding knee-deep. A few minutes later she led them out to keep them from drinking too much, then together they walked to the bottom of the trail where a spring tumbled over a rocky drop into a small pond. There they drank once more before retiring to a grassy patch to snatch noisy mouthfuls with loud chomping.

Sweating and dirty she slid into the water over her head. She came up to the retort of gunfire. It startled her. With a shout she raised her hat high into the air.

Mamie and her grandfather's single shot rifle were at work.

It was time to start on through the gulley to the other side. After securing the ropes used to tie their prisoners to their horses, she checked the men to make sure they were still alive, fed them each a hatful of water which they choked down hanging upside down, then mounted the mustang and headed out.

Gunfire followed her onto the plains that cut back into Oklahoma where homesteads were being settled. Gunfire, she hoped and prayed came from that old Winchester Mamie was such a hand with. Ahead hunched a soddy a couple of mules and a half-built shack of a barn near a plowed field.

Laughing, Sam walked her entourage closer. Fearing gunfire from the settler, she reined up, tied her mustang to a newly planted fence post and headed on foot toward the house.

"Hello the house." She waved her hat, shouted again. "Hello." Arms held out away from her body and the six shooter she wore at her waist, she strolled slowly.

A boy maybe ten or twelve ran from the back door. He carried a rifle, but it wasn't pointed at her.

"Paw says hold up. He'll be right out. Told me not to shoot you less you pulled a gun. You're not gonna pull a gun, are you?"

"No, I'm not. I'm a Deputy U.S. Marshal with three prisoners. Just want to sit and rest a while, get a drink and wait for my partner."

The boy stopped, yelled loud. "Pa, it's a U.S. Marshal."

From out across the plains rode Mamie, yahooing as she came.

"That's my partner. Tell your pa so he don't shoot. Unless someone's chasing her."

The boy peered into the distance. "Ain't nobody coming after her." He took off running toward the house. A man met him, and they ran back toward Sam. Just in case, she worked her badge out.

Held it up. "Sam Burche, Deputy U.S. Marshal."

The man eyed the badge, eyed her. "Why I ain't never seen no lady marshal."

"Now you have, sir. Now you have. And there comes another one."

BEYOND THE BADGE

I set about to find tales of those deputy marshals who bravely rode as they said, hellbent for leather into the jaws of death to fight for good. As always, more ink was used to tell the stories written for history of outlaws who wreaked havoc and fear over Indian Territory than was used to write about those who fought to uphold law in the vast lawless land.

Dates, names, and places are real. So are the tales of these courageous men and women who fought to clean up the west. At times trying to find stories of these heroic deputy marshals was difficult if not impossible. In putting together this story, I told everything that these fearless women were known to have done plus knitting the stories together with what wasn't known but most surely had to happen for them to have survived.

I found no more about Ada or F. M. French, or of S.M. Burche or Mamie Fossett after their adventures written here—not even photos. They appeared to fade into history, often with no more mention after fighting to help tame the West. As an author, I exaggerated where I could not find what happened next, only guessing how they must have survived in a wild west we can only imagine, or making up what they thought. But the truth remains, they carried out these adventures with pluck and bravery.

JUST AN ORDINARY DAY: JACE PERKINS

LED BY ONE of McDougal's hands, Deputy Jace Perkins found the agitated ranch boss waiting for him. Zach McDougal was a tall, lean man, who at the moment appeared much larger than he was, as if he had risen like dough in a pan.

"I tell you, Deputy, it was four of'em. I woulda run 'em all down, but they headed out in all directions like a startled herd. Time I got to what they was up to, it was too late." The irate red haired rancher whipped his horse gently with his reins and led Deputy Perkins, known as Perk to one and all, across the pasture to a downed steer.

Perk rose in his stirrups when McDougal swung from his saddle and stood over the butchered bloody animal, hands planted on his hips.

"This is what I'm seeing at least once't a month of late." Squatting he swung a gloved hand over the bloody haunch where the hide had been peeled back and several foot-long-wide strips sliced away.

Spitting a string of tobacco juice, Perk dismounted, checked out the evidence, then rose and took a look at their surroundings. "This land yours...?" He gestured a complete circle around the downed steer.

McDougal snorted. "Open range, sir. You're well aware of that. Cows can't tell when they cross over into the territory neither, so don't ask. Man don't deserve losing his livelihood cause cattle can't tell where them blamed Indians tread. And this ain't the first time. This time I seen 'em and can tell you who is doing this. I want you to run 'em down and get 'em up before that new judge. I hear he don't put up with thievery and such."

Perk scratched under his well-worn Plainsman and squinted into the afternoon sun. "You tell me who you seen, or better yet, point them out to me. I'll do the rest."

"You bet your last dollar I can do that. He and his crew runs in and outta the territory pulling his hi-jinks. Stealing, selling his ill-got goods such as this meat he carved off, or cattle on the hoof, sells his own people as slaves when he can lay a hand on some. It's time someone put a stop to his sort."

"You come into court and tell what you seen against them when I pull them in?"

"You betcha. Reckon that new judge'll hang 'em?"

Perk eyed the weary rancher, wondered what made folks come out here to this lawless edge of the frontier to settle. Then complain about how things was. Hard to fathom. "Well, I'll tell you, you don't see a man hanged for stealing. Only murder and rape carries that sentence. But he's a fair man, and he'll see to jail time if it's warranted."

"What's it mean, warranted? Them just law words to keep you from having to do anything?"

Perk spat out his tobacco, took the time to cut off another chunk and place it in one cheek. He wasn't beyond just sending this fellow on his way, but he got tired of folks thinking the law did nothing. After riding trail behind bawling cattle most of his younger life, he'd hired on as a deputy marshal. He intended to do his job keeping the law long as he could stand up and take another whack at some no-good who thought it okay to take what wasn't his. Then run off to Indian Territory with the idea he couldn't be caught over there. It was a new day of law enforcement here with U.S. Marshals and deputies riding with Judge Isaac Parker to back them up. And by Jiminy, he was proud to be doing his part.

"Naw. You witness the act, I'll do my job." In fact, he didn't even need a warrant if he saw the proof with his own eyes. Obvious someone was up to no good, this wasn't the first case like it he'd seen the past few weeks, and he was fed up. Usually no one saw anything. A fence rider or rancher just come upon the downed sliced up beef.

"We can light out after someone without a warrant gives the right evidence. Indians stealing from Whites makes it U.S. Marshal business."

"Oh, Marshal, it weren't Injuns. It was White men. One of my boys seen 'em. Clear as day, he's sure they was White."

Well, by God that made him all the madder. He was a decent tracker and in the mood. He'd bring these jokers down no matter. Nothing so big as that Cook gang what was hitting banks and trains and travelers right and left. Ever deputy in the country would like to lay hands on them. Did he wish he could run them down? Sure, but it wasn't likely. Meanwhile, he could maybe stop this bunch and the rancher's losses. Just another day.

"Well, deputy, you get these ole boys I'll come in to court. This is the fourth beef I've lost this way. Hell, they want a steak they could ask and I'd give 'em one. Don't need to take my entire steer. You run across 'em, we'll see if you'uns are worth your pay."

That was a laugh. Wouldn't take much to be worth his pay, but Perk let that go. He could end up traveling a lot of miles before he made his case and carried the owl hoots back to Fort Smith. But he was out here cause he liked the idea of fighting for the right side. And doin' it without eating dust on the trail or having a boss standin' over him crackin' a whip.

He bid McDougal good-bye and rode off headed for the first place he would look for his prey. You couldn't keep anything quiet in these parts. Thieves wasn't very smart, and they liked to brag. Bragging was a big part of success in getting a reputation and being a good thief. Hang around where thieves hung and keep quiet, he'd soon hear someone talking about who was stealing beef straight for eating rather than on the hoof. He didn't see farmers or other ranchers stealing a few cuts of meat off a downed beef. It more likely could be someone looking to sell some fresh beef steaks for a quick greenback dollar. Or a hungry gang camped for the night.

Not far across the Indian Territory border, Perk climbed down off his dun, tied him near a muddy pool of water and walked the rest of the way to Nials's Trading Post where no-goods liked to hang out. His badge concealed, he leaned up against a corner post, rolled hisself a smoke and lit up. If the thief who stole those slabs of beef wanted to sell it fast, he'd try to do it at one of the posts inside Indian Territory. They wasn't much law, and he'd turned a few good arrests there.

After a couple of hours of playing hide and seek someone rode in, Perk went inside. This called for more action. Nials gazed at him through eyes black as midnight. Once in a while he had a black girl for sale in the back room. Perk saw nothing wrong with that. He could make some money off buying one and reselling a few steaks here if he was a mind to. He wasn't. Deputy Marshals ought to have more good sense than that. Though there was worse things for those poor raggedy starving gals than being sold to someone who'd see they got at least a meal a day and a bed to sleep in for their return of favors.

He got the attention of the man waiting on his few customers. "Seen anyone coming through with some beef steaks? I'm looking to buy some for my boss that runs an eating place over to Fort Smith?"

The lean man ran a dirty hand through his hair. "Sell you some good goat meat. Ain't nobody got any beef that I know of."

"Don't care for goat meat. Boss don't neither. Sure no one bragging about bringing down a beef lately? If you had, I could pay a few bits to you."

"Naw, nothing."

The fella lost interest and went to a Native American who'd sauntered in. Started talking him up. "Got some good stuff here, just brought in this morning, brewed couple of nights ago. I'd take that there pelt you've got for this here jug."

The Native American pulled the pelt off his belt and handed it over without a word, took the jar of white lightning, grunted a thank you, and staggered out. Looked like he'd already found him some before he made his way in there.

The danged fool. Didn't have the sense God give a goose. Guess he didn't figure Perk for anyone but another thief. He slumped forward as if disinterested. Might as well take advantage of a good thing, dropped right in his lap. At least his day wouldn't go without pay at all. He watched until the owner of the post traded liquor to the Native American for his pelts. Checking to make sure no one else was in the post who might step in, he produced his badge, pulled out his six-shooter and crammed the barrel hard into Nials's gut.

"What the hell you doin', mister?"

"Arresting you, you no good idjit."

"What for, I ain't done nothing but carry out my regular business. Never even sold you stole beef."

A footstep behind him, but before he could turn back to Nials, someone crashed a half-filled fruit jar across his forehead. The stink of lightning choked him and burned his eyes. Knuckling at the fiery pain he stumbled toward the opening to gasp in some fresh air. The Native American who'd traded the pelt for whiskey fell on him and knocked him to the ground.

"You blamed idjit." He leaped to his feet and hammered at the Native American's shoulders. "I'm arresting him for feeding you that poison, selling or trading it to you is agin' the law. You are taking the wrong side here." He coughed out the words, shrugged his attacker aside, kicked out with the sharp toe of one boot, and came up off the ground growling like a danged bear.

He'd had enough, by God, when both the victim and the lawbreaker laid into him when he tried to do something on the right side. He ought to kick them both aside, wade out of there, and get on his horse and ride. He shed Nials and the Native American like ticks off a hound, scrambled for his gun and herded both of them into the back corner of the post where he tied their wrists to the corner post.

The Native American who had hit him in the head with the jar of whiskey stomped in the dirt and hollered. "Why in thunder you tie me up? I just saw you was in trouble and tried to help."

"You shut up. You're both going over to the Fort Smith jail and being charged with assaulting a Deputy U.S. Marshal. I'm fed up to here." He held his open palm below his nose.

Nials did his own hollering. "Ain't no judge alive going to bother putting me in jail. I didn't know he was a Indian. You're just wasting your time trying to trick me."

Even the Native American, who didn't seem to understand he wasn't under arrest for buying the liquor, but for attacking a lawman, showed his indignation.

Perk stabbed his forefinger in the complaining Native American's chest. "You'd be free to walk out of here had you not thrown yourself into the battle yonder."

Nials, who had been pretty quiet since the arrest, laughed. "You really think you can get us back to Fort Smith without getting yourself killed? Hell, man, there's two of us and one is a wild Injun."

Perk calmly checked the loads in his gun, then stuck it back into his holster. "Well, I don't know about that, but you both couldn't take me down here. Now, the way this will go is this. I'm gonna tie you together ankle to ankle and then you're gonna take one long trot back to Fort Smith while I ride in pure comfort on the back of that big old dun waiting patiently for me out there.

"You cain't do that, Marshal, that's cruel and inhuman treatment."

"The way I'm feeling now, I could get back without either of you. We might just have ourselves a hanging in the first tree we come to." Studying their astounded faces, Perk figured he'd gone far enough. He went to the post, untied the Native American.

"Now, you remember this. He cain't sell you liquor in the territory anymore, neither can any white man. He cain't steal your vittles, or britches, or your horse without going before Judge Parker. On the other hand, you can't go hitting a deputy over the head with a jar of whiskey or anything else for that matter. You tell all your friends that, will you? There's a new judge in town, and he don't brook law breaking from anyone against anyone. And he's got a whole bunch of us Deputy U.S. Marshals put out here to see the law ain't broke anymore. So go on, git fore I change my mind."

The Native American rubbed his wrists, shook his head in wonder, and grabbing up the pelts he'd originally traded for liquor, he high-tailed it out of there.

Nials glared at him. "You're gonna turn me loose too, ain't you? Hell, He didn't look like no Injun, I'll swear it in court and that namby pamby judge'll turn me loose for a few bucks. He always does."

Perk took a twist of rope off the back wall of the post shack and bent down to tie it around his ankles. "Hold still, you little bastard. I've had enough out of you. I'm gonna see you're charged with assaulting a marshal, attempted bribery, and taking part in a trade of liquor to a Indian. We got us a new judge, and he's gonna put you so deep in jail you'll be white headed when you get out."

He wrapped the end of the rope over the cantle and nudged the dun into a slow trot, just fast enough Nials could barely keep up without falling down.

Headed for the ferry to cross the river, Jace whistled Oh, Susannah. It was a song his horse particularly liked.

At the jail, he finished up all the paperwork, turned in his bill and signed his charge over. It was past dark when he left the courthouse and stepped into the moonlit shadow of the hanging gallows feeling pretty good. Oh, sure it was, just a little charge, but he was so blamed tired of hearing how the law didn't ever do anything but just parade around looking smart. A law had been broke so that would be answered for. And he hadn't forgot about the rancher's complaint. Tomorrow was another day.

BEYOND THE BADGE

This story was not written about a particular deputy, but to demonstrate how ordinary many of their days were as opposed to those where they were constantly in extremely dangerous circumstances.

SHE RODE FOR THE MARSHALS: ADA CURNUTT

ADA TOOK FOUR or five steps beyond the sign hanging outside the courthouse in Fort Smith, dragged her feet to a halt, and turned on the heel of her muddy boot to read it: *Signing up Deputy U.S. Marshals See Clerk Inside.*

Could it really be? Excitement swelled in her chest. She put her nose on the glass. Only a table and a few chairs sat in the lobby where men meandered around, some of them seated with pencil to paper. No women, but she would change that. The century would turn in a few years. Women ought to be prepared to turn with it. At least this woman planned to be ready.

In her head she carried a list of things she didn't plan to do in the next century. Laundry, cooking, mopping floors, looking after someone's children, and, oh yes, teaching, which had gotten to be a popular way for women to escape household duties.

She moved through a clutch of young men studying written efforts. Some shuffled away from her like she had a disease, others tried not to notice her presence. Treating her as invisible. She ignored them and stepped up to the table. One gentleman of an older persuasion sat there as if he had some notion what was going on.

He spotted her and smiled. Hmm. A nice face. We'll see how long that lasts. No women applying for the clerical job. Odd.

"Looking for someone, dear?"

He had a pleasant voice to go with the face.

She grinned and ran a gloved finger over a stack of applications, information penciled in. "Do you have a blank one? These all seem to be completed."

For a moment her question brought a silent look, then the earlier smile widened. "If you have someone who wants to apply, he'll have to come in himself. We like to interview briefly on first meeting."

"Ah, no. You misunderstood. It's for me, if you'd be so kind." She spread her hands. "And here I am."

For a long moment he looked like someone had told an off-color joke in public. He took a second or two to collect himself. "But... but you're a woman. I mean—"

"I think that's obvious. How'd you guess? Are women not allowed to apply or serve?"

He smirked.

She hated men who smirked but gave him a break. It didn't hurt his face.

"I reckon." He leaned forward to check her up and down. "Looks as if the britches fit you." The smart aleck remark grew into a friendly laugh.

She forgave him once more.

"If you'd care to send any one of these men outside with me, I'll be glad to show you how well I qualify. With or without britches. I can outshoot, outride, or outfight about any of them. Except maybe that fellow over there who looks like he weighs over two hundred pounds, in which case all he'd have to do is sit on me which leaves out the fighting."

The man stood and cleared his throat. "I would like to see your qualifications but as you see we have quite a crowd and by the time I reach your application the day will be gone. I'm afraid it's not women first in this case. Perhaps you could return tomorrow after you've thought this over." He held out a printed sheet.

"These are the duties we expect our deputies to carry out. Things have changed a bit since the early days when we took most anyone who could mount a horse and shoot a pistol. Even then never seen a woman. This is a job for tough-skinned men. You need to be real sure."

She peered past his hand at the list of duties, then snatched it. He appeared to be considering what she had to offer. "I'll be back tomorrow prepared to show you my abilities. I don't see any of those you appear to be interested in listed here."

He patted her hand. The man next to him chortled down in his throat. She jerked back the paper to keep him from grabbing it... or her.

"You do that, dearie." Again that smirk. This time he almost got his ears boxed for calling her dearie. But she left further reaction till the following day. Men could be such yokels.

She lived with her sister Cora and her husband Daniel. They had recently homesteaded on a small piece of land in Oklahoma. Time she arrived home, got Beckie's saddle and tack hung up, brushed her down, and turned her into the pasture, it was late. Her sister hollered from the front porch where she was cleaning up after pasting sheets of newspaper on the inside of the cabin. She carried a bucket and brush.

"Well, how'd it go? Were the Marshals eager to hire women today?"

"You can just keep on funning me. It may take me a while, but I'm going to get on with them if it kills me and them both. After what I saw today I think I can go at it from another angle. They have the messiest office. Applications are scattered all over the place. No order at all."

Cora studied her a minute. "Don't worry, I'm sure once they get to know you, they can't help but love you. So you'd settle for cleaning up after them?"

Daniel came in the back door, kissed his wife and hung an arm around Ada's shoulders.

"Show 'em that trick you do where you leap onto your horse while it's running circles in the barnyard, then shoot a hat off one of 'em's head. That'd do it." He flicked water at her from the wash basin. "I'm sure they need someone who can do that."

"Laugh all you want to. Both of you. I'm going to get hired by them before the week's out, you wait and see."

Cora tightened her lips and shook her head. "You two get washed up, supper's been cooking all afternoon. It'll be ready."

At the table, Cora passed Daniel a bowl of steaming beans and filled another. "I knew it was a mistake stopping to see that Annie Oakley gal when we went through St. Louis on the way here. If you didn't have any ideas before, you sure latched on to them then."

Ada crumbled corn bread into her bowl. "I didn't have any trouble with that one trick, now did I?"

"Well, it was a hand clapping finish when you slid off on to the ground on your behind." Daniel grinned at her.

"Yeah, well that dismount does need a little work."

Even Cora joined the laughter. Ever since Daniel married her, he'd taken to teasing Ada, and she enjoyed it as much as he did. Ma and Pa died of cholera when Ada was ten, and Cora had raised her. Last year, Daniel had stepped right into the family. Ada was grateful, but she was grown now, and ready to begin her own life. Despite the teasing, she wouldn't put up with them bossing her around.

Not for one minute.

Before sunrise the next morning, attired again in a pair of Pa's britches and one of his shirts, Ada rode Beckie to downtown Fort Smith, tied up in front of the famous courthouse and gallows where Judge Isaac Parker had held reign over the Western District of Arkansas since 1875. The 74,000 square miles, once policed by those men had recently been divided into smaller districts, but the deputy marshals still held sway over the law there, as did Judge Isaac Parker. If she didn't get the job, her heart would break.

The table had been moved in front of the courthouse, to accommodate a larger crowd. The man with the familiar face from the day before glanced up and held out his hand.

"Welcome, madam. I trust you are ready to outshoot, outride, and outfight our deputies. Well, I have good news for you. It seems that won't be necessary. The office in Norman over in Oklahoma needs a clerical deputy. And it's been decided a woman would be fine. Without any wrestling or shooting matches."

She threw out her arms to display her well-chosen outfit. "Do I look like a clerical clerk?"

Without a reply, she drew the six-gun strapped to her waist, took aim and shattered the glass covering of a street light across the way.

Her antics caused quite a ruckus, including the excited appearance of a deputy sheriff who informed her she'd get a bill for that. "We just had those lights installed a while back. You're blamed lucky I don't throw you in jail."

"Get the marshals to pay for it. They bet I couldn't do it."

Laughter mixed with whooping and hollering echoed from the men spilled over into the street. Several of those filling out applications crowded around Ada.

A tall, dark haired man elegantly dressed approached. "That'll do, young lady. You want to work for the U.S. Marshals stop this destroying our fair city. And we're Deputy Marshals, missy. Only one Marshal here and yonder is Marshal Crump inside there taking care of business." He nodded toward the courthouse.

One of the younger applicants snickered. "Put her in jail."

Another behind her. "Someone tell her she's a female, not fit for marshaling."

She took a step in his direction. "Why don't you tell me to my face?"

The man held out a hand. "Now fellows, let's not be hasty. I'm Deputy Marshal Heck Thomas, ma'am." He tilted his hat. "You might ride on over to Norman. It's true they're looking for a clerk to keep things straightened out in the new office there. Never said it had to be a man nor is it necessary you can shoot out streetlights. And the position is recognized as a Deputy U.S. Marshal."

Unable to hold her tongue, she squared her shoulders and stared up into his silent visage. "They hire me you can bet I'll be taking care of cleaning up more than an office." She held out a hand. "Ada Curnutt. Soon to be, uh, Deputy Marshal. Just cause I wear dresses don't mean I can't ride and keep up with the rest of you."

"Looks to me like you don't always wear dresses. We have no vacancies here for a woman, but you take this job in Norman and in no telling how short a time you'll be advanced. Just show them you can do the job. I can see how well you shoot. As a clerk, you'll work for Marshal William Grimes if he decides to hire you."

He looked her in the eye and repeated. "And you will be a deputy. A Deputy U.S. Marshal. From there, who knows where you'll go?" His crooked grin showed he didn't believe it at all.

She twisted her neck to gaze up at him. He might be pulling her leg. That's what men liked to do. Tease her because of her love of riding and shooting. She studied him closely to see if that's what he was doing.

His brown eyes sparkled. "Norman? That's a goodly ride off." A laugh from the small crowd.

He scratched his chin and stared toward the west. "Just keep right on riding that way. Ah, shoot, maybe a couple three days or more. Depending how fast that horse of yours is. Just south of Oklahoma City. There's a cattle trail all the way west. Signs once in a while to tell you where you're at."

She frowned, having no idea how far Oklahoma City was, but she'd find it. Just wait till she got home and told Cora and Daniel.

At the farm, she swung to the ground outside the barn and left Beckie standing to find her family and shout her good news. "And I'm leaving first light tomorrow."

"They hired you?" Cora stopped short of collecting an egg from the hen's nest.

"Uh, well, almost. All I have to do is show up over there in Norman."

"Almost? And you're going all that way by yourself for an almost? Through the territory?" Cora 's face took on a frown. "Daniel, tell her. Tell her she can't go. It's plumb foolish."

He smacked one of the cows on the butt, shoved her into a stall. "Tell her, Cora? Huh? When was the last time I told her anything she listened to? Well?" He peered toward Ada.

She opened her mouth to answer, but her sister stepped in.

"She'll get toted off by one of those outlaws you hear about. The ones they have all these marshals around to chase down."

"Well, Cora, your sister is going to be one of them, so I reckon she'll have to learn how to take care of herself."

Cora shooed a chicken off her nest and plucked up an egg. "The both of you, I don't know what I'm going to do with you."

"Cora, you're crying. Aw, don't do that." She put her arms around her sister. "Honey, 'member the night you come home and told Ma and Pa you were marrying Daniel and Ma cried and Pa got mad and hurried out the back door? And how you got so upset? 'Member that?" She pointed toward Daniel. "Look how good that turned out."

Cora buried her face in Ada's shoulder. Sniffing she nodded. "I guess, yes, but this is different."

"How? You'll get over this too."

"Cause you're going out there in Indian Territory to... to... oh, shoot."

"And so, here we are, the three of us." They stood in the barn laughing and hugging each other for the longest time. Later inside Ada helped Cora put supper on the table. Neither spoke.

Excitement kept her tossing and unable to sleep all night. Before the sun rose she was readying her saddlebags and supplies for the ride. Cora joined her in the kitchen, packing some biscuits left over from supper and slicing side meat from the smoke house out back. Arbuckle coffee, a pot, eating utensils, water canteen, and a bedroll were added to the bag Beckie would carry.

Cora took her sister's arm. "Why don't you hire someone to ride with you? I'm sure a young man would be glad to do so. Or better yet, go by train. Beckie could travel comfortably in a stock car."

"Sounds good, but the expense. I don't know if I could afford it." Daniel and Cora were just managing since settling on the land and buying a few animals to start the farm. She wasn't about to ask for money. "Besides, the way I love to ride, it'll be fun seeing more of the country."

Ada tapped her hand. "Now Cora, come on. Don't make me feel bad about leaving you."

"I know, I know."

Though she, Daniel, and Cora had come down from Ohio, this would be her first trip alone and that across parts of Indian Territory not yet wholly tamed. There would be places to buy things along the way, but buying things took money, so it was good to carry as much in the way of supplies as she could. What scared her more than making the trip was it was the first time she'd ever applied for work. She could do the job, but how in the world was she going to convince her family that this would be her life? Or beyond that. Convince the marshals?

WITH HER HEAD on her saddle, Ada gazed into a night sky, so splashed with stars there was little dark. In her brief life back east she had not much experience with living or working in the outdoors, though she'd always yearned for it. This outdoors appeared a way bigger outdoors than in Ohio. Someone said it was because the air was so dry everything, the moon and the stars, all looked closer. But this wide, exciting, if slightly dangerous, life held a wonder she could hardly believe. She would go out at night to check on one of the horses kicking up a fuss and Daniel would have to come looking for her. Only to find her entranced with the sight of the stars or the night fragrance or a clean breath of air. Sometimes she'd dance in circles reaching for the sky. This was the home she'd yearned for.

She tried to explain to her family that she was born to live here. The prairies and mountains, the trees and flowers and animals called to her. And therefore, riding for the U.S. Marshals promised a perfect job. Yet everyone claimed a woman's job was at home. They didn't seem to understand. But when Daniel bought horses for the farm, he asked her to pick out the ones that would be best because she had such an eye for their breeding.

On her second night out on the way to Norman she lounged on a boulder above her camp in the center of a wide treeless expanse. Alone and on her own, she could scarcely hold back her desire to leap about and shout with pure joy. Sleep crept up on her, but she fought it to watch a late rising moon dodge the stars. It was like being a very small fish in a huge bowl.

Staying up half the night caused her to sleep late. It wasn't till the sun's rays crawled across her face that she awoke to find a man opposite her camp, legs spread, a hungry grin on his bearded face. A movement fast as a snake and her hand lay over her gun tucked under the blanket. She'd shoot him if she had to, and it looked like she would have to.

"Move away." Her voice sounded weak, like she might be scared.

"Not yet, not just yet." He reached for his belt buckle and her heart leapt.

How had she let this critter sneak up on her? No time. No time. Do something before he makes a move. As if lying back to surrender, she slipped the Colt out and pointed it at him.

"Gonna do with that, little lady?"

In a flash, he jumped and dropped one knee on her wrist so hard she cried out, and gripped the gun till the cylinder cut into her flesh. How had he moved so fast?

She would not let go of her only weapon. Not if he broke her arm.

Sprawled over her stiffly struggling body, he mashed his elbow against her throat. His nasty breath, wet when spat through jagged teeth, washed over her face. She gagged. Maybe she could puke on him. Her stomach roiled. He sprawled one leg across her. She kicked his behind with one foot. The weight of his body stretched heavy along hers and pinned her down. Her frantic struggle to move ceased. Panic trapped her breath.

All that stood between them was wadded clothing. But he paid more attention to his need than her battle. The arm at her throat slipped away. Hands gripped his britches. He grew hard against her. He would wait no longer. The yanking movement freed her arm.

She had to do something. Now. Stop thinking. Do. Get loose before he has his way. A rock nudged at her wrist, and she twisted to get a hold on it.

By then, he really wanted his britches undone. With her wiggling around he must've thought she was as anxious as him. He dug under her belt with one clawed hand. She swung the rock hard and well-aimed, hit him in the temple. It made a terrible squashing noise. He cried out, collapsed as if dead. Not convinced she shoved him off. Rolled away and came up on her knees, gun pointed at his still body. For good measure, she scrambled to her feet and kicked him in the ribs. Relished the cracking sound under the sharp toe of her boot. Backed off quick in case he was tougher and faster than she thought.

He babbled something she couldn't understand.

"Where's your horse? You didn't walk here from wherever you're from."

Another moaning reply.

She was mighty tempted to truss him up and take him in to Norman. But why make a fool of sorts of herself? There were rules she didn't know, and she wasn't about to play arrest like she was a deputy or something.

"Guess I'll just tie you up good and leave you here, then. It gets mighty hot come afternoon, what with no water and broken ribs to boot. If I find your horse, I'll consider him mine for the trouble. Oh, and I'm on my way to Norman. I'll send a deputy marshal out to get you, if you're still alive."

She shoved on him two or three times but he appeared out cold. With one eye watching she packed up her things and went to saddle Beckie. Like an injured animal her prey moaned, scooted, scrambled to his feet, and lit out, darting across the prairie in a stumbling run. She shot at him two or three times, but he was fast on his feet and disappeared in a deep crevice. Her shots cut dust gobbets from the earth around him. Dang. It might be a good idea to practice some more shooting at running targets.

By the time she was packed up, dressed ready to leave without campfire or breakfast, the distant echo of a horse galloping away sounded. So her attacker was gone. Hope she'd taught him a lesson. Further, hope she hadn't made a mistake letting him go.

What if the folks in Norman found out about it and decided she wasn't worth much if she couldn't hold on to a single outlaw long enough to put him in jail? Worrying about it, she almost mounted up and headed out after the sound of his fleeing horse. But she'd never catch him. Had she failed a test already? All the way to Norman she wallowed the problem around in her brain, which of course didn't do her a bit of good. What she finally decided was to forget all about it and go on from there.

She camped outside Norman to save paying for a hotel room. It was early enough in the day to clean up a bit, put on the dress she brought and get on into town. Maybe find the court house and learn where she needed to apply for the job. If she failed in her effort, she could be partway back home, tail between her legs, by dark. Not about to give up, she fought the idea that she could always get a job in Fort Smith in the new school. The town had prospered immensely since Parker's Court had opened there and the deputy marshals cleaned up. Dismissing that thought, she rode down the main street of Norman.

The town was a bit larger than Fort Smith, and she got a feel for it by riding the length of the main street, then back again. The delay was no doubt to get up the courage to apply for the job. At a huge stone building sporting a sign for Oklahoma District Courthouse, she dismounted awkwardly in the dress, tied her horse to the hitching rail, and walked right in, just like she knew where she was.

Upper floors lined with windows let in brilliant rays of sunlight. Several men stood or sat at desks arranged along one side. Behind a waist-high counter a woman wearing a pinstripe dress with a black ribbon tie at her throat glanced up and smiled. A welcome expression.

Looked like it was a good thing she'd worn a dress today. The clacking of her boots across the marble floor made way too much noise. She was about to embarrass herself.

The woman gestured in her direction. "What could we help you with today?"

"I've come to apply for a job… the job as a deputy U.S. marshal… well, a clerk. A circuit clerk."

By the time she made it to the woman the words were all out, echoing from the massive walls.

She leaned on the counter, feeling like she'd run a mile. Breathing like it too.

The woman smiled wider. "Really? Where did you hear about the opening?"

"Marshal… no, Deputy Marshal Heck Thomas. He was in the courthouse in Fort Smith where I applied for a job as deputy marshal. He told me about it."

"You actually applied for a deputy's job? Really? What made you think you could… I mean only men fill that post, at least so far."

"I would like the job as deputy, but this opening here would maybe give me a chance to qualify for that in the future. That is if I could apply for it. I mean, you're working here."

This time full blown laughter. "I am indeed because my husband is Marshal Grimes, and when he needs help, I give it. This is the job that is open, for there are several reasons I cannot fill it anymore."

She moved to one side and lifted the counter. "Please do come on in. Where did you come from. Fort Smith? That's a long way off. Ride the train?"

"Oh no, I rode my Beckie, she loves long rides. She's a strawberry roan. I wouldn't dare go on a trip without her." Ada stepped behind the counter and took the chair the woman offered.

"Etta Grimes. You rode alone across the Territory, nights and everything?"

"Ada Curnutt. Oh, yes. I enjoy riding, especially over wide country vistas. My family homesteaded in Oklahoma Territory about eight months ago. I fell in love with the prairie and the idea of chasing outlaws and dragging them in to Judge Parker."

Etta chuckled. "It does take a little more than the love of the territory, but if you have the spirit and spunk, I'd say give it a try. However, this job, being a Deputy U.S. Marshal, would mean mostly paper work and keeping track of those outlaws you would like to chase. All sorts of records are kept, and it would be up to you as Circuit Clerk to handle that. Not much riding on the prairie." She paused, studied Ada. "All the way that far? And stayed overnight out in the open? My, you are a brave one."

"Oh, I really enjoyed it. Brave, I don't know about that yet. But I would be a Deputy U.S. Marshal. Right?"

"Yes, but Marshal Grimes would want to make sure you wouldn't take off one day chasing some outlaw and leave him suddenly without a circuit clerk."

"I wouldn't do that, but if he all of a sudden needed a deputy who could ride and shoot, why then, here I'd be ready made. I could show him how I ride and shoot if that's necessary."

Etta moved to another desk, thumbed out some papers and brought them to Ada. "Just sit down here and fill these out. When you're finished or if you have any questions, I'll just be in that office over there that says Marshal Grimes on the door. Have someone fetch me."

Ada's heart thumped so hard she could hardly breathe. While she filled out the forms, a conversation went on behind that door that was occasionally raised to where she could make out words. No way would she eavesdrop, but still when the argument concerning her arrival quieted down, she finished the final page and leaned back in her chair. She wasn't going to get the job. The man behind that door was against it. But she had presented herself as well as she could seeing as how she was nervous as a squirrel stealing nuts from an owl.

The door opened, and Mrs. Grimes came out followed by a large man with a healthy head of white hair. He wore a leather vest, neat pants, and white shirt with a five pointed silver star on the pocket. Had to be Marshal Grimes. Her heart stumbled.

With an effort to hide her disappointment, Ada rose to her feet.

Before everything could come together and him tell her she could not be a deputy marshal, the front door swung open letting in a brisk March wind and a tall young man she'd seen before. Maybe there was hope after all. This was Deputy U.S. Marshal Heck Thomas dressed in denim pants, a red shirt, and a well-worn Stetson, which he removed and headed toward Marshal Grimes.

She recognized him from Fort Smith. This was great. He'd cheered for her.

"Have you met this gal yet? That one yonder? I hope you've told her you'd give her a try. She shot out a street light over in Fort Smith without aiming."

Etta moved out of the way in time to keep from colliding with Marshal Grimes and the deputy striding across the floor.

"Aye God, Heck Thomas. As I live and breathe. Who'd you haul in this time? One of the Buck gang?"

The two pounded on each other a few times. "Seriously, I stopped by for one reason and that was to tell you about that very woman standing right yonder. Met her a couple days ago in Fort Smith and thought of you and this clerk opening. Girl wants to be a deputy, but you know how that'd go. Still, Circuit Clerk would make her a deputy and give her a chance. I'm all for given little women a chance, you know that."

Ada bit her lip. Little women, indeed. Oh well, she needed the bolstering. If the man hadn't been giving her a compliment, she'd have thrown the paper weight on the desk at him. Later, maybe, she'd get back at him, after she got the job and all.

"Come on over here, ma'am. Have you filled out that application?" Thomas waved toward her.

"Yes, sir." Papers in hand Ada scuttled toward the deputy. She must be red as a beet, hot as her face felt.

He turned toward Grimes. "See there, she can read and write. And shoot and ride too."

Marshal Grimes gave Thomas a long look, like he might tell him to butt out.

Etta saved the moment. "Why don't we go in your office, dear, where you can speak to Miss Curnutt in private?"

She wanted to shout, but swallowed hard instead and followed Etta and Marshal Grimes.

Before he shut the door, he turned. "Good to see you, Heck. Drop by anytime."

Once in the silence of his office, Marshal Grimes took the application from Ada. "Thank you, Miss"—he glanced at the paper—"Miss Curnutt."

"Yes, sir. You're welcome."

"Well, sit. Sit."

Etta stood beside a china pot. "Should I pour you some coffee?"

"Good thought, dear. You obviously think this might be a good idea."

"Well, I've done the work for a while." Her smile was sweet. "We are both women, so yes, why not?"

He peered at his wife. "But, dear, did it ever occur to you to race out of here in pursuit of some outlaws, shooting at them?"

Ada looked down at the floor. Oh, no.

Again everything went silent while Marshal Grimes read and sipped at his coffee. Etta patted Ada's shoulder. Finally, he nodded. "Okay, ma'am. No reason not to try this out, long as you understand, I tell you what to do, and you do it. None of that... well, that earlier stuff."

Joy nearly burst from her in the form of a yelp. "Sir. Yes, sir. You're the boss."

Etta laughed. "A good way to put it dear, you'll do well."

"I take it you live with your family." He sat behind the desk. Opened a drawer and placed her papers inside a file there. "You'll need time to find a place here and get your things carried over. So, say, by next Monday morning I find you behind that desk out there. Etta will show you which one and acquaint you with the office. Perhaps she can take you around town, help you find a place to live. How does that suit you?"

A true wonder she didn't faint dead away on his office floor. But she didn't.

IN THE FOLLOWING four years, Ada settled into her job. Deputies dropped in to tell stories about their adventures allowing her to relive them. An occasional visit to the court house, and she learned how that part of the justice system worked. Since the Western District had been split into smaller sections, trials in Oklahoma were not always held under Judge Parker. She enjoyed the atmosphere a lot, but there remained the yearning that one day she would ride the plains as an active Deputy U.S. Marshal. Deputies came and went, and she listened to their tales of close calls. The sad news of a deputy being shot or beat to death or thrown off a bluff often arrived. Over one hundred deputies were killed riding for the five-pointed star during her years in Norman. Yet she still yearned to earn the badge they pinned on her when she became a clerk. It was like she was play-acting a part by wearing it. Though those who knew her in Norman addressed her as deputy, she wouldn't truly be a Deputy U.S. Marshal in her own mind till she carried an outlaw in to the District and dumped him at Marshal Grimes feet.

March brought an early windy spring to the Oklahoma prairies. Ada bought a small house on the edge of town the previous year after renting an upstairs room in the hotel for three years. Each morning she dressed in neat black britches, a man's dress shirt and a ribbon tie. It wouldn't do to be called out and have to ride to fetch an outlaw in a dress.

That morning, in the fourth year after she was hired, she found the office locked and empty. Not real unusual but her heart always hammered when it happened. To think she might have been left in charge, with orders for her to arrest some owlhoot. In the mail under the slot of the door was the familiar yellow paper of a telegram. With shaking fingers she opened the sheet.

Read: Deputy Curnutt, Called out of town, Urgent you get a deputy to ride to OKC and bring in these outlaws soonest. Warrants and posters were attached for two men, Reagan and Dolezal wanted for forgery. I will be gone till tomorrow. Signed, Marshal Grimes

Heart slamming around in her chest she checked the small room where sometimes a few deputies gathered for coffee. It was empty. No one was waiting around anywhere. How far did she have to go to find a wandering deputy? They were supposed to check in even if they left again, but the check-in sheet was blank. It wasn't her responsibility to round up deputies. Showing up was up to them.

She hurried into the cloak room, gathered her bag prepared over three years ago for just such an emergency, opened the drawer of her desk and grabbed a travel voucher for the train. Buckling on her six shooter, she flew out the door and turned to lock it. Halted. Better leave a note. She went back in, scribbled a quick note for her desk and left again. Outside the door she stopped once more, looked up and down the street for a sign of any deputy. This was something she had waited on for four years and everyone knew it. She couldn't have anyone accusing her of jumping the gun.

The morning northbound train sat at the station, bell ringing, whistle hooting. Okay, had she done everything necessary, everything right? For a moment, she teetered on the edge of the boardwalk. Go? Stay? Okay, woman, this is it. Taking long strides she hiked up the street, crossed the tracks, and found the first open door of a passenger car. A conductor helped her up a step and inside.

"Good morning, Miss—uh, *Deputy* Curnutt. Going on a trip today?"

Caught unawares she studied him. Arnold Sizemore. She saw him around at the café often.

"Not exactly. I'm going to pick up a couple of prisoners in Oklahoma City." She could not believe she'd spurted the words. But she had, and she grinned at him.

"Well, you be careful, will you? We're proud of all you deputies around here. When will you come back? I'll watch for you."

"I should return on the evening train. I don't expect any trouble from these two. They aren't killers. Marshal Grimes is out of town and may not be back till tomorrow, so I'm doing this job. Didn't find a deputy about today."

He tipped his hat and showed her to an empty seat, punched her voucher, and smiled. You all are mighty busy here in Oklahoma, aren't you?"

"Yes, we sure are."

Ada sat back and stared out the window. What a day. She'd have to write to Cora and Daniel and tell them about her experience. They would never believe it. After all this time, she had at last been assigned to the field. Well, not exactly assigned, but it was fate that brought this about. At long last.

Heavens. What if Marshal Grimes had a cat fit over her going out alone? What if he fired her?

Passengers moved between the seats, each finding a place to sit. She had to calm down or something would go wrong. Before they could get off a deputy would probably jump aboard the train and insist he take the assignment, or something like that. But it didn't happen. A whistle, a hiss of steam, and they crept forward. At last, they were underway.

Serving warrants and delivering a lawbreaker paid six dollars. But that wasn't the reason she wanted the job. She craved the excitement. Not only that, she hungered to prove women could do this job. Sitting still all the way to Oklahoma City was impossible. On the edge of the seat. Scooting back. Eyes and nose close to the grimy window. Ankles crossed and uncrossed. Checking passengers who appeared to all be staring at her or deliberately looking away. Maybe they guessed this was the most exciting day of her entire life. On the entire trip she couldn't hold her knees together, they kept jerking with anticipation.

What seemed hours later the train pulled into Oklahoma City, and she sat stiffly for a moment, allowing other passengers to make their way out of the seats, down the aisle, and off. It took forever. She practiced her approach to locate the men on the warrants. Out on the street she checked her location, hailed a cab as the best bet to find who she was looking for. The men would be in a saloon, it was too late to be eating breakfast.

Climbing into the cab she showed the driver her badge. "A favorite saloon hangout for men on the run. Take me to each one in turn."

He cackled with delight and took up the reins. Clicked his tongue, and they were off. The drive followed a wide street filled with buggies, wagons, and horse riders. Finally, it cleared out some and on either side of the narrowing street saloons appeared.

She pointed. "That one, right there. Let me out and wait for me."

"You ought to be careful in there, little lady."

She nodded and stepped down. "I'm not a little lady, I'm a Deputy U.S. Marshal. You just wait here, please."

He touched the bill of his cap. "Yes, ma'am. If I hear an uproar, should I fetch a cop on the beat or hunt you down a marshal?"

Without replying, Ada peered over the swinging doors into the smoky dim-lit saloon. Overhearing plenty of the deputies discussing favorite haunts of thieves in cities and in the territory she would start with this sleazy place and chances are, sooner or later, she'd find the two she was hunting.

Just inside the door four men played cards with noisy joy. She stepped through the swinging doors and leaned over the nearest one's shoulder. "Know where the sheriff is today?"

He glanced at her, a little startled. In her outfit, hair under her hat, it was hard to tell if she were a man or woman. "Ain't in his office?"

"Nope. Sent me here. Got a warrant for these two." She shuffled out the warrants and posters.

The guy shrugged. "Ain't seen 'em. Nor Sheriff Harrelson. This time of day, he's walking and talking."

She backed out. The fourth saloon she hit pay dirt when she showed her badge to the man at the door.

He pointed into the gloom. "Them two. Been cutting up Ned all day. Wish't you'd get 'em out of town."

She tapped a couple more men on the shoulders. "Hey, fellows. You go back there and tell them two there's a Deputy Marshal out here needs to talk to them."

One of them peered close. "You a woman, you ain't no marshal."

"I'm both, you go tell them there's a lady outside wants to talk to them. Say I said to high tail it out here. Now. I'm prepared to deputize as many of you men out here as it takes to get my prisoners out of here and to the train station. Now go."

Men laughed and punched each other. Crowded around her making it difficult for her prisoners to fight their way through to her. When they did, they joined in the laughter.

Out on the sidewalk one of the forgers held his wrists out. "Little lady, you can cuff me anytime."

They still thought it a joke. Surrounded by a crowd of men she linked the two together before anyone could stop laughing.

The one called Reagan winked. "Where you taking us now, Deputy?"

Good thing they were forgers and not killers. She might have had a battle.

As it was she pinned the U.S. Marshal star to her pocket and pulled her Colt. "Sorry to break up your party, boys." The silenced men marched down the street to the train station.

Inside the depot she held her grumbling prisoners up against the telegrapher's wire cage. "I have to send a telegram."

The man peered at her, eyes bugged behind round glasses. "Yes'm."

"To U.S. Marshal Grimes, Guthrie. I've got your forgers. Sign it, Deputy Marshal Ada Curnutt.

There were more than a few women who served with the Marshals. U.S. Marshal Canada H. Thompson served from 1897 to 1902 as Marshal of Oklahoma Territory, and he had two female deputy marshals. They most often worked in the office, but they also did field work including serving writs and warrants and making arrests. These women were S.M. Burche and Mamie Fossett, who we covered in an earlier chapter.

Another of these brave women, who was appointed as a Deputy U.S. Marshal out of the federal court at Paris, Texas, in 1891, was F.M. Miller. At the time she was commissioned, she was the only female deputy known to work in Indian Territory.

History makes several mentions of her serving as a guard at the federal jail in Guthrie, Oklahoma under fellow Deputy U.S. Marshal Ben Campbell. She was also known to have accompanied Campbell on all his trips.

William H. H. Clayton (1840–1920) served as U.S. Attorney for the Western District of Arkansas, acting as Judge Parker's chief prosecutor for 14 years.

HATEFUL RATTLESNAKES: JAMES H. MERSHON

WITH BOOTS COVERED in dust, Deputy Mershon kicked open the door of his cabin. Arms loaded with saddlebags and a tow sack heavy with supplies, he stepped inside, squinted toward the shadowy corners of the cob-webbed cabin and butted the door shut. His well-worn hat tumbled off and rolled away, leaving a scraggly trail across the dusty floor.

You'd think ten years'd be enough, and this place'd tumble right down, but it wasn't, and it didn't. No matter how much cleaning and coming and going, and raining and wind blowing, the place never looked any better or worse. Maybe he'd take a little time to brush down the webs and sweep out the powdery settlings. Couldn't even see through the only window.

Ah, well, maybe there'd be time before he had to light out and serve a warrant or chase some no-good into the territory. As if being chased, a lizard slithered across the floor headed for the light under the door. He bent forward, dumped the armload, and came eye to eye with a slit-eyed viper. Coiled and swaying, the snake studied him, broke the silence with a deadly rattle. Right there in his house. A warning went off in his brain, a sound so loud his ears rang.

Fear no sooner roared through his weary mind then the deadly rattle shot his heart into his throat, where he swore it stopped beating. Just stopped, by God. He stumbled backward, slammed up against the wall and slapped at his empty holster. Hell of a time to drop his six-gun off at the smithy. Firing pin. And the Winchester leaned up against the outside door. An ignorant man totally unarmed.

Stumbling backward, clawing at the wall and the axe that belonged there, his fingers found the axe. It tumbled from its hook slammed on the floor. That damned snake held close. Rattler. The only thing in his life he feared. Not guns or men holding them. Just such as this. The deadly snake was ready to strike, its warning bounced around the empty room. Anger heated his face. Never could stand those sidewinders. Sneak up on a fella, not caring a damn they could give him a heart attack. He froze as if caught in a blizzard.

Well, John, do something even if it's wrong. Gunfights, fisticuffs, wrestling he could handle. Not this.

Coiled to strike, the fat intruder leaned back, shook the rattles till it was all he could hear. With a shout, he jumped sideways. The snake struck so violently that when it missed, it tumbled from its pose. Must've knocked itself silly cause it slithered off, shoved its way out the door as if clubbed.

He could only lean against the door frame and tremble. Well, not shaking from fear so much as anger that the nasty intruder had dared take up residence in his home. More-so, anger at himself for not being able to shake loose this baffling fear. Anything in this world he hated, it was a snake. He could stare down the barrel of a .45 aimed between his eyes or kick the shit out of attacking wild dogs, but snakes.

Good God.

He hugged himself, shook for a minute or two, then grabbed the bucket and made for the well where he drew out cold water and, with shaking arms, poured it over his head.

He gasped, his teeth chattered, and he stumbled into the glimmer of a setting sun to warm up a bit. "Danged stupid snake, anyway." He spit into the dirt. "Would scare anyone."

As a deputy marshal who had been one of the few survivors of the Going Snake Wars that took down near twenty of his peers, he had dodged bullets and fought some of the meanest Cherokee in the Territory. Why worry about a big old snake? Such a fear of a ground-crawling creature was senseless. He'd think he was over the reaction till here came one of his enemies again. He'd rather they carried a gun than those deadly sounding rattles and a venomous bite. To admit his fear was even worse than the fear itself.

The sidewinding trail of the fleeing reptile left the vicinity of his doorstep and vanished into clumps of waist-high grass. He stood there a while staring out across the waving prairie. With a holler, he scuffed hard at a pile of dirt as if stomping his enemy. Who had by now gone on his way.

"Teach you to come around messing with me." His shouted voice broke the silence of the late evening. There was no one there to hear him. No one at all.

Later, kicked back on the porch, drinking coffee, and watching stars in a midnight black sky, he laughed at himself. Who ever heard of a grown man acting like that? It was such a female thing. Actually, he'd known women who could walk right up on a snake and cut it in half with a hoe. Must just be a plain old, in-built fear. Probably dropped on his head as a baby. He'd heard of such things.

Because he'd be home a couple days before picking up his next warrant, he spent the next one cleaning and checking for places snakes could wiggle their way in—behind the washtub in which he took an occasional bath, under the corn husk slats of the bed, behind the woodpile back of the stove. All good hideouts.

By evening, he'd had enough of brooms and was ready to go to town. After pursuing a wanted over much of Indian Territory and nothing to show for the effort, he looked forward to a cold beer and some company. Maybe some of the men would be in town tonight. Or if not, he'd find a shapely gal.

Ace High, his favorite saloon, beckoned with bright lights, piano music, and male laughter. He reined Tipper into a gap between two red duns, slid off, and looped his leathers over the hitching rail.

One foot on the boardwalk brought him in line with a tumbling Native American who knocked him down followed by another who leaped over him. On his hands and knees, John scrambled out of the way, caught the one still standing, and toppled him off into the water trough. One of the horses took umbrage at being interrupted and reared on both hind legs, a front hoof coming down on his target's flailing arm. A loud crack followed by the fellow's shout made it plain it was broken.

Someone grabbed him and dragged him to his feet. "Ever time you come to town, all hell breaks loose, Mershon." The man wearing a sheriff's star turned to the downed man. "You'd better have your friend take you over to the doc, son. Looks like you won't be holding fights with folks for a while." He then pulled Mershon inside through the swinging doors. "Come on, I'll buy you a drink."

Mershon laughed, gestured toward the two Native Americans. "Ain't you gonna arrest them?"

"What for? Might haul *you* in if you weren't wearing that marshal's badge. Just a regular Saturday night in Fort Smith. And what in thunder you doing in town? Hadn't you ought to be out cleaning up the Territory so the good judge can hold another mass hanging?"

"Nah, figured you'd miss me if I didn't drop in once in a while and see how the law is really enforced."

The small lawman pounded him on the back. "Let me buy you a beer and explain how we in Arkansas take care of our outlaws."

He followed his friend through the lamp-lit saloon where they grabbed a table toward the back. He wasn't staying long, but there'd be time to have a beer or two before Julie performed her act on the stage that sloped a bit along one wall.

He'd been away too long without a night in her bed. All the women in Indian Territory were either dirty, mean-lipped, or both. Not that he blamed them much, the kind of lives they lived. Plenty were black Freedman slaves with no place else to go making their way the best they could.

But, hell, he couldn't save them all, and he wasn't much for rescuing the helpless. Let them fight for every bite and breath just like he had.

He took a long sip from his mug of beer. After more than a month riding untold miles of Indian Territory searching for the worthless Christian Gang and getting nowhere, he needed this break.

The long-legged Julie danced, shook, and wiggled her way to the center of the stage. He leaned back and took a good look. That would do him, do him just fine before he dropped into Marshal Yoes office first thing Monday morning and began his hunt all over again.

Sheriff Smith set down his half-empty mug. "So how'd the hunt go this time? Those ole boys still slipping away? I don't figger why you don't just shoot 'em 'stead of trying to bring 'em in alive."

"You know the judge. He don't take kindly to killing. Prefers we have a trial. The American way, you know."

The sheriff spurted beer from his mouth with a huge laugh. "Yeah, like hanging over sixty men since he arrived? That's the American way? No one ever heard of such a thing till he got here and went to work. Now, I ain't saying I don't agree with how he's doing it. The Territory needs cleaning up in the worst way, but it's beyond me why he has such a fit when one of you deputies just hangs your catch to save bringing him back."

"I'll talk to him about that next time I see him."

"Thought you was after that mean-ass Christian bunch."

"I am. But going to get up a posse and do it the right way. District'll pay for wagon and pack horses so we can pursue and catch 'em like we ought to. We don't snare them we'll find us some others. I'm sick and tired of returning empty handed."

On stage, Julie kicked her legs high, and he clapped his hands.

She did look mighty good tonight, but then he'd been gone a long time. Just about any woman might do.

Smith laughed. "Can't say as I blame you about her. She's about the purtiest gal in Fort Smith. Now, you'd better finish your beer. Looks like she's waiting for you. She must be pretty good."

Jed downed his beer. "She's a woman, ain't she?"

His friend's chuckle followed while Jed rose and went to fetch the dancer.

WITH THE RISING of the sun, Deputy Marshal Mershon dismounted outside the courthouse, back on duty. It paid to be early or be stuck with missing Marshal Yoes, who was pretty adept at taking care of business.

He didn't get far before Judge Parker spotted him as the clerk at the courthouse unlocked the doors and swung them open. The judge gestured toward him and smiled. "Good to see you, Deputy. Sorry to see you back empty-handed."

The court clerk came to the open doors and raised a hand toward Parker. "Okay, thanks." The judge nodded toward Mershon. "See you soon, one would hope."

Crossing the alley way, Mershon approached Marshal Yoes's small office and tapped before stepping in.

"Jimmy. Hoping you'd be by today. Heard you were back in town."

Mershon grinned. Nothing ever got by this man. "Hear you have some warrants. I'm ready for another. Lost track of the Christian Gang again. They're slippery as eels. Course, I'll get them one of these days. Meanwhile, what else do you have? Maybe I can come back with a prison wagon full next time."

A large, handsome man dressed impeccably, Yoes laughed heartily. "Tell you something. Next time you go out after a wagonload, I'm tempted to tag along."

"Yearning for a little adventure, huh? You're welcome to join me. Hear you have something interesting for me in the meantime, though."

"Saw the judge, did you? Yep, I'd like you to take this one. It's getting old, and I'm afraid the killer will die before we can hang him. That would be a darned shame."

"Come on in and set down. I know you'll enjoy this story."

Both men had become acquainted over the past years they'd been associated with the Western District and the U.S. Marshals Service and knew how each enjoyed a story, often the gorier the better. Especially when the criminal was made to pay for his dastardly deeds.

"Goes back a ways, and I'll cut it short. A horse thief named Stephens took up residence in the Arbuckles with a young girl calling her his wife. It wasn't long before he fell in with a bad negro name of Henry Loftus and a bully of a man name of Martin Joseph. Henry had a good brother named William, and he and his people did everything they could to get Henry to go straight. Nothing doing.

"So back in April, Henry Loftus, Stephens, and Martin Joseph decide to steal a bunch of horses grazing nearby. Stephens takes his pretty wife along on the venture, and they leave her picnicking in the valley where Henry and Joseph have strung a rope corral for the stolen horses. For some reason known only to the sleeziest minds, while in pursuit of the horses, Henry sneaked up behind Stephens and shot him in the back leaving his body there to rot."

Yoes held up a hand. "Oh, we weren't to get the gist of the whole story for a while, but it's all known now. So after killing Stephens, Henry fetches this bully Martin Joseph, and they ride down and tell pretty Missus Stephens that her husband has been hurt, and they take her quickly up the mountain, where they proceed to rape and misuse the poor girl till she's lying on the ground begging for mercy, then they shoot her."

Mershon shuddered and shook his head. "Where does all this evil doin' come from? I swear I never thought to see so much killing and torturing till I took up riding the Territory. And what's so surprising is it's Whites and Blacks doing most of it. I figgered on fighting me some wild ass Indians, scalping and skinning and such, seeing as how it's Indian Territory." He took a breath. "So, how did anyone come to know about this?"

"Well, they didn't for a while, and it was the goodness of Henry's brother, William, that finally brought it to light. He is as fine a man as Henry was bad. Anyway, Henry got good and drunk, and he blabbed to his brother what they'd done to that beautiful girl. And that they'd tossed her and her things into a deep hole in a cave up there."

Yoes stared off into space a moment as if gathering his thoughts. "William and Henry had a terrible fight over it and Henry, he died. Hit his head on a rock." He slapped both hands on his desk. "Well, I've got to go. I'll fill out a warrant for you so you can chase after that no-count Joseph. He probably hi-tailed it into the Territory somewheres."

Mershon took the paperwork that included a rough sketch of Bully Joseph, thanked Yoes, and told him he'd see him in a few months. They both had a little chuckle over that, but it really wasn't that funny, just a way of erasing the ugly story. Folding the warrant into his shirt pocket, he left to begin a search for men to ride posse with him. At least he'd found someone besides the Christians to chase after.

Oh, well, it was the job he'd chosen, so he hadn't ought to complain. He'd been doing it for nearly ten years, and he'd probably ride into his grave chasing some ornery bastard who thought the world owed him all he could steal or kill.

After leaving Marshal Yoes, he visited three local saloons to pick up some men to ride with him in his search for Martin "Bully" Joseph. At the Bent Horseshoe, a dusty young cowpoke approached him, stuck out his hand.

"Name's Jarvis Norton. This here's my brother Colt." He took a boy's arm and nudged him forward. "Got that name cause my pa said when he bust outta Ma, 'ain't he a purty little colt?' He ain't but fourteen, but he's a tough rider. And we'd work for just half what you'd pay two. We're itching to get back at Bully for killing our pa."

The over-talkative young man looked fit and the boy could be handy for his small size because of the cave they might have to go deep in. Both were kind of shoddy and looked like they could use work in the worst way.

"I pay my posse a penny a mile each. The two of you settle for that?"

The man nodded.

"How come Bully to kill your pa?" Though tempted to hire the two, Mershon didn't want someone on a vengeance hunt. He could lose control.

"They got into it over some steers Bully stole. After Pa died, we lost the ranch. I'd give a pretty penny to help hunt that no good down and that's the truth."

Mershon studied the sturdy young man's expression. "Well, I reckon I can give you that for the help providing you look out for the boy. Keep him in hand. He shoot that six gun on his belt?"

Jarvis nodded. "Taught him myself."

"Also teach him to be wise what he shoots at?"

"Yes, sir, I did. My pa came back from the war." He glanced at his worn boots. "Ma died while he was away, but I held on to the ranch till then. Bully hadn't stole those steers we'd a kept it too. Pa was a good man, taught us the same. We'll do right by you."

"And the law, son. Do right by the law, no matter what." He'd give these two their penny each, couldn't see it any other way.

The spark in the young man's eye showed a desire to do right. Clearly he wasn't that much older than his brother. Probably not even in his twenties. Two boys left orphaned and homeless by Bully Joseph. More good reason to catch the son of a bitch.

They shook hands, Jarvis pumping right hard. Probably needed the money bad having lost his ranch. "You don't happen to know anyone else who might go along? I'd think as bad as this ole boy is, there might ought to be three of you to stand with me."

Jarvis didn't, and two more saloons later Mershon was set to just go with the two. But he wasn't happy about it.

By the next morning, all were outfitted with what they'd need for weeks on the trail. The Marshals Service would pay for renting a packhorse plus six cents per mile. He'd have to pay the posse out of that so maybe they could do with Jarvis and his brother. He was already keen for the adventure to begin.

The third night out in the middle of Chickasha country they camped near a small settlement of Native Americans living in shelters built of willows from a nearby creek. A Chickasha lawman name of Gray Cloud was spending the night with his wife and her people. While the men shared a pipe around the campfire, the conversation worked around to Bully Joseph.

Gray Cloud laughed bitterly. "A truly bad man, that Bully. He killed my wife's sister when she was not yet a woman. He was trying to take her up on the mountain. She ran off from him."

Mershon blew out smoke and handed the pipe on to the brave next to him. "This man has piled up the killings. He'll hang. The young girl's murder and rape alone will assure it. The rest will pile weight on the scales of justice. And believe me, Judge Parker believes in justice. Why didn't you get in on it when he killed your little sister?"

"I was off the other side of the Territory in the posse chasing after Blue Duck. Time I returned I could not find him. He is a white man, but I have been looking off and on since. Had I found him first I would have carved the flesh from between his legs." He grinned showing white teeth, something not often seen in adults. "I would be happy to oblige when you catch him. He could still hang from your judge's gallows without balls."

"You know I can't let you do that. But I *can* invite you to the hanging."

The Chickasha tossed a rock into the fire sending a shower of sparks high in the sky and said nothing further.

Mershon rose and stretched. "Believe I'll turn in, we'll leave by sunup tomorrow."

The silent Jarvis and Colt mumbled their good nights and followed him to where their blankets were spread.

Mershon settled his head onto the seat of his saddle and stared up at the stars, flickering in and out through smoke from the dying fire. He'd have to keep an eagle eye out tomorrow to make sure Gray Cloud didn't track them. If the lawman got the chance, he'd do more than geld Joseph. And once he was done, there wouldn't even be a body to tell the tale. Not that he had much against that, but hanging was the legal and white man's way to punish someone like that cruel animal. Trouble was, they had to run him down first. Men like him, though, had a way of leaving a trail. They couldn't stay out of trouble or bragging about it.

Five hard days of riding, and they ran into their first break at a post run by a bowlegged, rheumy-eyed white man who said his name was Hutch. He told them there was a deputy by the name of Spencer nearby who might know something about that Bully fella. He had set up a camp for a few days and had been in twice.

"Ye might find him yonder." His wrinkled voice was little more than a whisper. Good thing he pointed toward the north and a well-traveled trail.

Mershon led his posse out of sight of Hutch's post where he reined in. "I figure he's selling liquor to the local Indians and is real anxious to be rid of us. I want the two of you to ride on up the trail. See if you can come across Deputy Spencer. Find out if he's interested in joining us. I'm gonna stay here and watch that old coot. I see what I think I will, we'll pick him up on our way back after we find Bully. I brought plenty of long rope. He can follow us to Fort Smith on foot."

Jarvis chuckled. "Hey, I think there's a bear yonder. Be right back."

Colt stared at Mershon in disbelief. He took off his battered hat and pushed back long greasy hair before settling it once again. "Ain't Injun business for that Gray Cloud lawman?"

Mershon squinted in the kid's direction. "Not as long as the old man is white, it ain't. Indians is free to drink it if they can get it. We just can't sell it to them."

The kid shrugged. "Seems sort of unfair to me."

"Up to the Chickasaws. They lay down the law for their people. We can't interfere."

"What if an Indian kills a white man?"

"You ask too many questions, kid. You go relieve yourself with your brother and get on and do what I say. If you don't run across Deputy Spencer by noon, come on back, and we'll be on our way into the Arbuckles. Our man's gone back there to disappear. I feel it in my bones, hearing the way he hightailed it into that country once before."

"Okay, boss. Your say so. We count the miles we ride?"

"Hell, yes. Find a sign post somewheres to turn around at if you don't find him. You'll be headed for Texas going west. Stay vigilant, and don't get caught. Tell Spencer if he wants to go with us into the mountains to find this yahoo, to come on. From what I hear of him, we can use an extra gun."

He watched them out of sight, feeling for the two young men. They weren't alone in their plight, for plenty of families had been torn asunder in this wild country. But he'd like to think he was helping them a bit. One never knew. Hardship turned some into stronger men, but turned others onto the wrong road. And oddly enough, the best of life meant the worst of results. He'd seen it go both ways.

Before the noon deadline was reached he watched the old buzzard in the post sell liquor to several Native Americans he recognized from the Chickasaw he'd visited with the night before. The older ones had smoked with him, now here was the sumbitch preying on the younger men. Way too much.

Tying Tipper and the pack horse out of sight, he drew his six gun, crept back on foot, and stepped through the door. "Throw your hands up, you old bastard." Without waiting for the three Native Americans to react, he waved the six shooter in the air in their direction. "Drop that poison and get out of here. Now. Hear me?"

The young bucks startled, whirled as if not sure. Mershon fired a shot and one of the jars burst spraying the cheap rotgut all over the place. The overpowering odor nearly made him drunk. The young men took off in three directions. Hutch staggered as if to escape through the back. The next shot shaved Hutch's left ear, and blood spurted to mix with the spilled liquor. The old man must've thought he was a goner for he hunkered forward and wrapped both arms around his head. The sounds that came out of him were nothing short of whimpers.

"You old fart. Selling them boys that filth. I ought to pour it down your throat till you choke to death."

Hutch dropped to his knees. Blood dripped off his arm and made a puddle with the liquor in the dirt floor. He cried out a plea. "Leave me be. I can tell you where that fella is you're looking for. Just don't hit me no more."

Sheathing his gun, Mershon yanked the old man to his feet. "Bully Joseph? You know where he is? You tell me now, or I'll shoot that other ear off, you crazy old coot."

"I said I'd tell you. You done went past his place. He's living in an old shack back down the road toward the Chickasaw's place. Been there a while now. Said he's feared of going to the hanging place for what he done."

"Damn. We rode right past him. Did the Injuns know where he was?"

The old man's eyebrows raised, he shrugged. "If they did've, they'd have shot him dead for what he done to that little gal of theirs. Nope, he's been laying way low after he come here."

Mershon whopped him over the head with his hat. "And you willing to help him hide. How long's he been there and you knowing it and not telling Gray Cloud? He's liable to scalp your ugly hair right off your head."

Hutch shivered all over so bad Mershon almost lost hold on him. "Don't tell them, please don't."

He slung the old bastard to the floor once more. "I'll make a deal. You promise never to give nor sell them so much as a drop of liquor, and I won't tell them you knew where Bully was."

Hutch crawled back to him, grabbed his feet and gazed up, tears and blood and dirt mixed on his old wrinkled face. Mershon almost felt sorry for him, but not quite.

"I promise, I promise, I do."

He stared down at him. "Tell you what you're gonna do." The old man shook his head yes. "Get on your feet, and I want you to pour every bit of that liquor out here in the middle of the floor. Do it now."

For a moment it looked like Hutch would say no, but when Mershon took a step forward with both fists cocked, he crawled to his stash of liquor and began pouring it out, crying like a baby the whole time. When the deputy was sure every drop was emptied, he took out his stash of Sulphur matches. "Git out. Go on now and run."

Hutch's eyes grew large, and he crab walked out of the old log post, stumbled to his feet, and legged it down the trail.

Gagging on the whiskey smell, Mershon snapped the head of the match across his thumbnail, and when the flame flared, he tossed it onto the puddle in the floor, turned, and skedaddled. With a whoosh the soaked earth caught fire. Without a word, nor did he look at the retreating post owner, he climbed on Tipper and rode toward where he sent the two boys. Best if he brought them back before riding down to the shack Hutch had told him about and picking up the killer Bully Joseph.

When he settled in the saddle, he noticed the four Native American boys hiding in the cane alongside the small creek.

"You stay away from here, you don't need to be drinking that stuff. It's poison." Not sure if they understood, he shook a fist and spit on the ground.

They laughed and ran back toward their camp. Chasing each other like kids. Damn that old bastard. They were just kids, and him willing to sell them that swill.

Riding the trail, Mershon relaxed in the saddle, but he kept an eagle eye on his surroundings. Outlaws would never leave a lone rider alone for long. Right now, the land appeared pretty flat, but that was misleading. Ahead, the trail occasionally dipped enough to keep a rider out of sight for a spell. Then, like this very moment, what looked like hats would rise into the wavery heat and soon men, then the horses they rode would appear, indistinct at first. Winchester clear of the scabbard he reined in and drew a bead on one of the two.

"Stop where you are." No sense waiting till he could see the whites of their eyes.

"It's us, Marshal. Me and Colt. Hold off."

He whirled the rifle back into its leather. "I ain't a marshal, boy. I'm a deputy." Without replying they rode on up, and he turned to join them. Looks like you didn't run across Spencer."

"We did. He's wanting to join us and will be along shortly. He's packing his goods. Been out a while, looks like."

That could cause a problem. Mershon didn't want to wait til that old fart he sent skedaddling had time to change his mind and figure Bully could be the more dangerous of them all. If he warned him, then they'd be tight, and he wouldn't have to worry should Bully get away. He had to grin at the thought. A word he'd learned from Yoes and had been waiting to use it. Liked the sound of it. Besides mulling all this gave him time to think of the best way to go on this.

"Come on, men. We've a job and the quicker done the safer. Spencer can catch up if he arrives in time." He whipped Tipper with the end of his reins and loped away without further explanation.

Jarvis and Colt raced up alongside the bouncing pack horse. Good boys. Didn't need to ask why. Just come along. Leaving a trail of dust, they rode past the old man's empty post. The shack where Bully was said to hide was barely visible in some puny trees. He hauled up before leaving the trail. Signaled his posse to get down. Bent low, the three of them approached the shack. A window on the back seemed the only egress save the sagging front door, so he sent Jarvis there and kept the boy with him. He'd need some instruction before they went in.

Lips close to the kid's ear he gave his orders. Then proceeded to carry them out. While he stood out of sight beside the opening, Colt crept up to the sagging steps, kicked in the door and dropped to his stomach right there. Mershon filled the opening, gun drawn. It worked just like he figured. The surprised prey jumped out the window. Hunkered in wait, Jarvis clubbed him in the head with his pistol butt and when Mershon and Colt went around the shack, he was sitting on the unconscious man.

"Worked right well, didn't it? I'll tie his arms behind him before he wakes up, then we can celebrate. I was afraid we'd have ourselves a real battle with a bully like this one. You boys done just fine."

Jarvis grinned and slapped his brother on the back. "You didn't expect no different, did you, Deputy?"

Mershon shook his head and sighed. "No, son, I guess I didn't. Now let's get this yahoo back to Fort Smith. You got yourself a horse, Mister Joseph? If not, it's a long walk."

"I don't think he heard you. Maybe I hit him a bit too hard."

"Nah, you can't hurt someone as mean as this one. Go see if you can round him up a horse. After all, how would a horse thief not have a horse?"

Colt ran off to see if their prisoner might have an animal around somewhere. Mershon dragged Bully to his feet where he swayed for a few minutes before getting steady. He pushed him forward and heard a rider coming down the trail. "Take this no good, Jarvis. And watch him."

Shoving the man away Mershon drew his six shooter and watched the rider approach. "Hold up, mister. Right there."

The man did as he was told. "Deputy Marshal Spencer here. You Mershon or should I draw down on you?" He swung a leg forward over the cantle and dismounted without taking his eyes off Mershon.

"Whoa, good to see you. We had a real wild one here, but we took care of him. Me and my two boys here." Mershon holstered his sidearm and stuck out a hand. "Good to see you. Sorry about drawing down on you. A bit nervous about who might be coming. This man's known to run with some pretty bad boys. Reckon they're all dead and gone by now."

"Who you got there?"

"Let me introduce you to Martin "Bully" Joseph, wanted for the past few years for back shooting, rape, horse thieving, murder, and just about everything else you can think of."

"Well, congratulations. How you getting him back?"

"I've got a packhorse yonder. See you have one too. Maybe we could load everything on one and let him ride. Or, hey, we could make the sumbitch walk. It's only fifty, sixty miles to Fort Smith."

That brought a laugh from everyone. Colt came back leading a scraggly looking paint. "Didn't find no tack, Deputy. Jest this Indian pony."

Mershon reared back and pointed. "If that's the best you can steal, Mister Bully, then you can have it. I've heard those ponies give a right uncomfortable ride."

The kid laughed. "Maybe we ought to just tie him down across its back."

Hilarity built as Mershon proceeded to do just that. In a good mood everyone mounted up and headed for the trail.

Before they rode far, Mershon spotted the old man from the trading post sprawled along the edge of the trail. Well, hell, he'd have to take him in, too. They ended making room for him on one of the pack horses. He probably didn't weight more than eighty pounds.

They might could make it back to Fort Smith before pure dark if they hurried.

MARSHAL JAKE YOES looked up from his desk in time to see Deputy Mershon escort two prisoners into the courthouse across the street. The man had proven to be a very able deputy since Yoes was appointed U.S. Marshal for the district by President Harrison. Wonder who Mershon had brought in. There were ten to twenty warrants out at any given time, some more than ten years old.

Yoes went back to his paperwork. The reports would eventually go through him. Sure enough, the next morning he was approached by District Attorney Clayton.

Yoes invited him in and poured them each two fingers of whiskey. Once they had sipped, said their hellos, and relaxed, he got down to business.

"Who'd John Mershon bring in yesterday evening?"

"That's what I came over to speak to you about. He'll be here in a few minutes and the tale needs not be told twice. By the way, how's business going? You really have a job what with all your hotels and stores along the railroad. Must keep you real busy. Don't know how you handle all that and marshalling too."

"It's tough sometimes. But I have family to run most of them, the others are managed by trustworthy people. You know my dad was a merchant before me, and he taught me a lot. I couldn't pass my days without those stores and hotels to keep up with."

The door creaked open before the conversation continued, and Deputy Mershon peeked in. "Busy?"

Yoes rose. "No, come right in. Been expecting you. Saw you ride in yesterday. Curious who you had."

"You're not gonna believe it, but it's Bully Joseph."

"Bully...? *Martin* Joseph? I was hoping as much one of these days, but... after all this time how did you find him? Or was it purely a lucky accident you ran across him?" Yoes grinned.

"A little of both." He told his story briefly and included the old liquor peddler as well. "I think if the judge hadn't decided to send someone out once more with a warrant for the Bully, he'd stayed lost till one or the other of us died."

Everyone chuckled. Clayton interrupted the joviality. "There's a problem, Jake."

"What? He looked in good health so the deputy here didn't... uhm... *damage* him too much."

"No, not that. We have no evidence and all the witnesses to what Bully did are dead. I need something before we can go to trial with this man."

Yoes frowned. "He shot a man in the back, raped his young wife, killed at least two more men, caused the death of another, and we can't get a guilty verdict from our judge? I'm confused."

"I need something that we can bring in for proof. I understand William Loftus knew where Bully and William's brother disposed of the woman's body and her clothing. If I had those to present at trial, I could get the man hung. He raped the woman so her body where he said it was would be enough for the hanging without proof of any of the other deaths."

Mershon rubbed his chin. "I'll go after it. Take me some deputies. Already got two real good boys who are anxious to help me hunt down criminals. And Deputy Spencer is willing to go along in the posse. Where did this William say his brother disposed of the body?"

"Let's see. It ought to be here." Clayton paged through his file. "In a cave up on Arbuckle Mountain. In a fit of guilt or bragging, Henry Loftus took his brother William up there and showed him, but the family was too scared to say anything because they were afraid of Bully—er—*Martin* Joseph. He's meaner'n two painters with their tails tied together. Now that we've got him I'm sure William will talk. I'd bet he might even guide you up there now Bully's in custody and can't hurt him."

Mershon nodded and grinned. "I'd be pleased to do this. I want to see that awful killer hung."

A BLISTERING SUN climbed higher in the sky sticking Mershon's clothes to his skin. He wiped his face with a dusty bandana. Made it worse than it was, all gritty and such. The kid came up beside him, trotting his small horse.

"Slow him down, son. A man can't do without his horse, but his horse can do without him."

The boy laughed. "Never heard it put that way before. Sorry, I'm tired of riding in the dust of the others."

"Well, I reckon it's about time we stopped for a bit. That tree line up there will have some water if I recall. We'll rest a while and cool everyone off. No big hurry since we're not after men but evidence. You and your brother could've stayed home if you'd wanted." He said it without thinking. The two didn't have a home far as he knew.

The boy remained quiet.

To change the subject Mershon glanced toward Deputy Spencer. "Now that one, he's got him one hell of a horse, ain't he?"

Colt didn't laugh, but he turned to study the long-legged Appaloosa. "Well, seems to me like he 'bout needs him one like that, else his feet'd drag on the ground." He leaned toward Mershon and spoke low. "Lord did you ever see such a huge fella? And that Appy must stand sixteen hands at least. I'd need a ladder to climb on his back."

Mershon exploded with laughter. "Clear he needs a big one, though."

Spencer must've overheard cause he laughed, too. It was enjoyable riding with men who had a sense of humor. Sometimes by himself he'd ride for hours without a word or reason to so much as chuckle. His horse didn't have much of a sense of humor. The kid sure did like living, considering his tough upbringing.

Jarvis hollered at the boy, and he dropped back where he and his brother had an intense conversation. He hoped the kid wasn't chastising his brother for being too friendly with the older men. He'd make sure to find out and set it right.

The leader, William, held back his horse on the increasingly rough trail. Everyone did the same, looking to him as a guide to the mysterious cave. On the steepening trail the horses' hooves kicked loose pebbles and rocks into the holler below. Behind them the two boys rode, having a low conversation he couldn't hear.

Eying the tree-strewn green landscape, quite different from the flat prairie they'd left behind, he mapped out in his mind the twists and turns. Always good to know the way out in case something happened to the guide.

To his surprise, the next rest stop William settled with him and Spencer and spoke about the situation. "I never figured my brother Henry to turn bad. He was brought up good, like the rest of us. Sure is a wonderment what causes men to turn sour. Our folks was real good to us, though we had to work hard. But who don't these days?" He stared out across the string of green mountains spilling into the territory from Arkansas. "Ah, hell. Reckon I'll go fill my canteen. Best do the same."

Mershon watched him walk away. "Reckon he still feels some guilt over Henry's death after their fight. Not good to be responsible for the death of a brother."

Deputy Spencer took up the conversation. "Wonder how long it's gonna take to clear the Territory out so it'll be fit for settlers? Judge Parker is cutting a wide swath through the criminal gatherings. If the government leaves him alone, he'll clean this place up. I hear they're hoping to open this land for settlers, but they're still looking to us to do our part. Only two hundred of us riding hard and fast is supposed to catch all thousand or more and shovel them into his court house. I been doing this ten years, and it's like dipping water with a fork. Funny how we was brought in to make it safe from the Native Americans and turns out it's these bastards we're hunting."

Mershon followed William into the scant shade made by a scattering of sassafras trees. "This looks like a good spot to cool off these animals and ourselves.

Colt rode his pony into the water.

"Don't let him drink too much now, son."

"I know, Marshal. Pa taught me some about horses before he went off to fight the Yankees."

Jarvis smiled. "Some folks can't help being a pa."

William carried his dripping canteen to a fallen log where he sat apart from them. Man was having a hard time getting friendly. Perhaps he felt they looked upon him badly for what his brother had done.

Spencer pondered the earlier discussion for a while till they'd all drank and were relaxed in the shade. "You want to know what I think, I say hang 'em all high ever chance we get."

"Yeah, too bad that ain't legal." Mershon cut a fragrant twig from a sassafras tree and stuck it between his teeth.

Spencer snorted. "Yeah. Too bad. Takes too much time to haul 'em in, have a trial, turn half of 'em loose for us to catch again, and finally hang the other half."

"Be even worse if they hung someone who didn't do nothing. That's precisely what Judge Parker said. Said worse to hang the innocent than let the guilty go."

All the same, Mershon couldn't help thinking something more needed done to rid the territory of such violence. Just how many outlaws had Spencer strung up on some tree hundreds of miles from Fort Smith with never another word heard about it? Plenty of rumors about deputies doing just that, but he couldn't bring himself to do it, though there were times he sure as hell wanted to. Sure didn't appear to do a whole lot of good.

The subject didn't come up again and after a while they moved on.

They didn't stop for overnight till the sun sunk behind the hills throwing darkening shadows across the prairie and the air cooled some.

William scoped the land. "We'll not make the Arbuckles tonight, but maybe tomorrow, so we might as well lay out here along this stream."

Mershon joined everyone in agreement and made camp under some ragged trees. The blowing wind whispered through the leaves and cooled their sweating bodies. The two boys stripped off and jumped in a hole of crystal clear water. Soon they were laughing and splashing each other turning the stream muddy.

Lost in thought, Mershon relaxed on a boulder.

After Spencer took care of his huge horse, he came up behind him. "Remember being that young?"

"Not sure I ever was. Sometimes I think I was born old, or at least grown. Everything I remember is working at one thing or another. Went west on the Cherokee Trail with my dad when I was but ten years old. Cared for the horses and cattle all the way to California, then started panning for gold with my pa. We came back to Arkansas a few years later as broke as when we left. There was always something, then Pa died, and that left me on my own. Those were crazy years. Nothing scared me, and I near got killed a few times. Didn't realize it till I got old enough to know how easy it is for a man to die. I consider it a blessing I was scooped up in the deputy marshal search or I might be one of those outlaws we're chasing. Or dead somewhere."

As usual, William settled down a distance from the two deputies and stared silently into the campfire lending nothing to the conversation.

Mershon studied Spencer a moment. "Did you ever marry?"

"Shit, no. The life I live ain't nothing to ask a woman to accept. Not many women would be able to. You?"

"Almost, before the war. I come back, and she was married with two little ones. That was enough for me. At the time, it broke my heart, but I recovered." A burning in his eyes denied the truth of that statement.

In the darkness cast by thick woods, William made himself a bed away from the rest of them. Wonder if the man regretted what he was doing, maybe felt like he was betraying his brother by leading the way to the hidden evidence. Nothing he could do about that. We all had choices to make and then had to pay the consequences or gain some good from them. Might be a right fine idea to keep an eye on their guide, should he decide to turn tail and run or make them somehow accountable for his past losses.

A whippoorwill sang its melancholy song. Soon an owl chimed in asking who of the large night bird. When he awoke the next morning, the owl's question was his last memory before falling asleep. William's bedding was gone, and he hurried to his feet.

Damn the man. How would they ever locate the cave? He'd seen to it they had a rough sketch of the route so perhaps they could find it. Still, he disliked folks who didn't keep their word.

About then, splashing and shouts echoed from the creek. The boys must be up and about. Anxious for a good cool face wash, he stomped his way through the knee-high brush to see William, Jarvis, and Colt immersed up to their necks in the water hole, naked as jaybirds.

Spencer came up behind him. "Looks tempting, don't it?" Before Mershon could answer the other deputy peeled out of his clothes and jumped in with a huge howl.

"Come on in, Mershon."

Hell, he might as well. Clearly they weren't going anywhere till everyone was out and dressed. He stripped from his clothing and waded in. It was cold, no doubt bubbling from a spring deep in the earth. He lowered himself till the water was just under his chin. Too bad he didn't have some of his Ma's lye soap to scrub the dirt from his wrinkles.

Jarvis and Colt splashed everyone for a while, laughing all the time. Be nice to have such a happy attitude. Considering what those boys had been through in their short life, it was sort of gratifying to see their horseplay.

Colt was the first to climb out. "I'm so hungry my belly thinks my throat's been cut. What we got to cook for breakfast? I'll start a fire."

Jarvis followed his brother. "Let's eat the rest of that side meat fore it gets any greener. You old men relax, we'll fix this 'un." The boys laughed.

It turned out the two of them were pretty good cooks. They produced corn dodgers and fried side meat floating in rich gravy.

Sitting around the campfire enjoying breakfast, Mershon licked a gravy smudged thumb. "I'll hire you boys right on the spot to follow me with a chuck wagon and see I'm fed. This is larruping good."

Jarvis laughed. "Heck, Marshal, you can't afford us."

Even the silent William got a laugh out of that. The canopy of trees trapped a pleasant smell of smoke from the campfire.

All were jovial while they packed and headed on up the mountain. Must've been because they were nearing their goal.

William led the way. "We'll make the cave today if nothing happens. Be best if it's early afternoon and plenty of light down in there. I brought along some candles as it seems to me it was really a deep, deep hole where he threw them. Been a while since I was up there. Anyway, we may need some candles to find what we're looking for."

Clearly he avoided putting words to the discovery they searched for. It was on all their minds.

"How we going to bring up the—er—body or bones or whatever is left?" Mershon felt kind of silly asking the question, but such a rescue wasn't something he'd ever thought about.

"We all got rope and blankets, that won't be too hard to manage." Spencer appeared confident.

Well, sure, that made sense. In all his years of riding the Territory looking for and capturing law breakers, he'd never run across something like this. He wasn't really looking forward to it either. No telling what might be hiding down in the cave or the well, for that matter. Snakes, the things he hated most, loved dark holes. He shook his head at his ridiculous fear. A grown man who never ran from anything... well, *almost* anything.

William instructed that they leave the horses in a flat meadow before they reached their destination. It seemed everyone was used to obeying William, and Mershon didn't mind that much. William went to work digging supplies from his saddlebags. The candles, a box of Sulphur matches, and untied the bedroll from behind.

"Someone needs to bring another bedroll, too, and all the rope we've got. Need to make sure we don't have to come back after nothing."

It was amazing how quickly William took over once he was in familiar terrain and knew what was needed.

Colt hastened to gather what else they might have to have. The boy was going to be a right helpful hand soon. Might could talk him into coming along as a deputy on some manhunts. Keep him from ending up going the wrong way.

Didn't take long to see why they walked and left the horses. The path on up the mountain was made for goats. Sometimes the posse actually crawled through narrow openings on hands and knees. How in the world would they haul out a body?

At last, the terrain flattened out into a larger meadow abloom with golden daisies. From there, they gazed in awe out across the wide expanse of Indian Territory. Almost like you could see forever. Birds spread wide wings and soared below them, casting their shadows over the distant plains. William looked around as if puzzled. Mershon followed his gaze. Damn, if he'd got confused and brought them to the wrong place, they'd be up a stump.

Their guide made a loud noise and trotted forward, rocks tumbling under his feet. "Here it is. Growed up some since we was up here." He went to hacking away at low brush sending dead leaves and dust flying everywhere. He coughed and brushed at his face.

"Might could've brought an axe or something." Jarvis went to help, diving right in and clearing a path like he might be anxious to see what they come after. Soon the way was cleared to a large cave opening under the overhang of a bluff. "In here. They put her in here."

Easy to see why he brought candles. Not ten feet inside the hole, and it was pitch dark. The ground dropped from underfoot real fast. Startled everyone into grunting.

Holding back with his heels, Mershon muttered under his breath. A warning would've helped. Maybe he'd wallop the man on the head.

"Okay, boys. Hold up, we're at the hole. Mind where you step till we get some light."

"A little late with the warning, Will."

Colt came stumbling up behind Mershon, and he reached out in time to keep him from running right off the edge.

"There's a shelf over here where we can put everything till we get organized."

"Lord God, how'd they find this?"

"An old outlaw hideout from before the war. Men scrambled all over these hills hiding out from their enemy, whoever it might be."

In the dark, he could only tell who talked by the sound of their voice and what they had to say. "Still doesn't tell me how your brother found it."

"He didn't. He came up here with Bully. No telling about that sumbitch."

A match scratched, put off a Sulphur smell, and flared to light. William continued lighting a few candles till shadows crawled up the dark walls. A slight movement in the air caused them to dance like spooks.

William carried his candle to the edge of the hole. "Down here is where he said he throwed her and her things. Poor little gal. I still can't stop thinking about it. Maybe after the judge gets done with her we can have her a decent laying out."

"Good idea. First let's figure how we're going to bring her up here."

Jarvis approached, his eyes in dark pockets. "Colt don't weigh much. He could go down there, take a look and see what's what."

Colt hollered. "Yeah, hey, yeah. That'd be fun."

"I don't know if I like that. He might fall and get hurt. I'll go down. Ole Spencer here, he's too big. It'd take ten fellows to pull him out of there."

"Naw, ought to be me." William shuffled his boots on the gritty surface. "It's my brother had a part in it."

Mershon got busy tying the rope into a loop he could wrap around his butt. "While you argue about it, all of you back off yonder and wrap up in the other end. I'll only take a quick look, and we can decide what to do and do it right. Just lower me down right easy."

He waited till Spencer, William, and both boys had a good grip, then backed off the edge, feet walking down the wall. He was maybe ten, twelve feet down, when he heard it. Surely couldn't be what it sounded like. Maybe he was just nervous in the dark after his earlier run in with that blamed rattler in the cabin. Anyway, his butt clenched and his feet hunted for purchase. It was the distinct rattle of a snake, one possessed with a dozen or more of the things.

Dragging in a deep breath he stopped trying to walk down the wall to listen some more. Okay, he was just being silly.

From above Colt's face lit by candlelight peered over the edge. "You okay, boss? Okay?"

"Yeah, fine, let me down a bit more. Slow, though."

The face above disappeared and the rope lowered him a couple of feet. There was no imagining it this time. More than one of the devilish rattling, hissing things. Not one or two either. "Pull me up." His shout bounced around in the dark. "There's rattlers down there. Snakes of all sorts. Hissing and rattling. God, pull me up." Hollered words leaping about over each other. He might never live this down, but he could not go into a pit of snakes, not if they told jokes about him the rest of his life. "Get me out of here." He swore he must've walked up that wall without any help.

Once they pulled him back over the edge he dropped to the floor, gasping for every breath.

Spencer slapped him on the back. "You okay? Can you breathe? Dang I thought you had fallen in or something. You need to just sit there for a minute? Did you get a good look so you can go down and gather everything? You'll need a few candles and—"

"Hell, man. I'm not going back down there. It's a snake pit, pure and simple. Bet they're knee deep, every sort of viper known to man. I could smell them, hear them, all but see them." He dropped his forehead in his hand. "No, sir, I'm not going back down there. Sorry. Shit, I'll give my riding fee to whoever brings her out."

Spencer reeled up the rope. "I'll go down there. We need her bones and whatever's left of her clothes, the picnic things. Cain't let that man get away with this. No way. After this long her bones won't weigh but a tiny bit. We got another rope? I'll take it and a blanket down with me, make a bundle you can pull back up. There's bound to be a boulder in here somewhere we can tie this one around, and I'll skedaddle right on up here. Did some mountain climbing as a boy. Got pretty good at going up and down a rope. It's easy if you know how. Better not to sit in it, like you done."

"Spencer, I'm telling you there's snakes down there. A bevy of 'em. You'll get bit and die."

"Ain't a snake living I'm afraid of. Got this." He whipped his large knife from its scabbard on his waist.

William tugged on Spencer's arm. "He's right. The judge, he don't want any of us dying to get that stuff."

"Maybe not, but I'm telling you I don't want that killer to go free after what he did to that little gal and everyone else he killed. I can't even think of it." He took the longest rope from William and tied it around the biggest boulder near the deep hole. "Now, when I get ready to send everything up, throw down a blanket and another rope. I'll signal when it's ready, and you bring it up."

"What about you?" Jarvis sounded near tears.

"Hey, kid, don't you worry none. I've climbed ropes and walls steeper than these most all my life. I'll find plenty of footholds in these old rocks. It'll be like steps." He sat down, toed off his boots, and peeled off his socks. His feet gleamed white in the candlelight.

Jarvis tied a rope to one of the blankets. "Reckon this is big enough for everything?" Everyone agreed it was.

If he could've dug himself a hole and crawled in it, Mershon would have. What was he, anyway, a coward? No doubt he could've come back up that wall just like Spencer planned but not with snakes after him. The idea paralyzed him.

The large deputy marshal tested the knot holding the rope secure around the boulder, he made an odd looking knot around one foot, and stood on it with the other foot. Then reeling backward, he threaded the rope out through his hands and feet and lowered himself over the edge. He disappeared into the darkness so quickly Mershon ran to see if he'd fallen, but in the fading light of the candles lowered himself deftly. The darkness swallowed him up.

"Go ahead on and drop that other rope down, Jarvis. You and Colt hang on to the other end tight so it don't fall in."

For a while it was quiet in the black hole. From below first came the sounds of struggle followed by cursing the like of which Mershon had never heard. Surely to goodness, the snakes had got that big ole boy.

"What's happening? What'd he say?"

Mershon shouted into the hole. "You okay down there? Don't let them snakes get the better of you."

The only reply was a series of echoes and more cursing and more echoes.

"I reckon he ain't bit dead." Colt's eyes reflected huge in the light. "If he was, he couldn't make all that noise." He leaned down and held his candle low as he could. "He's a coming up. I think... I mean, yep, here he comes. But...."

The kid scrambled backward, dropping the candle into the abyss. The large deputy exploded out of the hole as if shot from a gun. Around one arm was what remained of a fat rattlesnake, another hung dead around his neck. In his belt was the knife he'd brandished earlier. He kicked his legs and bare feet clear of the wrapped rope.

Breathing heavy he turned to Jarvis. "You can draw that blanket up now, boy. I got her tied good. Not much left, so she don't weigh nothing. Be watchful it don't have any hangers-on. Here take this just in case." He whipped out the knife and gave it handle first to the boy. One more round of explosive cursing, and he unwound a rattler from around his arm slung it across the cave, then did the same with the one around his neck.

As if mesmerized, Colt and Jarvis stared at the huge man slinging snakes off like they were dirty shirts.

Sweat pouring, he pulled one from his waist. "Save some for supper if you don't mind. They're right tasty."

Mershon couldn't take his gaze off the deputy. It was the strangest thing he'd ever witnessed, and he thought he'd seen everything.

Later that evening, they sat around a fire eating beans and flame-roasted snake and talking about the weird occurrence.

Mershon glanced up from his plate. "You still think you want to be a Deputy Marshal, Colt?"

"I believe I'm gonna have to think about that, Deputy. I'm gonna have to think hard about it."

No one laughed any louder than the huge Deputy Marshal Spencer who Mershon would forever think of as the snake skinner.

Martin Bully Joseph was sentenced to be hanged after the evidence brought in by Mershon's posse was presented to the jury, and he was found guilty of the heinous crime.

THE SHADOW OF DOUBT: MARSHAL MAPLES & NED CHRISTIE

NED CHRISTIE ROSE early that morning, his mind on the council meeting to be held in the capital city of the Cherokee Nation, Tahlequah. Talikwa to the Cherokee. People would attend from all over the Nation to air complaints and listen to what the council had decided about some important issues regarding the plans the United States had for the nation. A meeting of the bicameral Cherokee National Council was comparable to a session of the United States Congress, just not as large.

Something Ned Christie despised about the fate his people had met was the lumping together of the Nations of the Cherokee, the Creek, the Chickasaw, the Choctaw, and the Seminole. Worse, all lived in what was called Indian Territory. Now the United States planned to take over the territory and make it a state, the same as the white man's Arkansas or Texas.

Arriving a day early in Tahlequah, Ned joined a friend to have a few drinks under a shade tree outside town. Meanwhile, Deputy Marshal Dan Maples arrived in town and began asking about Bill Pigeon. He then went to the same place Ned had procured his whiskey to get himself a drink. Ned soon drank too much whiskey and fell asleep under a tree. His drinking friend staggered off toward town.

Sometime later, as Deputy Marshal Maples rode across a creek, a man stepped from the trees, pointed a gun, and shot him twice, killing him dead.

It didn't take long to blame Ned Christie, who had been lying alone in those same woods sleeping off too many drinks. No one could say where he was.

Cherokee Statesman Ned Christie. He was charged with the murder of Deputy U.S. Marshal Dan Maples, on May 5, 1887, in Tahlequah, Indian Territory.

According to many history experts, Ned Christie was framed by a group of Cherokee who wanted to join the United States and thought Christie was a rabble rouser. They decided things would go much better for their cause if they saw him blamed for killing a Deputy U.S. Marshal such as Maples.

When news of the killing reached Fort Smith, Judge Isaac Parker sent out five men to capture that murdering Ned Christie and bring him back dead or alive.

Though most historians think Christie was innocent of that crime, that was not the belief of the judge nor some others of the time. The Cherokee was pursued for five years, though there is no record he ever "rode the outlaw trail." During the time he was a wanted man he continued to live with his wife, Gatey, and their son, Arch, near Tahlequah in his fortified double-walled log cabin while working to make life for his people free of the white man's domination.

As it turned out, this was a feat not easily accomplished. Under Judge Parker's orders Deputy Marshals kept up a constant pursuit of Christie following Maples killing. Time after time they'd think him cornered, and while they shot up his hideout, the man would escape. Famous lawman Heck Thomas once got a shot off at the well-known Cherokee. It wounded Christie in the face and sent two

Deputy Marshals and Posse pictured after a fight with Ned Christie in the Indian Territory, November 1892. Back row (left to right): Tom Johnson, Bill Smith, John Tolbit, Abe Allen, Wes Bauman. Front row (left to right): Captain G.S. White, Charles Copeland, Paden Tolbert, Heck Bruner, Dave Rusk. Courtesy of the National Park Service.

bullets into his son Arch Christie's chest. His wife Gatey helped Ned and the wounded Arch escape the law once again. During that battle Ned Christie was wounded and killed his first man, and that weighed on him terribly. With the help of friends, the family hid out in a cave where the two wounded men were doctored by Old Wolf. It was then that Christie vowed to never speak a word of white man's tongue again.

After two years of unsuccessful pursuit led by Heck Thomas against the wily Christie, Judge Parker asked well-known Northwest Arkansas entrepreneur, then Marshal Jacob Yoes, to choose a replacement for Thomas and sent a posse out once more to hunt down the "murdering Cherokee outlaw Ned Christie." Thomas wasn't one to fail in his duties.

Meanwhile, Christie wasn't lying around idle. His home had been burned to the ground by pursuing lawmen, and he and his friends began to rebuild, this time adding double walls of logs all the way around. In the end, what they built was a fort, and it was christened Ned Christie's Fort. Old Wolf burned his medicines to put up a protective circle, and the family moved in. Near the front door were Ned Christie's guns—cleaned, oiled, and loaded.

On that same day, Dave Rusk, the marshal chosen to go after Christie, and his seven deputies gathered. All were well mounted and heavily armed. They also took with them a wagon loaded with ammunition, food, and other stores. Rusk attacked the Christie Fort with all he had and a long battle ensued. In the end, Rusk limped away with the survivors, yelling into the air filled with acrid black powder smoke, "I'll be back, damn you, I'll be back."

And sure enough, at the end of four years of freedom for Ned Christie, Judge Parker sent Rusk back once more to bring that "thieving, dirty Cherokee outlaw in, dead or alive." But once again, the marshals failed when the dynamite they tried to use on the fort lost its fuses and refused to explode. The posse had no more stomach for continuing the long gun battle with Christie and deserted. So Rusk's dream of doing something the famous Heck Thomas couldn't do, and thus becoming famous, died.

Back in Fort Smith, Judge Parker put pressure on Marshal Jacob Yoes to end this and have Christie brought in, dead or alive. He was tired of his best Marshals and Deputy Marshals coming back empty handed and defeated by one lone Cherokee.

At the end of his rope, Marshal Jacob Yoes called in Marshal Paden Tolbert, explaining that Judge Parker absolutely, positively insisted that Ned Christie be dealt with. Tolbert declared he was the man for the job. He spent several weeks recruiting the best men to accompany him. One would be Rusk because he knew where Christie's Fort was located. Then Tolbert sent a special order to Coffeyville, Kansas for a small field cannon with a four-foot barrel. He wanted it mounted on a heavy wooden carriage that would stand up under the trip into the wilderness of Indian Territory.

He declared "he would blast that Cherokee outlaw to hell if he had to, but he would bring him back to justice in Judge Parker's court." He and his men waited at the train depot in West Fork for the delivery of the weapon plus the wooden crates that held forty bullet-shaped projectiles and enough ammunition and dynamite to destroy Fort Smith itself.

The posse, numbering twenty-three, lit out from the small Arkansas town on the West Fork of the White River, and after a cumbersome trip dragging the cannon, crossed the border into the Cherokee Nation. One of the members of the posse was Sam Maples, the son of the slain Deputy Marshal Dan Maples. He had a special reason for riding the trail in pursuit of the man he believed killed his father. He wanted to put a bullet in the killer.

On a cold November night, the sky crisp and clear, Ned Christie sat outside his cabin alone. For the past twenty-six hours his people had performed the stomp dance counterclockwise around the sacred fire that was said to have been kept perpetually burning since it was carried west over the Trail of Tears in 1839. Ned's wife and son were a part of the festivities.

Soon after Ned went in the house, the dogs began to whine and scratch at the door. He sensed something bad was wrong and rose silently, went into his shop, and cut locks from his hair in preparation for the dark times he believed he would soon face. Once shorn, he walked into the woods and buried the bundle of hair in a deep hole. Back in the house he took out his best suit and a white shirt and laid them out carefully. He must dress for this moment. With his hair cropped short, he looked different, older perhaps. Or maybe it was the knowledge that this time he would not escape the white man's ire that darkened his handsome features.

Outside, Marshal Paden Tolbert and his posse had surrounded the Christie Fort. Tolbert was a good and honorable man, and did not want to kill the man he'd been sent to capture. He wanted to take him back alive. But despite the marshal's urging Christie to surrender and leave his fort, Christie refused to surrender. With a heavy heart, Tolbert ordered the forty-pound cannon brought to bear. His shouts of Fire! roared into the still night, and one after another the projectiles slammed into the fortified walls of the cabin. The ground trembled underfoot. One cannon-ball stuck in a log, then fell out. One after another bullets bounced off the thick walls of the fort. It was almost daylight with no surrender in sight before Marshal Tolbert ordered his men to empty one of the wagons. Taking out all the dynamite, he tied the sticks into a huge bundle, lay it in the wagon, lit the fuse and set the wagon loose on the incline to roll into the fort.

Gatey and Arch and a few close friends who had remained with Christie in the cabin, escaped out the back way. Ned Christie survived the explosion and raced from the ruined fort, a Colt in each hand. As he ran into a hail of gunfire, Wes Bowman, who had hidden behind Christie's shop, stepped out and shot him in the back of the head. Sam Maples put several more shots into the body, as he'd sworn to do to avenge his father's death. To Paden Tolbert's dismay, the Cherokee outlaw he'd wanted to take back alive lay dead at his feet. He ordered the men to remove the back door of the fort from its hinges. They strapped the body to it, and placed it in one of the wagons for the ride home.

The slain Cherokee "outlaw" was put on display in Fayetteville before the long trip down to Fort Smith to report to Judge Isaac Parker that the man so long pursued by his crack team of Deputy U.S. Marshals had been captured. Dead. This is probably one of the single longest pursuits by marshals of one man in the annals of Judge Parker's court. And the irony is that in all probability they were after a man who had done nothing but to be in the wrong place at the wrong time and have the wrong enemies.

BEYOND THE BADGE

At the beginning of this book I promised that the stories would focus primarily on the U.S. Marshals and Deputy Marshals rather than the outlaws they pursued. The story of Ned Christie is an exception. Modern research suggests that Christie may never have been an outlaw at all. Because Cherokee blood runs in my own veins, I felt compelled to include his story and acknowledge the historical debate surrounding his reputation.

Christie was long portrayed as one of the most colorful outlaws in the Indian Territory, but the historical record is more complex. He was a Cherokee patriot and a member of the Cherokee National Council who opposed continued encroachment on Cherokee lands and worked to defend the Nation's sovereignty. Those political tensions likely contributed to the accusations that followed.

The chain of events that branded Christie an outlaw began with the death of Deputy U.S. Marshal Dan Maples. Maples left home that morning with four men to arrest Bill Pigeon, who was wanted for murder but was widely regarded as a medicine man and not considered especially dangerous. For that reason, Maples allowed his teenage son Sam to accompany the posse. The encounter that followed ignited a five-year conflict to capture Christie and drew several brave and honorable U.S. Marshals and Deputy Marshals into the pursuit.

More than a century later, in 1993, investigators with the Washington County Sheriff's Department broke up a theft ring and recovered a single-action Colt revolver believed to have belonged to Ned Christie. The weapon had been stolen from a collector near Lincoln, Arkansas, and remained hidden for many years after its original owner passed away. While it adds little to the historical record, the discovery stands as one more curious footnote in the long and controversial story of Ned Christie.

SWORN TO THE STAR: IKE ROGERS AND JOHN DAVIS

August, 1893

MARSHAL CRUMP STUDIED the two wanna-be deputies, each of mixed Black/Cherokee blood. Judge Parker preferred this mix in his Deputy Marshals because they knew Indian Territory and the places best to hunt down law breakers.

Since Native Americans referred to Blacks as black white men, it surely must mean there existed a bit of distrust between them. So who was Crump to say different, not being from this place? However, he had to consider Parker's belief, though it would be a while before he came to trust most of this cut of men. Considering the country's history, trust between Whites, Blacks, and Native Americans was tenuous at best. No matter who did the trusting. As far as putting them to work as deputies, it might not make a difference to Judge Parker what tribe they were from, but he, by God, wanted to know anyway.

Though Crump hated to admit it, coming into Parker's court direct from the Arkansas Senate was a tough change for him. The President had only appointed him for this job as U.S. Marshal because of his work in politics and him being a veteran of the Confederate army. He wasn't sure that qualified him to take charge of deputies, many of whom had never trod the trenches of bloody battle. Perhaps his time served in the war would help when it came to dealing with men like these. Then again maybe not. The judge would have to trust his judgment.

U.S. Marshals had been around a long time. Way before that blasted war, and still the government hadn't assigned them specific duties or given them uniforms. As a soldier, he worried about that a lot. Could be a good thing seeing as how it kept outlaws from recognizing the deputies. What would keep them from shooting each other he had no idea. With no training in chasing down the worst of humanity and bringing them to justice these fellas made up sort of a hodge-podge of a poor man's army. No telling how many of them would be killed in the endeavor.

The smallest of the two men standing before him, willing to lay his life on the line for God only knew what reason, stepped forward and introduced himself.

"Name's Ike Rogers, and I have my Freedman papers." Pride flashed in his eyes.

Crump studied him. Should he ask to see his papers? Perhaps not. Wasn't that what the war had been about, so such papers would be unnecessary? That was only a portion of what that war was about. Hadn't the South fought for their freedom to establish states with their own laws? Hadn't they lost as an enemy of the North's economy?

Crump looked up from his desk. "It's fortunate for men such as you that freeing the slaves was a side-effect of the North's prevailing in that war." He waved away Rogers's puzzled expression. "No need for the papers. It's a new day in America and there's a wilderness country itching to grow."

Rogers frowned, clutched the papers as if they were being threatened. "I didn't steal them. They're mine, suh."

Ill-tempered, he waved loose fingers at the man. "I'll look at them then. Maybe make you a colonel right off."

Rogers stuck out the creased paper, proof of a freed slave, a man of unproven mixed blood with no real place to go but a white man's battlefield. Thunderation, for now, his duty was to hire as many deputies as he could to replace those already killed in the effort. What the hell did he care about their knowledge? They'd end up in the territory, blood mixed in the killing fields till it made no real difference what color their skin or tongue their culture.

He was truly making too much of this. Just do the job of Marshal given by Judge Parker and let someone else sort out the results.

Rogers lay down his paper and put his finger on the word swear. "Why in thunder would we swear? Ain't that something decent folk don't do is swear?"

John Davis, the larger of the two, nudged his elbow into Rogers's ribs. "It means we promise, idjit. We promise to chase after and catch all the sons a bitches we can else we won't get paid nothing." He grinned at Crump. "Ain't that the truth, Marshal?"

Crump nodded and sighed, looked over the men's papers. Just so they'd understand he went through all the rules posted on the wall for everyone to see.

How much the job paid, what was expected of them, and so on. After all, he had known it wouldn't be lawyers and senators applying for a job that was clearly so dangerous and paid next to nothing. A blamed monkey with a gun could accomplish about as much as these fellows.

After swearing them both in, he pulled open the desk drawer and took out the badges the government finally got around to making for these guys stupid enough to walk into the jaws of death for no rhyme nor reason.

The men eagerly took the badges and looked them over closely. Dear God, they were excited to get the work. Jobs must be scarce in the territory.

"Never laid eyes on one of these." Davis ran a dirt-rimmed nail over the five pointed stars, then the lettering United States Marshal around the enclosing circle.

Crump couldn't help but smile. "You men are fortunate again. Up till a little while back men made their own crude copies out of silver coins. Now you understand, you are deputy marshals, but all the same U.S."

"Must be lots of Marshals though, ain't they? Considering the importance of it and all." This from Rogers, but Davis spoke almost over him.

"How many of us is there, Marshal? Deputies, I mean." Davis appeared to take over the conversation, speaking decent English as most Cherokee did.

Crump squirmed. Should he explain that these two would replace two bodies lying dead somewhere? Perhaps they would go on to the same fate? Claimed or unclaimed by buzzards from the sky. When some were killed, others were hired to keep the number up to 200.

Nah. That might make these two throw down their badges and run. Maybe not, but he dare not lose even so few.

It probably wouldn't make much difference to history in the long run, that only one Marshal was appointed at a time He likely would never leave his office to chase after the law breakers. But wasn't that the way things always were? Those in charge never walked into danger. It was his job as Marshal to keep track of all the crimes, and those who were captured or being chased and hire replacements. The courthouse paperwork took much of his time. For that matter, him being appointed after serving in the Rebel Army against the United States probably meant more to him than it would to history. Still that war, like all wars, was in the past as far as history was concerned, though he would never forget it. He shuddered at a violent memory of cannon fire and bloody fields, and let it go.

These men signing up to pursue those who were evil beyond belief had to be tougher and meaner than the filth they chased after, or they wouldn't survive a week in Indian Territory. How long these two would last out there was anybody's guess, and he dare not let himself care one way or the other. He fingered the corner of an arrest warrant for a brutal killer who had little reason under the sun for committing such vicious murders.

The new deputies' names printed crudely on paper might mean something one day or they might not. He tilted his head to read them. John Davis—Cherokee and Ike Rogers—Cherokee Freedman. In other words, a slave no doubt set free by his owner before the war.

"Well, boys, there's the wanted poster and a warrant for this man's arrest. He was reported near Tahlequah across the border from where he butchered these two folks. He's avoided capture for months now like he senses lawmen. Worse, he's bragged about it all over the territory. I'd suggest before you start your job you pin those badges underneath your jacket or inside a pocket so he don't see you coming. He runs, you go after him. It's up to you to bring him back to Fort Smith. He's probably still in Indian Territory, they all hide there. If he still has the gun he shot those folks with, you bring it back for evidence. Or anything else of value to the courts." As if they'd know that.

"Don't go running your mouth to your fellow tribesmen if you want to keep upright. Be smart and don't talk too much. And we've got others out there so don't shoot one of our own."

"Or let one of them shoot us, huh, Marshal?"

"Exactly right, uh, Rogers."

"Ike, everyone calls me Ike. Say, do we bring him back to you, Marshal?"

"No. Deliver him to the courthouse in Fort Smith with your warrant. That pays two dollars plus six cents a mile. Pay attention and make yourself available, and you can pick up extra change delivering papers, or prisoners, or serving summons."

Ike took hold of his companion's leather shirt. "Come on, let's get us some supplies and git to work. Daylight's burning, and I'd like to be over the border before dark. There's bad 'uns to chase down." He turned to Crump. "Say, how do we measure the miles we git paid for?"

Crump handed him two paper rolls. "These here maps. Each take you one and keep track of your trip. Keep a good record of your travels, and you won't have any trouble settling your mileage on delivery. Work together or set out alone."

Outside the door the two hauled up for a minute or two and took measure of people on the street. Made some remarks to each other. For a moment he watched them. Would he be looking at their corpses the next time he saw them? He shrugged.

If they stayed together, they ought to do okay. Less money but safer. He wanted them to, and that was strange since he'd come into this looking at it as just another job to be done. Still, with what awaited them, it was hard to say if they'd make it or be carried in belly draped over a horse one of these days after someone found their bodies splayed amid tree limbs.

First time since the war he'd actually thought of what it would be like to keep sending men out into certain death. He'd grown blamed tired of it during the war, and he'd passed that trial, but this... this was different. Men kept coming to sign up, some of them so young they surely still had their milk teeth, all untrained in the many ways of killing. All the worst ways. Anxious to fill the ranks of deputy marshals, most of them were not sure what they were getting into.

In his first month, Parker and his new marshal, D.P. Upham, appointed by President Grant, in July of 1876, had signed up two hundred, and in the seventeen years since Crump was appointed Marshal, more had come on. Granted, some just gave up and wandered on to something else, often without uttering even a goodbye. And too many already were buried somewhere. God help their lonely souls.

OUT ON THE street Ike Rogers joked around with John Davis while each checked their gear and the fit of their rigs. Ike's horse, a red dun he called Red for lack of a better idea, shouldered away the black speckled mustang belonging to his companion before the men climbed on their impatient animals. Davis appeared to be the friendly sort. Asked Ike to call him John right away.

"So you reckon we can join up for this first job? Maybe get along. The prairie can get weary riding alone. Poor Dominecker there"—John gestured toward his mount—"gets tired of my palavering and kicks up a fuss. Still ain't half-broke, but I like him that way."

Ike chuckled. "I 'spect if it gets wearying, I can do the same." Relieved, he joined his companion. "Long as he don't kick me in the head."

Exchanging friendly remarks with the likeable John, Ike trailed him toward the mercantile. It was good to pal up with someone as smart as John, especially when it come to talking white man's lingo. He discussed the value of the coins spent on beans, bacon, Arbuckle coffee, and cornmeal, arguing friendly like with the big man over amounts and choices. It was important they form a friendship, and Ike welcomed the possibility. It would help them survive what was to come.

On the way out of the store, John picked up a copy of the Fort Smith Mirror and stuffed it under the latigo 'neath his saddle. Maybe he'd read and explain some articles out of it to Ike, who found most of the white man's stories confusing.

Together they divided their purchases evenly on both animals' backs.

John tied the leathers tight. "Ever done anything like this before? I mean chasing out after some outlaw?"

Adjusting his heavy bags equally, Ike gazed off toward the territory. "I've already rode with Reeves in a posse he got up last winter. He's been a deputy for a long while now. Smart man even if he do be Black. It was riding with his posse that convinced me to sign up as a deputy myself. Best known Black working out of Fort Smith. We work hard, we can be good as him. Not many of us doing this job lest we have Indian blood. Reckon a little of both won't hurt us none, now will it?"

He took the folded warrant from his shirt pocket and spread it in the seat of his saddle. "Probably a good thing if we team up. Seemed okay with the Marshal so reckon we can both get paid when we bring this one in."

John chuckled. "I wouldn't count on that. Probably have to divide the pay."

"Why is it Whites never do what they say? It says a fifty dollar reward is offered. Don't seem much for a man who killed two people, does it?" Ike examined the wanted poster, his fingers crackling over the drawing of the killer's face. "Reeves told me the posse divides that there reward, us deputies don't get none of it. It's give by the railroad or such, and we don't work for them."

John nodded. "That's true. We work for Marshal Crump." Done with packing, John slid the folded newspaper free of the leather strap and opened it up. "Listen to this from the newspaper. A man identified as Abner Johnson, from the Choctaw Strip, hid behind the well in front of his neighbor's house till the farmer came out. Then with no further thought or warning, raised his gun and shot him in the face. When the farmer's wife ran out screaming, he shot her. The bullets tore into her stomach. She was alive when people showed up. Before dying of the horribly painful wound she described the man who she recognized as someone her husband had sold a cow to the week before.

"This here says it was as brutal a killing of the innocent as has been seen recently. This reporter would hope when the man is captured, Judge Parker will see fit to dangle him from a rope on the gallows. Sure makes that cow worth a lot, don't it?"

Ike glanced at John. "That don't seem rightly fair. Us not getting the reward."

"May not be, but we took a job, and we get paid for it. One has nothing to do with the other. Come on, let's get on the trail. We need to make camp in the Territory and be hunting by sunup tomorrow. We can be in the strip before dark and track this man down if we find someone who knows him or saw him."

To John it seemed simple, but not so to Ike. "Wait a minute. How do we know where he run to?"

"It's called detecting. Reeves said they all go into Indian Territory to hide out. Besides, he's from Tahlequah, and folks go home to roost." Without turning to look at his companion, John headed west out of Fort Smith.

"We'll show his picture to the ferryman crossing the river. He might've seen him or know someone who has. We got to start somewhere."

Glad to have partnered up with John, Ike growled into his beard and spit tobacco juice into the muddy street. Seemed like a hell of a way to start a job. "Never did like boats. Appears downright strange to have to ride in one in the middle of Arkansas."

"Only way to get across the river lest you want to swim it." John took over questioning the ferrymen. Flashing his badge, then spreading the wanted poster showing the crude drawing of Abner Johnson, he fell into a friendly conversation with each one, addressing them by their first names as if he'd known them a while. Luck came with the third man when he docked, unloaded his passengers, and quickly peered at the creased paper.

John put a finger on Abner's squinty eyes, then crooked teeth. "Easy to take him for someone with a mean thought or two, ain't it? Looks like he might be ready to bite someone's head off and spit it out."

The ferryman scratched his thick thatch of dark hair. "See a bunch a folks in a day, so cain't say for sure. But he sure does resemble a fella who crosses nearly ever day to work on the docks."

"You point us to him and be right, there's fifty dollars on his head. That is, if we catch up to him."

Ferryman scratched his tangled hair again. "Fifty? That right? Got to share it with you and your partner there." Again nails digging behind an ear.

Ike stepped back a bit. Could be he had bugs of some sort in that tangled hair. "Nah. Don't seem to be the way it works. We deputies get paid by the folks who hired the judge. They wanting to clean up the Territory. Time to get rid of everyone thieving and killing honest folks."

The ferryman looked amazed. "Sure bout time too. Why just last week one of the men working here got bonked on the head and robbed. Never seen anyone come around about it. Some of the men working on the docks are robbed a lot. Can't even get home with their pay. I'd be happy to see this 'un caught, and others too. Good idea that, paying good money to us who help the law." He grinned sheepishly. "Not that I'd have to get paid to help out."

"Is he over there on his job today, do you know?"

"Nah, it's been a couple days since he crossed." The ferryman appeared disappointed he couldn't steer them to Abner, or maybe just sorry he couldn't collect any money for his capture?

Ike pulled on his partner's shirt sleeve. "He is probably on the run. He will not be coming back to work what with a poster going around."

"No, but he might go home. If not, there is folks there who knew him."

To Ike this sounded like the smart thing to do. "Good thing we paired up. Two heads thinking is way better than one."

"Tahlequah is a long two days ride from the border. We ought to push the first day so as to arrive not all tuckered out when it comes time to arrest this feller."

Ike shifted in the saddle. "Best if we check any Indian settlement or post on the way. Make sure he does not change his route."

The hot sun crossed the sky slow as a snail on a rock. Here and there where a small creek meandered, a few scraggly trees nodded in the still air. Despite that they needed to get to their destination, Ike suggested short stops whenever they found water, shade, or both. Davis did not object.

Sitting on a boulder watching the mounts slurp water and muddy the creek where they'd already gotten their own fill, Ike studied the craggy silhouette of his partner. Hard to tell his age, but he was curious.

"Ever been married, John?"

"Almost, long time ago while I still attended church." Davis pitched a small pebble into the dirt at their feet. "I fell away, and she took up with another man."

"Oh, yeah? I never got the calling myself, despite the white men bringing their Christianity to our people."

John chuckled. "Funny you dodged talking about a woman and went right to church."

"I sort of figured being tied to religion would bring me to a lot of rules I could not obey. I am having none of it. I much prefer dealing with the spirits of our people. They are more forgiving."

"So I guess you never looked at another woman or entered a church."

Ike was silent for a minute. "No, but I spent a lot of time talking with God. I prefer his sense of humor. Come on, we need to be moving."

Swinging a boot into his stirrup, John glanced at Ike. "Sometime I want you to tell me about God's sense of humor. Have to say I never noticed anything funny about how he lays out life."

Two days later Ike reined in on a rise above a small farm. "Ain't this where we was told that murder occurred? Even if it ain't our horses is exhausted. Let's go on down and check it out. Careful like, in case our killer is hanging around. An empty place is a good hideout."

John slid off and dropped the reins to the ground. "One of us needs to stay up here while the other goes on down there and checks things out just in case. If he ain't hiding here, there may be something down there to show us where he might be."

Ike leaned forward without dismounting. "Like what would we be looking for?"

"Oh, a letter from back home, something bought at a local store we might check out. I'll go if you would rather." John studied the horizon.

"Nah, I will go. I am good at sneaking around. Hide with the horses yonder in that copse, and I will creep on down. See what I can find. You know how good we are at creeping. Us Indians. Keep an eye out and a trigger finger on that rifle. You are the good shot. If I need you quick, be ready to fire." Ike's eyes sparkled.

John nodded, picked up both animal's reins, and led them into the brush covering. "Do not worry. I can hit a mite on a flea at one hundred yards and not take the hair off the dog's back."

"Sure hope you do not have to prove that, my friend." Ike muffled his laughter and headed down the hill, one fist around his six-shooter.

Coming up on the back of the house where a small horse corral sat empty in the afternoon light, he crept bent over till he made it to the bottom of a window sill. There was no glass in the square opening within the logs. He slipped off his hat and raised cautiously till his eyes reached the bottom. Inside proved to be dark with only one other window in the small single room. A narrow cot slumped in one corner and a potbellied stove sat halfway along the wall toward the front door.

Time to get inside. Back against the logs, he took a step and something zinged through the window and past his cheek so close it ploughed a furrow in his skin. The burn might as well have been a fiery stick, and he gnashed his teeth. Could not help but think about what he had said about God's sense of humor. He liked to make a feller think he was doing just fine, getting along in this world, and then He would come along and knock him silly. Or in this case, set his skin on fire.

Hand cupped over his cheek, he whirled in time to see the shooter's shadowy movement from the back of the house out into the open, rifle pointed at him. "Don't try nothing. I'm good with this thing."

His partner up on that hill claimed to be even better. He sure hoped he was. But he was a long way off. And what was he waiting for?

Maybe he could talk this man down. "You always shoot visitors without finding out what they want?"

"When they sneak up on my house armed like you doin'."

"Sorry, I was looking for John Davis, and you ain't him. Place looked empty, so I was about to go on my way when you took a shot at me. Right un-neighborly, I have to say. You don't happen to know where John lives?"

Come on, John, shoot this sumbitch. It was like waiting for a circling stinging bee to land.

"Never heard of him."

The man straightened, gestured with the barrel of his rifle. "Get on over here." He raised the gun. "I figger you might be looking for me."

"Nope, said I was...."

The guy took aim like he was going to shoot and Ike broke off. What in hell you doing, my friend? Now is the time to prove that shooting talk was not just bragging.

A shot went off. Not sure where it came from, he squinched his eyes shut, ready to meet whatever might await. Another one followed practically on top of the first. The man made a low-down strange sound. Ike dropped to his knees in case he'd been shot and did not know it. He scrabbled for his six-gun, came up to see the man crumpled to the ground. In the background Davis rode toward him, leading Ike's horse and yahooing.

In case the man wasn't dead, Ike half-crawled half-walked to the body, Colt ready in case he moved. Reaching him, he held a palm over his mouth. No breath.

Davis skidded to a stop, the horses' hooves kicking up dust and gravel. "You okay? Hey, you do not have to worry, I shoot someone he does not get up again. Sorry it took a bit after the shot, got my damned foot hung up in the stirrup getting down off that wild mustang to find a good prop for the rifle."

Ike dropped to his butt in the dirt. "Thought I was a goner. Sure a good thing he ain't as good a shot as you are." He took off his hat, stared with amazement at the hole through the crown. "The bastard had another shot at me, same time you shot him."

"Wait, he took that shot? Hey, I thought it was your signal for me to get moving, and me kicking loose of the stirrup. Danged right he ain't as good as I am or you'd be dead."

"You know what I think, John?" Ike wiggled his finger in the hole in his hat. "I believe you ought to tame that horse, or maybe give him a better name. What the hell does dominecker mean anyway?"

"It's a rooster. Had me one as a kid. All black and white like ole Dominecker here."

"Well, that explains it. No horse wants to be called rooster."

Laughing, Davis dropped into the shade alongside Ike, who fell into discussing every moment of the day.

Pretty easy to be plumb happy to be alive and able to talk about it. The sun lay on the horizon before they rose, dusted off their britches, and went about checking out the scene.

John gathered up the man's Winchester. "Just in case God does have that sense of humor, we'd best make sure this is the man we come over here after."

"We be in trouble if he ain't?"

"Nah, not really. We'd still have one to catch. But he tried to kill us and that ain't allowed, seeing as how we're Deputy U.S. Marshals. I read it in the papers Marshal Crump had. The attempt does not amuse the hanging judge one bit."

There was no question, even though the drawing on the poster was crude, the unusual shaped nose and crooked teeth were just right. By the time they ran down the outlaw's horse to haul him in on, Ike was cussing up a storm.

"I'm too wore out to start back till morning. I sure didn't want to spend another night out here, but looks like we have to."

John laughed. "I warned you about God's sense of humor."

BEYOND THE BADGE

Uncounted mixed blood deputies, as well as Black deputies such as these two, rode the 74,000 square miles of the Western District. It is said thousands of outlaws were captured or driven from Indian Territory during Judge Parker's reign. At least 163 deputies were known to be killed during that time, though how many lay uncounted and going back to dust is anyone's guess as records were not always kept.

After working under Marshal Crump for two years, Davis was killed in August of 1895. He went to serve an arrest warrant on Sam Butler for robbery and murder. Davis received a tip that Butler was living with his mother near Claremore in Indian Territory. On Thursday, August 1, Davis reached the Butler's house around eight p.m., however Butler was waiting under an apple tree, and when Davis was in range, he fired hitting him in the stomach. The shot knocked Davis off his horse. Despite being mortally wounded, he crawled to his feet, grabbed his Winchester, and returned fire. He fired one last spectacular shot hitting Butler in the chest killing him instantly. Davis lived for another hour, dying just as doctors arrived.

Deputy Isaac (Ike) Rogers was related to Oklahoma humorist Will Rogers He worked with Deputy Bass Reeves often and with Deputy Rufus Cannon in the Choctaw Nation. Many of the outlaws that Rogers assisted in handling were later tried in the Fort Smith Courts. Rogers was not nearly as distinguished as Reeves or Johnson, and there are those scholars who feel he was less than dependable. As a deputy, his most famous effort was his part in the capture of Black Cherokee outlaw Crawford Goldsby, known as Cherokee Bill, the last man to face the gallows under Parker's reign.

Read the adventures of Marshal Crump and Deputy Marshal Isaac Rogers re-enacted later in The Wild Capture of Cherokee Bill.

A DANGEROUS DECEPTION: H.D. FANNIN

A NEARBY CLEAR stream offered welcome shade from the blistering afternoon sun. At times, Fannin flat-out thought of turning in his deputy's badge, leaving Indian Territory, and lighting out for the Rockies. To ride Buddy through belly-deep snow, to dismount and cool off in an icy pool. Yeah, and freeze his ass off bedded down under a saddle blanket on a windy January night.

That was funny enough to bring a laugh, and it did from way down deep. Buddy joined him with a curious snort. Hell, he was anyone's fool to even think of leaving this job. End up riding drag on a herd of dogies bawling or stampeding mindlessly, running over each other, dumb as they are. *Nah,* he'd done that once when youth made it possible. It'd kill him today.

Damn. Best if he quit thinking altogether, or he'd forget how close he'd come to biting the dust chasing a whole gang of owl hoots. But standing over one he'd downed, seeing the look of loss and anger, hearing the shout of despair with the realization that it was over. Now that, he needed as much as he needed air to breathe and a horse to ride.

Fannin always figured he had a choice at that point. Haul his catch in to the hanging judge or put a bullet through his toothless grin. So far he hadn't chosen the latter. Sometimes he rode into the night chasing after a wanted outlaw, other times he was so used to being out and about he went on whether in search of someone up to no-good or just plain enjoying riding under the stars.

Buddy raised his head, the long yellow mane blowing in the wind. Skidding to a sideways halt he pawed the ground, kicking up rocks that splashed into the water around a bobbing bundle. Dismounting, Fannin sat on his heels and tipped his Plainsman back with a thumb to get a better look. But he didn't really want one. A decomposing body rode the flowing water, caught in a tangle of twisted limbs. A long blonde braid floated out from the head. Above, dangling on a thin twig, something glinted from a golden chain. He worked it loose with callused finger tips. It held a tiny heart. Fury tightened his stomach, and he squinted into the sky a moment, then tucked the necklace in his shirt pocket. *Dear Lord, what could have happened to a girl of such obvious standing? Killing a child. God damn it.*

Staring down, his swallow painful, he shook his head. Got hold of his feelings. A dead body, that's all. How unusual for him to discover a corpse. Most of the time he went out in search of the killers after a poster or warrant was issued.

With a gentle touch he worked the body loose and lay it in the grass. Expensive store-bought clothing remained together. He'd been around ladies enough to know the difference in that and flour sacks stitched by hand while supper cooked. She wore one high-button shoe. He brushed a tear away to keep from looking at the small bare foot. Gritted his teeth against a muttered curse. Damn anyone who would do this to an innocent girl. He tucked her beneath some underbrush

Rising, he mounted the disturbed palomino. Turned him toward a squatter's shack slumped low in the distance. Doubted anyone there was missing the unfortunate victim, for she come from a better-off family than one living out here would be. Still he had to begin somewhere. That meant the man plowing the field with a mule.

He dismounted, wrapped the reins around a fencepost and climbed over the barb wire. A bullet zinged past his ear, its passing like an attacking wasp. He jumped. Turned to check Buddy, make sure he wasn't hit. Couldn't he go anywhere without being shot at? Wary, he held both hands open away from his body. Faced the armed farmer.

"Deputy U.S. Marshal H. D. Fannin, sir." He hated having to identify himself here in the Chickasaw Nation. Doing it or not, either way could get him shot. Was a matter of his own judgment. Chances of the fella plowing the field also being an outlaw were rare.

The mule waited shielding the man who now held a rifle by his side. "Show your badge, mister, before you come closer."

He had no desire for a shoot-out, but he never wore the damned thing. Spent too much time in Indian Territory, and it was best not to be known as a lawman by most of the worst kind living here. The whole bunch of 'em sent signals from one high spot to another over the rolling plains, warning of the coming of a man with a badge. Finally. he pawed it from his britches pocket. The silver, five-pointed star flashed in the sunlight

The rifle lowered. "Come on ahead. Tell me what you need."

He obeyed, kicking through lumps of red earth turned up behind the plow. "It's a terrible question I have to ask, sir, but do you or any or your neighbors know of a young woman missing in the past few months?"

The farmer pushed his straw hat sideways to scratch his head. "Not here, Marshal. And we don't fraternize with neighbors much, we live so far apart in dangerous territory."

He rarely bothered correcting folk's mistake of calling him Marshal. Didn't reckon it mattered too much that he was a Deputy Marshal. The small tracts of land permitted by the Nations to squatters were scattered here and there near the Arkansas border. Fannin had no interest in that. It was a Native American problem. He wanted to identify the body, even worse he couldn't just ride on. He had to find her killer. The urge was ingrained in him.

"You hear of such, tell them to get in touch with the U.S. Marshal's office in Fort Smith. Appreciate you don't mention seeing me here today. I'm taking her remains in."

"Thank ye for the same courtesy, sir."

"Welcome." Fannin strolled back to his horse. It paid to have the mutual aid of those not interested in killing lawmen 'cause they themselves often existed on the edge of the law.

He'd bet the girl lived with a well-to-do cotton farmer along the river. No doubt their daughter. There folks grew and shipped cotton and earned a fair living. Oddly enough, their slaves had stayed on as a work force after the war freed them. There was no place for them to go. He couldn't leave her there, this heat would do its worst on her. With dread, he returned to his task, unpacked a bundle of tow-sacks from his bedroll, spread them on the ground, pulled on gloves, and began the grisly work of readying her small body for transport to civilization. The remains tucked inside two burlap bags, he secured them behind his saddlebags. Buddy didn't like the idea, snorted and crow hopped away as if he could avoid the smell.

Fannin cupped a bare hand over the horse's nose. "Settle down, Buddy. You've carried worse." He swung into the saddle and squeezed with both knees. Buddy neighed and kicked. Fannin allowed it considering. With patience, he heeled the large palomino into a slow walk which he kept up all the way to Fort Smith.

The condition of the body meant it was bound to come apart. Still maybe the coroner would be able to identify what had killed her before Fannin lit out in search of the filth of humanity who'd caused it. There was nothing on the ground around her to give him a clue, but what with the recent rains, there wouldn't be. She was probably dead when she was tossed in upstream.

Back in town, he found Coroner Slack and presented him with the poor little thing. Because he would go after the sumbitch that did that to her, he hung around to learn what the man found out. The wanted would simply be listed as unknown killer, but he needed a warrant from Marshal Boles. The only other clue to who she might be or where she might have come from was a ring caught by the knuckle-bone of the third finger of her left hand. Possibly to signify she was engaged. Which could mean she was fairly well off. And the locket. Very few girls wore engagement rings or gold necklaces in Indian Territory. And she was white.

The coroner laid out the remains with great care. "I'll do my best with her. "

In spite of being around death, Fannin would never get plumb used to seeing the young butchered like this. He left the coroner with the dreadful smell clinging to his clothing and the hair in his nostrils. No matter the source, a fella had to earn a few bucks else he couldn't eat. No matter, though he'd catch the bastard. He stopped in at the barbers for a badly needed cleaning up.

Inside the door, Ernie, the bald man cutting the hair of old Mr. Simpson, looked up. "Wowwee, I can tell what *you're* after. I'll order you up some hot water, it'll just be a short time. Would you mind waiting outside, H.D.? I'm afraid you'll drive away all my customers."

Fannin looked around the near empty shop. "Would sure hate to do that, Ernie. But I do smell better out in the open air. Ever wonder how someone could take up being a coroner?"

Ernie glanced up through thick white brows. "Nor a deputy, either, H.D. Nor a deputy."

That brought a hearty laugh from all three men.

"Maybe after your bath you can tell me about it."

"Might ought to. I need to identify a girl that was killed, and I'm hoping someone will know she's missing. I been over in western territory after that Buck gang, so I need caught up. I'll come back in, and we'll talk. You get around town a lot."

Ernie waved a straight razor in his direction. "Good, but if you don't mind...."

"I'm gone." He slipped outside and sat on the bench to wait for his bath water to heat. No surprise no one sat down to visit with him though a few nodded. That was fine with him. He had some deep thinking to do.

Half an hour or so later, scrubbed clean, he returned to the barber shop to get a haircut and shave to finish off his once-in-awhile bathing. The old man was asleep in the barber chair, snoring softly. Fannin hated to awaken him, but he cleared his throat and touched the man's shoulder.

"Oh, hey, H.D. How was your bath?"

"Pretty good. Buddy'll thank me for losing all that grime and the stench."

Ernie chuckled and patted the worn chair. "Well, set down here, and we'll take off another pound or two." The barber shook out a cloth, tied it around his neck, and went to work on his shaggy hair. "Say, you wondered if I'd heard anything about someone being missing. Come to think, they was a little gal." Ernie tapped his lips with clean fingers. "Lord if I can remember her name. Memory ain't what it once was. But you go on over to the paper, they'll be able to tell you. Reckon you found her?"

"Aw, 'bout made me sick. I've seen lots of dead bodies and am sort of used to it, but this little gal, well, she couldn't a been very old. Barely grown. Found her in the creek just over in Chickasaw Nation. Not an Indian or a Black. Could tell that much."

"What was a White gal doing over there, you reckon?"

"From the look of her, I'd say she got dragged over there by some no-good. Clothing sort of quality not like a whore. She wore a purty ring on her engagement finger, and I found a gold necklace hung up on a nearby limb. Some rich farmers lives in the Nation along the river. She might've come from one of them, but they'd be out looking for her, surely."

"Sounds awful. Those dirty outlaws do their best to have their way with innocent gals."

"Well, I'm going over to the newspaper office when I'm done here and see if they know anything. I'm getting Singleton to run it in the paper, see if anything pops up. I intend to catch this sumbitch. I'll tell you one thing, this ole boy that did this better not even raise a lip to me, or I'll just hang him from the nearest tree."

"Huh, and who would blame you either?" Ernie stopped snipping, removed the cloth, and powdered Fannin's neck with a soft brush.

The sweet odor hovered in the small shop. "Owie, that smells good."

Ernie laughed. "Yeah, good idea you stay away from the saloons tonight, you're liable to get chased all around town by them purty gals."

Fannin thumbed a coin onto Ernie's countertop, spread his fingers through the new haircut and slid his hat on.

"I hear anything about that gal I'll let you know, H.D."

Civil War veteran Thomas Boles (1837-1905) served as U.S. Marshal for the Western District of Arkansas from 1881 until 1889.

Fannin crossed to the far side of the street to check a board posted with a few notices. He'd go on to the Marshal's office and see if there was a wanted. But he doubted that very much. Folks didn't tend to go to the local law in search of a missing loved one. That was for posters issued on robbers, thieves, marauders, public killers, gangs, and the like. If he found someone with an idea who this gal was, he could get started hunting for witnesses first, then the ones who'd done this horrific thing. He dropped in on Marshal Boles, who was excited and ready for him. "H.D., I hear you might've found the Devere girl. I was just fixing to get on over to the coroners."

"What do you know about this? I didn't find a poster."

"Haven't been able to get one done up that anyone can identify, H.D. She disappeared a couple weeks ago. The Devere family searched for a while before coming in to report it. Seems they were told originally she had eloped with some good looking fellow, a Creole cowboy from Texas, who'd been courting her for a while. Finally, one of her friends come out and said she was scared of what this ole boy might've done to her. We only just got the story about him such as it is. I'll go down there with you and see what we've got. Our artist can make a drawing from their description of the boy. Knew him by the name of Jason Labreu. Doubt he goes by that now. Everything's behind still yet since we only have this one's story."

Boles grabbed his hat from the rack above the door.

Fannin followed him out and down the street. "This is dreadful. No one in the family will want to see the remains I found. It appears like she's been laid out in the sun to bake, then tossed in the creek. Some animal's got to her face. I'm telling you, that family don't need to look at this."

"My God, what makes some people so treacherous?" Boles stomped along the boardwalk. "I hate to have to tell the family. They live off out near Chickasaw Nation along the river there. Name of Devere. I'll make out a warrant if you're planning on heading out to go after him."

"Blamed right I am. Quicker the better. You get everything drawn up and try for a sketch of this wastrel. I'll get the sumbitch. I want to speak to the family, find out more about what went on. Maybe find a witness or two. For what he done, I may not come back with him. Oft times makes me want to just carry back a pair of ears."

"Don't let the judge hear you say that."

"Yeah, well, then maybe I'll haul his ass down to the coroner's, and he can see what I found. He might change his mind."

"Best that's not said either. He's more than a fair man."

Fannin nodded. "I know, but sometimes hangings plumb too good for 'em. A hanging from some other parts would suffice how-some-ever."

"It's my experience men like that just don't give a damn what you do to 'em. You'd be wasting your time. Get packed up and ready to go. I'll have everything you need done by late this afternoon. Go on out and talk to these gals and the family. Maybe they have some notion where he might be headed so you'll know where to start."

Fannin got directions to the Devere farm from a man hauling a load of cotton toward the river docks. As he expected, it was a plantation style house surrounded with fields of the blooming plant, the boles white as far as the eye could see. Black workers lined the rows, bent like life-sized clothes pins. Plenty of money there. Easy to see why Labreu picked on their daughter. He'd get the story fast as he could and get moving. No sense them knowing the way their girl had died. Bad enough she was dead."

He introduced himself to the farmer who strolled out from the huge barn when the dogs took to barking.

"I've come about your daughter, Mister Devere. I understand she's been missing, and we have a body. She's down at the coroner's. She was carrying a necklace we've been told was hers. I'm so sorry to tell you this."

The man looked like he'd been pole axed. Fannin reached out to grab his arm before he staggered to the ground.

"Was it that no good that took her away from us? That worthless no good? Has he killed my girl?" Devere sucked in a breath as if he'd been kicked.

Fannin stared out across the prairie. "I don't know. We've been told maybe Leona ran off with some cowboy name of Jason Labreu. If he done it, we'll get him."

The father's eyes filled with tears. "You find him, you do me a favor and bring him to me first. Could you do that?" His fingers tightened on Fannin's arm, and he went on without waiting for a reply.

"I'd rather you didn't bother my wife, she's suffering something awful from Leona's disappearance. You talk to our boy Ned, yonder." He gestured back toward the barn. "He's the one knew who she went off with. Please, I need to go in now and be with my wife. If you'll excuse me, sir."

Fannin shook his head. "Coroner Slack will bring her to you whenever you're ready for the burial. You, nor the family, don't need to see her."

No way to imagine what the man's pain must be like. Maybe he would drag what was left of Labreu back here for him to finish off. Then they could both get some satisfaction out of their revenge.

THE STORY HE heard was bone shattering. Fannin found Leona's brother Ned inside the suffocating barn stacking bales of cotton.

"I wanted to talk to you about your sister. Do you know Jason Labreu? What he looks like? We need to find him." He couldn't bring himself to tell the kid about his sister yet. Maybe he could get a better description if he waited.

"What's he done? We warned Leona. Her friend Lizzie found out right away what kind of dirty dog that man was. He tried his charms on her first, but Lizzie was having none of it."

"Do you know much about him?"

The lanky kid shook his head. "Downright pretty boy from over Texas way and, despite our warning, he charmed poor shy Leona until we couldn't even reason with her. What's happened? Why you looking for him?"

"He's wanted by the U.S. Marshals. But we need to make a drawing of him."

"I can help you with that, I surely can." The boy described Labreu down to the color of his hair and that he was tall and muscled like a fighter... ice blue eyes that look right through you like a bullet."

Fannin drew a long, deep breath. "Son, I'm sorry to say, but we found your sister's body."

Ned kicked the wall with a heavy boot. "Dang, should've run him off once we saw what he was up to, but it was too late. Leona was lost to us."

Gagging, the young man turned away to gather himself. "Poor sweet little Leona. She didn't know what men like him could get up to." He could barely speak the words, but he stuttered on. "I wanted to take him out in the barn and whip the thunder out of him, but he was a big ole boy with lots of muscles. Told me once stay out of it or he'd have my head. I didn't doubt for a minute what he meant, but I shoulda done something anyways. All I did was try to get her to stay away from him, but she wouldn't."

"Why didn't you say something to someone?"

"I did, but it did no good. She was so smitten. Accused me of having the same thoughts about Lizzie was why I accused Jason of it.

"After a while of them going places, you know like church and picnics, we found out she was spending time in the woods with him. Once, she came home hiding tears and her dress was torn. She told us she had snagged it on a tree branch and wouldn't tell us why she was crying. The next day she was wearing a diamond ring, said they were engaged, but we were to tell no one. We only saw her a few more times. She had bruises on her face once. Another time her lip was swollen. He said that sometimes when she didn't pay attention to what she was doing, she fell down. Promised he would take real good care of her. They were going to elope. Bragged that he could easy get a job with one of the squatters in the territory and no one could ever find them. I wish to thunder I'd a got Pa's gun and snuck up on him and killed him. I wish I did." He turned and tried to hide a sob. "Poor, poor baby sister. Are you sure it's her?"

"Yes. I'm so sorry."

"No, no, no. He told us he loved her, and she loved him. Did he do it? She admitted in private to her friend Lizzie that sometimes he lost his temper but afterward he always brought her flowers and candy from the mercantile. What has he done to her? How do you kill someone you love? We never saw either of them again. I thought they really had eloped."

"I'm sorry, son. Real sorry. Looks like he's gone and murdered her."

Ned turned away. Hammered the wall with a fist. "I wish I'd killed him, that's all I can say." He dropped onto a cotton bale, face in his hands.

Fannin rode like lightning back to town. Prodded by what he'd learned of this man, he would leave as soon as he laid in supplies for a long stay in the territory. He'd find Jason Labreu or not come back. He sounded like the perfect specimen of a man hiding an evil heart. From what he'd bragged about getting a job with squatters and never be found, that's where he'd be. And so would Fannin, on his knees weeding cotton patches till he found the bastard. A pretty boy wouldn't be hard to find in the cotton fields.

Marshal Boles ran Fannin down at the mercantile putting together his goods.

"Got any ideas where he might be?"

"I'm sure he'll be working at one of the squatters places."

"He'll take out he hears you're coming after him."

"He won't hear."

"You won't be a deputy on his trail then?"

"Nope. He'll look up from hoeing a cotton patch and there I'll be, and he'll never see me coming cause I'm gonna be hoeing right alongside him. Do me a favor and don't put out the drawing our artist sketched of him. He just might be somewhere and see it. I don't want him to know we have any idea what he looks like."

Boles stuck out his hand. "Take 'er easy. See you when you get back." He turned, halted. "Bring him with you, H.D."

"I'll do my best. But either way I'll get him."

A HOT SEPTEMBER sun baked the back of Fannin's neck, but he kept right on a'hoein'. Took lots of rows and months to plant and grow cotton. The calluses in his palms had hardened and stopped bleeding. Across the row was a tall handsome fella he'd been working with for near a month after dogging his trail under several names. That was fine with Fannin, for he'd chase the sumbitch to hell and back if he had to. He'd gone under a few false identities these past months himself. Finally found Labreu at work a few miles out of Thackerville in Chickasaw Nation. His man carried a Winchester strapped to his back at work or at rest, giving Fannin no chance to draw down on him.

He tried everything to put the man at ease. Slowly befriended him, shared meals, and a room, and bed. After the remainder of the summer picking and baling cotton together he resorted to telling him a story of how he'd killed a man over in Dallas and how he'd got away with it by hiding out here in Indian Territory. Gave him some gory details.

His pal was real quiet for a long time. They'd shared all kinds of stories before but never a murder one. One that would put Fannin on the gallows should he be caught.

Laying in their bed that night, Labreu, going by Charles Ringer, convinced he could trust his new friend, finally confessed his own murder of the Devere girl. Almost like he was bragging to outdo Fannin.

"I held her under water till she couldn't breathe no longer, then for good measure choked her till her neck broke under my hands. Bitch, talked back to me."

All was quiet for the longest time, then Fannin, in his role as Dutch Muller, said, "Well, I believe you outdone me, you sure did."

It wouldn't be long before Labreu got to worrying about what he'd done. He might back-shoot Fannin, so he had to be quick. It was now or never.

The following night, after the call to supper, both men stood in line at the wash basin to splash their hands and faces with water. Chuckling at some action of another worker, the ever vigilant Labreu, who normally slept with his Winchester at night, stood the rifle against the wall to wash up, leaving Fannin in line behind him. What he'd waited for, the unguarded moment.

Without a second thought, he wrapped his palm around the stock of the bastard's rifle. It slipped through his grasp and his finger trapped the trigger.

Too late, Jason froze to stare into the barrel of his coming death. Fannin studied the expressions that twisted his face. Fight or surrender. He cuffed him without a struggle.

BEYOND THE BADGE

On the way back to Fort Smith, the prisoner found what he'd waited for. A chance to run when the blare of an oncoming train distracted his keeper. Too bad he ran in front of the speeding locomotive, thus cheating the gallows. According to regulations Fannin paid to have the body buried. Well, almost all of it.

Deputy Marshal H.D. Fannin represents one of the early Deputy U.S. Marshals with a talent for going undercover to get his man. Today this is one of the many important jobs of Deputy U.S. Marshals who wear no uniform.

THE FINAL CAPTURE OF CHEROKEE BILL: HECK THOMAS & IKE ROGERS

HECK WORKED HIS way through the noisy late-night crowd gathered in the Broken Spur Saloon. He didn't turn to make sure his two friends, Heck Bruner and Burl Cox, followed. They were in a tizzy to discuss what had happened in that fouled up mix-up in the Territory. And mostly figure out how to shift the blame for losing the notorious Cherokee Bill right when they almost had him. That blame was open for grabs.

He headed for a table in the corner to commandeer and grabbed one even though he had to run some drunks out of it. Serious business had to be discussed away from the courthouse, astir lately with exciting roundups of straggling members of the infamous Cook gang.

Someone at the bar shouted curses at a companion who promptly hit him over the head with a glass. By the time the fight was carried outside into the street, Heck was seated against one wall, with Heck Bruner in the corner, and Burl Cox on the other wall. All yackety yacking over who did what and who didn't. Despite his ill feelings against the ever-slippery Cherokee Bill, he chuckled at poor Bruner who looked as if he'd been sent home in disgrace.

"Good you got our backs to the corner, otherwise someone might shoot us." Bruner's low grumble carried beyond to the next table where a hot game of Texas Hold'em was underway.

One of the cowboys let out a chortle, then tried to look innocent. Thomas laid a hand on Bruner's tensed arm. "Leave it be. We ain't got nothing to prove."

Henry Andrew "Heck" Thomas (1850–1912), alongside fellow deputies Bill Tilghman and Chris Madsen, is credited with capturing more than 300 fugitives.

"That we're afraid to turn our backs in case the place might be bursting with outlaws doesn't say much for the power of law here in Fort Smith, does it?" Bruner had been mostly ill-mannered since missing a shot at Cherokee Bill. It was said he outdid the most cruel of gang leaders in the Territory for wicked doings. This time he'd shot a man in the gut and was gone, becoming the first man to escape from the Fort Smith jail.

Before their butts could settle comfortably in the chair seats a sultry gal hurried to be the first to serve the deputies.

"Bring us three dark lagers, Sis." Bruner beat Thomas with the order, so he followed up by showing three fingers. "Soon as you can, bring three more. It's been a hell-bent thirsty day."

The sparsely-clothed gal, name of Maggie Glass, smiled and touched her fingertips to his whiskery chin. "You bet, Marshal. Anything else I can get you?" She took her time rubbing full breasts along his shoulder. Bruner watched her go. Eyed him. "Looks as if you've got a bed for the night."

He kept an eye on the girl out of sight. Was she just looking to get something from him, or did she know something he didn't?

"D'rather sleep in mesquite with a side-winder. No time for dilly-dallying as long as that devil Cherokee Bill is back on the loose." He slapped a hand flat on the table, startling the other two who jumped. "It don't say much for Marshals who can't even trail and catch one lone wolf."

Cox, who usually kept quiet in the company of the two better known lawmen, spit a brown arch of tobacco toward a spittoon nearby, hit right on, grinned, and wiped his moustache. "Ain't every one criticizing our performance loud enough without you telling it too. Sides, he sure as hell ain't no wolf. He's worse than a sidewinder too. God's creatures ain't to be insulted by putting 'em up beside that varmit. Weren't me who missed the first shot at the bastard." He glared at Bruner.

His target aimed raised brows. "Don't be so blamed cantankerous, Cox. I'm the one ready to spit rocks. I'm aware I shoulda put one through his head when I had the chance. Don't let on you don't get thirsty and saddle sore once in a while. Hush your complaining and relax. We'll be back out there soon enough. Besides, who's to say Bill won't drop in here for a drink? We might look up and there he'd be. Ready for us to get the draw and fill him full of lead."

"Somehow I doubt that." Cox came back.

"Yeah, but you don't know it for sure." Bruner sent a sharp stare over the crowd, as if Cherokee Bill might be there this very minute. Of course he wasn't, and Bruner went back to his grousing "And I don't want to hear no more from you or I'm apt to drag you outside and show you I can shoot straight."

"Will you two shut up your palavering?"

Fed up with their yapping, Thomas checked out everyone in the place. All he wanted was to drink his lager in peace, then get back on the trail. They'd been after the escaped outlaw for days, weeks, hell, it seemed forever. Ever since Cook led a bunch of his gang on the first ever breakout from the Fort Smith jail.

Bill Cook, the leader of the infamous gang, was thought to have headed for Mexico, and the leftover gang members weren't doing so well with the exception of Cherokee Bill. He couldn't be kept locked up long. Since Judge Parker slapped high rewards on their heads the jail was filling up fast. When there was money to be had, the public was quick to give information to deputies, then keep an eye out to help catch the fleeing owl hoots.

"And the sumbitch goes to see his sister, giving us the only chance to get him, and we mess it up." Bruner stuck his nose in the mug and slurped aloud.

"S'cuse me, son. It was you out there taking pot shots at Cherokee and missing. I ain't getting in on the blame for that." Be damned if he would. He offered Bruner a dark scowl.

"In spite of over two hundred deputies, Indian Light Horse troops, and other lawmen swarming the Territory, we can't put one little ole creepy crawly out of business. Should've shot him dead the first time he took off out of jail. The way things look he can't be kept long enough to hang."

While his friends were sincere about seeing Cherokee hang, he himself was determined to be one of those who rounded up the outlaw.

As the exasperated judge said, "Bring him in dead or alive, just bring him in."

Dead would suit him just fine. And he'd bet it'd suit Bruner too.

He wasn't sure about Cox, who shared out the three mugs the girl set down on the table and offered an opinion. "I don't think we're going to ever catch Cook. We've seen the last of him. Shoulda shot the son of a bitch when we had the chance."

Thomas didn't remind him that Bruner had tried that and missed altogether.

He took a long drink and wiped his mouth in the crook of his arm. Seems everyone had an opinion about Cook. "Mexico can have him, far as I'm concerned. Some's been as far as West Texas to bring those bastards back here to be sentenced. Seems since he visited his sister over in Nowata, he might do it again. What if he just came back and hunkered down on her place with her? What if he was that smart? Wonder if anyone's keeping an eye on the place since Bruner botched it."

Crawford Goldsby, aka "Cherokee Bill" (1876—1896), in an undated photo with his mother, Ellen Lynch.

"Aye, God, do you have to rub it in?"

His old friend had to feel bad about that, so maybe he ought to back him up. Just as he was about to say so, Maggie dropped a glass, and it shattered.

A customer cursed her, another leaped up, knocked his chair over and socked the curser flush in the mouth. His target staggered backward toward the table where the three sat.

Thomas rescued his mug, stood out of the way, and took a long drink. Always easy to find a fight in this danged saloon.

The stumbling man landed in the middle of Cox and Bruner, pinned them in the corner.

Normally a calm sort of fellow when not annoyed with his own self, Bruner scrambled from underneath the pile. Thomas contemplated helping him, instead stepped aside to watch the altercation.

Bruner dived for the drunk who was still upright, and propelled him into a group of card players. Unperturbed by the fight, they had persisted on continuing their poker game.

The table and money scattered everywhere and the card players entered the fray.

Surprised at his friend's actions, he grabbed two men and slung them in opposite directions, then waded into the middle of the uprising.

He needed more than a good fight to clear the cobwebs from his brain. Breaking a trail through knots of battling men, he slung open the swinging doors, barreled across the boardwalk and into the street, where he stood staring up at the moon.

Just getting himself some air helped. Maybe he ought to howl at that old moon. Nah, he was getting too old for that kind of nonsense. Instead, he staggered to his horse, led him down to the livery stable and after seeing to the dun, curled up in the hay in the same stall and went to sleep.

The light of dawn and a slamming door awoke him to find his two companions asleep in the hay close by, their horses in stalls. Odd how they must've got there, considering the barroom brawl he left them in. Maybe that had cleared all their heads, rid them of their doubts so they could ride out after Cherokee Bill one more time.

He left his buddies groaning awake and rode back to the courthouse where enough lawmen were gathered to let him know something was up. He couldn't believe what he was hearing. The news traveled like a Texas cyclone. Cherokee Bill had been brought in by two deputies and a posse, and this time some of the best guards available were hired to make sure he stayed caught.

Sorry it hadn't been him who caught the fleeing outlaw, Heck Thomas lingered long enough to get the whole story from the very deputy marshal who caught the wily Cherokee.

DEPUTY MARSHAL W.C. Smith's story took Thomas back a few nights when Smith and Deputy Marshal Ike Rogers sat in the very saloon he and his friends Bruner and Cox had occupied the previous night. In fact, it could've been the same table. Smith elaborated on his tale.

THAT PRETTY GAL brings us some of that sweet lager we've ordered, and she and Ike act pretty friendly.

"Hey, Ike. You spend time with that pretty little thing back in her crib?" Smith asked him after she left.

"Hell, no. That'd be what do you White's call it? Incest?" Rogers replies. "Even we half-Cherokee know better than that. Maggie's my cousin."

We laugh and enjoy our drinks for a minute. What he says next is what starts the whole thing.

He says, "Her and Cherokee Bill used to have a thing though. They were crazy about each other once upon a time."

Smith took another drink or two, and got to wondering. What if they're still doing it?

As if he'd said that aloud, he goes on. "You know, Maggie stays with Bill's sister off and on. They're still friends. They used to meet there now and then, Bill and Maggie. Don't think they still do, though."

Smith stared at him for a long while. "You've known this all along and never thought to mention it?"

Ike gave him back a stare. "Sure, what difference could it make to anything?"

"Ike, you idjit. You call Maggie over here for a minute. Let's talk to her."

"About what? She don't know nothing about him and where he's at."

"You call her over here," Smith said. "Let me do the talking. Don't interrupt, you understand?"

He looks at me like I've been drinking more than a glass of lager. I wave toward her, and she heads our way. "You go along with this, you got it?"

Cherokee Bill posing with his captors in Nowata, Indian Territory following his capture in on January 31, 1895. Left to right are #5) Zeke Crittenden; #4) Dick Crittenden; Cherokee Bill; #2) Clint Scales, #1) Deputy Ike Rogers; #3) Deputy Bill Smith

She arrives, chest bouncing out of her outfit, and grins down at him. He glares at me.

"Well, introduce us, Ike. Go ahead." I nudge him.

First, I think he's not going to do it, but he gulps down another swallow and obeys. "Maggie Glass, Deputy Marshal Smith." He grins as if he's accomplished something smart and leans back in his chair to watch the two of us.

"Hello, Miss Maggie. I'm pleased to meet you. I'm about to help you earn a good deal of money, and you won't hardly have to do much at all."

Her eyes glisten. "I charge six bits for a roll in the crib. I don't do much at all, but you'll enjoy yourself." She puts her sweet hand on my leg, you know close to… well, uh….

I break in. "Ike here tells me you're cousins, so I'm willing to help you out. If you can do just one little thing for me, I'll see you get five hundred dollars."

Her eyes nearly pop out onto her cheeks.

"Sit, darlin'," I say, and she sits… hard.

"You know Cherokee Bill, in fact I understand you were once sweethearts. If you can get him to visit you at his sister's place, I'd like to talk to him."

She's already shaking her head. "What are you going to do to him?"

"Nothing. We just want to see if he knows where Bill Cook might be. We don't intend him no harm at all. It's Bill Cook we're after, sweetheart. Surely you've heard that."

She chews a fingertip. "You promise you won't hurt Bill? And I'll get five hundred dollars?"

I take her hand and nod. "Just be sweet to him, so he'll meet you there. That's all. Don't tell him about us, or he won't come cause he's afraid of us. He thinks we'll hurt him, but we won't."

Well, we talk her into it and arrange everything. She leaves him a note in a place she always contacted him, and we hunker down to wait. Figuring he will be real cautious it might take days for him to check her contact place. But he must've been anxious to see her. Turns out he's staying with his sister and just happens right away to find her note in a knot hole on the backside of the barn where they always left notes.

He shows up at her place the very next night.

Damn me, if he ain't cautious. I thought we'd never get him. He stays awake all night, sleeping with Maggie and his gun. Yeah, even when him and her is fiddling around, he's got it between them, finger on the trigger. She's a mighty nervous Dove, I tell you. He finally gets it on, and we think we'll take him, but shit no. I ain't never seen one man concentrate on two things so close in my danged life. Anyway, it's daylight before he finally lets down his guard to go piss in the yard, and we take him without firing a shot.

Good thing, too, cause Maggie is so scared by this point, she's fixing to tell him we're there.

So, in the end me and Ike Rogers capture the most famous outlaw ever to ride in the Territory. This time the judge says he's hired the best guards available to see the little devil don't escape.

HE FINISHED TELLING the story to his two friends. "And *that's* how Cherokee Bill was finally captured by Deputy Marshal W. C. Smith and Deputy Marshal Ike Rogers, all before we could ride back out and do it ourselves."

Bruner spit tobacco juice and eyed him. "I hope they can hang on to him long enough to hang him." He laughed at his own joke. Thomas didn't think it was one bit funny.

BEYOND THE BADGE

A few miles southeast of Old Fort Sumner on January 11, 1895, one might imagine the ghosts who looked on as New Mexico officers closed in on the very house where Pat Garrett killed Billy the Kid, to take the more infamous Bill Cook into custody without shedding a drop of blood. Cook was sentenced to forty-five years in prison.

After at least two escape attempts, Cherokee Bill was hanged in Fort Smith on March 17, 1895. Two years later, on April 20, 1897, Deputy U.S. Marshal Ike Rogers was shot and killed by Cherokee Bill's brother, Clarence Goldsby, at Fort Gibson, Indian Territory.

FOUR DEPUTIES, TWENTY HORSES: HECK BRUNER

POKER BEING SOMETHING to do while waiting to decide who to chase after next, Heck Bruner joined his deputy buddies Frank Jones and John McCann in the Broken Spur Saturday night. Before he could deal another hand Bill Tilghman stormed through the doors.

"Can't believe my eyes," Heck joked. "Just as we could use a fourth hand and in comes the busiest danged deputy in the Nation." He raised and waved his hat. "Hey, Bill. You got time between manhunts to set in on a hand before you go out on the trail again?"

"Nah, I just picked up a warrant and to be truthful I could well use some help. My old partner, Heck Thomas, is out on some wild chase. So I reckon this Heck will do just fine. Looks like you boys could've got together and picked a different name for one of you. Heck and Damn, for instance." All three joined him in laughter.

Bill went on. "Truth be told, I'm here to get some help on this warrant. Marshal Yoes saw you fellas come in here, and he wants us all to go out on this one. Says we need to show up in force and put an end to this horse thievery"

"Must be bad if you ain't big enough to put it down." Heck bit the end off his cigar and took his time lighting it. Squinted through the cloud of smoke. He liked Tilghman fine, but hell, his reputation made it hard to ride out with him. Sometimes he attracted trouble like a pile of dung draws flies. He allowed Jones to ask what was up.

Across the crowded room, two men argued loudly over their tab, and one of the gals squealed with delight when a customer smacked her bottom.

Tilghman raised his voice to be heard over the noisy bunch. "Well, it seems Doc Bland stepped deep in trouble when he fenced land in the Creek Nation. Just 'cause he married a Creek citizen don't mean those Injuns are going to leave a White man alone."

Jones laid down the deck of cards. "I heard some about him. Ain't he been fighting horse thieves day and night?"

"Hell, what'd he expect? Injuns think all horses is theirs for the taking, then he goes and starts raising them right in their midst. Fool built his place in the heart of the Creek Nation. Now he's lost a bunch of mares. Comes around begging us to help run them down. I reckon it is our duty, but those horse thieves could be hard to convince."

"Well, he's having all kinds of fits about twenty-nine head of mares disappearing. Granted that's a bunch of good horseflesh, and I can understand his being upset, but—"

"But, I'm in the mood for a good old fashioned chase." Deputy Jones didn't let Tilghman finish. "Beats sitting around losing all my money at the poker table."

"Losing, hell," McCann said. "You the only one ever goes away winning." He rose and grabbed his hat off the wall. "Well, what're we waiting for?"

Laying down his rare winning hand, Heck joined the other deputies shoving their way through the elbow-to-elbow crowd. You'd think some of these customers would have something better to do than hang around a saloon half the night.

"Let's go get us some horse thieves."

Out on the street, fires kept the town well lit, the smoke filling the air with the thick smell of coal oil.

At the hitching rail, Heck climbed on his spotted Appaloosa and followed the rest of the marshals down the middle of the street. Wavering shadows of the four men climbed eerily up the buildings.

Bland's ranch lay on the Cimarron and the ride to reach it would take most of the night, so he settled into his well-used saddle. No telling what they'd find or who might be lying in wait along the way to cut them down. That's what made marshaling so exciting.

Their horses trotted across the wooden bridge outside of town, hooves clattering in the dark silence. The dirt road wound through a thick stand of trees that filtered the light from the watermelon slice of moon.

The four talked among themselves in a soft drone of conversation. Heck relaxed and let the others visit. He liked to listen sometimes a lot more than say

Arkansas native Eli Hickman "Heck" Bruner was a Deputy Marshal in the Western District from 1880 until his accidental death by drowning in 1899.

anything. Tilghman was an intelligent man with lots of knowledge about stuff he had no feel for. Still Heck liked him a bit more than the stoic McCann and Jones. He would never have admitted it to any of them.

Best of all, though, he would've picked these men over a lot of others when caught in a gunfight. Not a one of them would turn away from a battle. Would stand tall till the very end. A fella never knew when his ride might be his last. So he wanted to go down with others who shared his stern belief in the law.

The ride to the Bland ranch continued on through the night. The moon crossed the sky and sank behind the horizon. He drank deeply from his canteen and hung it back on the cantle. Beside some large boulders, he reined in. The others followed him, dismounted, and relaxed while the horses snatched a few mouthfuls of prairie grass. All were content to sit on the scattering of boulders and enjoy the silence, broken only by the animals' noisy chewing, their discharge making small plopping sounds on the ground.

After a while, he rose and stretched. "Reckon we better head out. It's still a long ride."

With a general murmuring, denim rubbed on horsehide and saddle leather, boots hit the stirrups, and bodies settled into the saddles. Off in the woods something scuttled through dead leaves. A deer maybe, or fox, or family of coons. Water chuckled over rocks close to the road.

Heck closed his eyes and enjoyed the familiar night sounds. How in God's name did some folks live shut up in houses day and night? He'd climb the gallows before he'd settle for that. He couldn't imagine any life but the one he had.

To the east, beyond a slight rise, the sky brushed a purplish stain into a lavender glow that painted the distant plains. Their four silhouettes bobbing from ash to shadows approached the town of Choteau.

Bland's ranch sprawled off to the north, and they rode wide of the settlement to keep from meeting up with anyone who might carry news of the four arriving Deputy Marshals.

Ahead, a wide wooden gate with a large B on top announced they had arrived. A board fence marched east and west and out of sight. In the tall grass pasture, a small herd of horses grazed, raised their heads to neigh greetings. Before the deputies could reach the house a rider met them, his rifle butt propped on a stirrup so the barrel slanted toward the deputies.

Heck drew up along with the others, not anxious to get shot by mistake. Tilghman called out and rode to meet the man, a Native American dressed like a white man, and then signaled them all to approach.

"Come to the house. Doc is waiting for you. He is happy so many marshals could come." The man spoke with the sing-song Native American accent familiar to so many in the Creek Nation. "We hope you can stop what is happening. I do not think the Indians are doing it."

Naturally he wouldn't, but Heck left his judgment till he saw more evidence of the theft. At the hitching rail everyone dismounted and stretched. The horses tossed their heads and settled down.

Doc Bland stomped out the door, letting it slam behind him. "About time you got here. Follow me, you can see where they brazenly come right up to the barn, herded them out and was gone while we slept." Bent forward he hustled along while continuing to talk. "I followed a ways, then grew fearful they'd lay in wait and pick me off. So I come back here till you arrived so's we could go together. Ned White Horse there swears it wasn't Creek nor any other Injuns that stole them. He's my wife's brother, so he'd say that. I'm not so sure. They ain't been too happy to have me and my ranch on their land."

The Native American on horseback shot Doc a shriveling glare but said nothing.

Heck and the others led their horses and followed the old rancher.

Walking beside him, Jones muttered out of the corner of his mouth. "Whut the hell did he expect?"

"The man has the legal right, marrying a Creek woman." Heck wished Jones would leave his opinions behind.

But he wouldn't. He went on. "Just cause he's got the right don't mean he has to be so foolish. Dammit, you got to consider these Injuns been treated ever which way but good by white men for years now. We pen 'em up on worthless land, feed 'em rotten meat or none at all and expect 'em to be grateful for whatever rations we allow. Then we think we're entitled to live on that same land. Wouldn't surprise me if they ain't eating some of them mares, hungry as they probably are."

Shooting Jones a dirty look, Doc Bland hauled up short and pointed at the churned dirt a good ways from the barnyard. "See here where they headed off that-a-way. They had to break through the fence out there somewhere. Drove my herd into the creek and took off northwest. A feller cain't track even twenty horses running through a rocky creek bed."

Tilghman spit tobacco juice between his boots, then squatted and ran a finger over a deep hoof mark. "They gotta come out sooner or later. And when they do, we'll be right on their trail."

Heck went down beside him, studied the tracks that led into the creek. "That Jones don't shut up I'm gonna shoot him."

Tilghman, known as the best shot by far among all the Deputy Marshals, chuckled at Heck's remark. He often rode with Madsen and Heck Thomas. It was said he was truly reluctant to shoot anybody. The three were close friends. They were known as The Three Guardsmen all over Indian Territory. How they earned that name puzzled Heck.

Doc Bland insisted on going along on their pursuit, so they waited while he put his goods together and rode out of the barn to join them. He wished the old man would remain safely at his ranch and let them take care of this.

"Hope he don't get hisself shot, maybe even killed. We could do this without him." Heck mounted up but didn't voice his opinion to the rancher. It wouldn't do any good anyway.

By the time they rode beyond the broken fence, with still no sign of the herd leaving the wandering creek, high noon had passed and Bland was slumped in his saddle, drenched in sweat, his face red from the heat.

"Why don't you send him back?" Heck frowned to show his worry, yet he would leave the decision up to Tilghman, who carried the arrest warrant and thus was in charge.

The deputy finally replied. "Afraid he'll fall off his horse and drowned with no one around to help him. We can rest up a bit and have some chow yonder under those trees. Maybe he'll feel better then."

But Bland wasn't feeling any better as they gathered everything and prepared to head out after eating some biscuits and jerky. He staggered to his feet and McCann caught him before he hit the ground. Heck helped support him to a fallen tree and sit him down.

Jones watched from astride his horse. "We could just leave him here and pick him up on our way back. He'd be okay."

Though Heck hated the thought, the man was right. The rancher couldn't go any farther. "Doc, we can finish this while you wait here for us. You'll be fine. There's plenty of water and shade. We can each leave you some of our rations." He glanced at his companions, and they nodded. All but Jones who turned and walked away.

What was wrong with that man? Didn't he have any compassion at all? It took hard men to ride this trail, but to survive it also took some caring. Ignoring Jones's reaction he reassured Doc some more and convinced him he would be okay.

Not even an hour or so after leaving Doc, they ran across cut-up ground headed east where the herd finally exited the creek. It must've been ten miles or more that they followed the tracks left by the twenty horses. Ahead appeared a small rundown shack with a log barn huddled together in the center of the wide prairie. Typical for the barn to be a much sturdier structure than the house, seeing as that's how they made their living. Hiding and sheltering stolen livestock was all important. Out to one side was a slab corral crowded with the herd of fine looking mares. Doc didn't have to be there to identify them, but Jones went up on foot to check the brand.

He soon returned with the news that the animals carried Doc Bland's mark.

It was near dark by then, so Heck suggested they lay back till dawn. "Just as soon not start something where no one can see who they're shooting at. We'll go in at sunrise, arrest them, and drive the herd back to Doc's. Tilghman can then serve his warrant and be grateful to us for the help."

A low chuckle moved through the group. It was customary to share earnings in such a situation, but it wasn't required. Tilghman would do what was right.

In the fallen darkness, they retreated into a copse of trees and made dry camp so no fire would be spotted from the house. After eating the remainder of their biscuits and deer jerky, they turned in.

Bird song warned of morning before the sun peeked over the horizon. The sky glistened with a rosy shine when Heck awoke. Wishing for coffee, he wet his whistle from his canteen, the water having grown tepid overnight. The four horses were tied on a rope line between two trees, whinnying in reply to the penned-up herd nearby. In anticipation of a battle, his heart slammed against his chest. He could hardly wait to challenge them. In his experience outlaws who stole anything, valuable or not, were quick to shoot at anyone who attempted to hinder their success. Even men wearing a badge.

Crouched low he crept from one sleeping man to the next, making sure each was ready. Then waited for Tilghman to take charge.

The deputy was quick to do so. "Jones, if you could go around back in case there's a window, me and Heck will take the front and McCann you check both sides but stay ready to lend a hand if they come pouring out the front openings."

They surrounded the shack, and when everyone was in place, Tilghman shouted. "Inside the house. U.S. Marshals. We've got you surrounded. Come on out."

At their feet a shot cut dirt, then another and another, aimed at no one in particular, just making a statement.

It ceased and a man yelled. "What do you want, anyways? We got a family in here. We ain't coming out. You gonna shoot us and our kids?"

Heck exchanged glances with Tilghman, who hollered back. "Send out the women and children then. Don't want to shoot anyone, but you have to come out. Them horses out there ain't yours and the owner wants them back. Come on out here right now. Who is that in there, anyway?"

"Frank Shelby, that's who, and them's our horses. You got no right accusing us of horse thieving." Gunfire erupted from the two front windows. Heck and his partner ate dirt and returned lead, cutting chunks from the ramshackle house. Out back, McCann yelped. Must've shown hisself. There was no sign of Jones.

Heck cursed under his breath. Gunfire continued from inside, chopping clods of grass all around them, the deputies quick to return it.

"They must be barricaded good in there." Heck shouted to the others. "We're getting nowhere and neither are they. This could go on till we all run out of ammunition."

McCann came stumbling around the house. "Ain't no windows back there. One of 'em snuck out a side door around the corner of the house and got me in the shoulder. I never seen him."

"Where's Jones?" Heck wouldn't be surprised if that one had took off, seeing his attitude about Bland.

"Hell, they're just gonna keep shooting." Tilghman said. "Think we need to do something else. Before we run plum out of ammunition, let's retreat into the woods. We can hold them off from there till we think of something." He glanced up. "What the hell is that? Looks like something on fire out back."

Smoke poured into the sky, followed by flames that licked high in the air. A screaming woman ran out the front door carrying a baby, followed by several smaller children yelling their heads off.

Heck and the others stopped shooting, when two grown men and a couple of younger boys burst from the burning building. But he shouted anyway. "Inside, come out with your hands up."

Jones came running around the house. "Everyone out? I figured that would work. Good thing I had me some matches."

So that was where Jones had got to. But how did he get that big a fire going?

Rounding up the men and boys, Heck was too busy helping Tilghman tie their hands behind them to ask. What would they do with the family? Kids, a baby, the woman, who continued to scream while watching the house collapse in upon itself.

"What in thunder did you do, Jones?"

Short of breath, the man gasped out his explanation. "That wagon out back? I put some hay from the barn in its bed, set it on fire and pushed it agin' the back of this place. Didn't take much for them old boards to catch and burn.

Put a stop to the shooting right away, didn't I? Anyone out here need a hand?" He grinned great big.

"Naw, we're good as gold, Jones." McCann turned away from the man. "Bout time he done something besides complain."

"I didn't know if I had any matches or not. Then when I found some, I thought they had got wet. Almost never got one to light. Good thing that hay was dry, huh?"

"Okay if I shoot him now?" Heck glanced at their leader." Jones would continue with his bragging all the way back. He wasn't the kind of man a feller took to a long trail ride.

Always the patient one, Tilghman grinned. "Best if you hold off on that, at least for a while. Good thing he didn't set the barn on fire too. Let's see what else is in it, like tack, so we can saddle some horses to carry our prisoners back. Be a shame if they had to walk all day getting there, wouldn't it?"

Heck shoved one of the men, who stumbled forward and gave him a dirty look. "Oh, I don't know as how it would hurt these here thieves to walk a mite, long as the woman and her kids got a ride."

BEYOND THE BADGE

Though horse thieving in most western movies is a hanging offense, that was not true in Judge Parker's court unless murder or rape were connected, but the horse thieves paid a price nevertheless in time served.

William "Bill" Tilghman, Jr. (1854–1924) was a famed lawman, gunfighter, and politician. As a Deputy U.S. Marshal, he helped capture Bill Doolin and dismantle his gang.

THE THREE GUARDSMAN: BILL TILGHMAN

THE BADGE CAME off easier than Tilghman figured it would. The city of Perry could well do without him now that law was duly established. The door slammed open and Heck Thomas stepped inside the office.

"Well, we going or staying?" Heck went to the desk and dropped his badge on top, turned to smile. "You still going after Doolin?"

He smiled back. "You're damn right I am. Him and that Wild Bunch still raising hell, even though Marshals are after ever one of them. It's Bill I want, the bastard. Cut off the snake's head."

"You and me, we're still Deputy U.S. Marshals, even after taking care of the law here for a while. I'd say, we'll be the ones to cut off that head, so to speak." Heck went to the gun rack and took down his Winchester. Turned to Bill. "Well, I'm packed."

He followed Heck's lead, fetched his rifle, and led him out the door and down the street toward the livery where their horses and tack were waiting.

HECK THOMAS ALWAYS spoke the right words. A good friend since the two of them became Deputy Marshals back before the Cherokee Strip Land Rush in '93. Even then, Heck'd joined him in his foaming at the mouth over taking down Bill Doolin. Both were intent on breaking the back of that outlaw's Wild Bunch wreaking havoc across Indian Territory.

He squatted close to the fire and held out bare hands to the heat. "Damn February weather gets cold enough to freeze off a man's balls."

"Looks like you'd didn't warm the right things then." Laughing Heck dropped his saddle as close as he dared to the flames. "I was hoping to find better shelter from this blamed storm. Maybe an abandoned soddy or a rancher's shed."

"Where you reckon he's gone to? We ain't cut his trail in days."

"I'd say we head for Nowata where we can bed down in a livery till the worst of this is over. We won't run up on that bunch out in this storm. Six bits says they're in some rancher's barn. These folks are either scared to death of the Wild Bunch or being paid off by them. Can't much blame them. It's the onliest way for them to keep their families alive in the Territory."

He was right of course. Irritation at failing to spot some sign of the gang's members rose in Tilghman's gut. Bones popping, he stood, dragged his saddle over to the fire, flipped open his bedroll, and curled up in it. Dancing flames painted weird pictures till he closed his eyes.

Early sunlight woke him. Only trickles of smoke curled from the coals, the burnt wood smell hanging in the air. He gathered dried leaves and small twigs, knelt to blow on them till they caught, then steepled larger limbs to build a crackling morning fire. In a nearby shelter of trees, the horses nickered and stomped the ground.

He stretched and moved around to awake his friend. Maybe today or the next they'd run across a trail, some evidence that would lead them to Doolin and his gang. Winter out here would soon turn to spring and the chase would become pleasant, or at least comfortable. Until then, he would endure whatever he had to.

IN THE SPRING of '95, he sat across from Heck Thomas at a poker table in Guthrie and checked his cards. Three Aces and two Jacks. Another winning hand. Just as he pushed most of his money into the pot, a shouting and yelling broke out. Several deputy marshals shoved through the double doors up front.

Chris Madsen, and a couple of deputies he didn't recognize, bellied up to the bar with loud laughter. "We're buying for the house," Chris hollered. "We been busy ridding the Territory of filth."

Amid the noise he made out the names they tossed about. Tulsa Jack and Bitter Creek. "Killed the two of 'em back in April and last week damned if we didn't run across George Newcomb and Charley Pierce. Cut them down too. Thinning out that blasted Doolin gang."

He gathered up his winnings, bundled them in his bandana. "Come on, Heck. Let's get over there and find out more about this. Where those fellas go so does Doolin. First we've heard of any of the Wild Bunch in months."

In fact, he'd about lost hope of them still being in Oklahoma anywhere including Indian Territory.

He shoved his way alongside Heck to the bar next to Deputy Marshal Chris Madsen just as he did some more bragging. "Slowly but surely them devils is being wiped out."

Ordering a drink, he addressed Chris. "Any sign of that son of a bitch Doolin? We been riding and looking off and on for a couple of years. He's doing one fine job of hiding out."

"Hey, hiya, Tilghman. Heard you was still on the trail looking for him. We hear tell of him once in a while. Found these two running from robbing some poor rancher over in the Territory. Last month's when we caught up with Tulsa Jack and Bitter Creek. You know, these old boys won't sit still for being captured." He slapped the bar and Heck jumped. "They insist on being killed, and we obliged them. Reckon they fear the gallows over in Fort Smith."

"Can't say as I blame them. Between you and me, I do not intend to drag Doolin back there either. I'm planning on shooting him where he stands. Cause you know he'll come out fighting. Catching him means one of us don't walk away, and it ain't going to be me."

"Know the feeling. I took a posse with me. You alone?"

"No. Heck Thomas is with me, just there." He nodded toward his friend a ways down the bar enjoying his free drink.

"He's a tough man. Good at his job." Madsen lifted his glass as if to salute Thomas who returned the gesture.

After drinking and playing cards and visiting until late that night, Madsen searched Tilghman out. "Good luck. I'm going on my way now. Looking for "Little Bill" Raidler. Heard he's been spotted over near Tahlequah. Don't reckon some of them Indians would be hiding him out, do you?"

"Can't imagine they would. I've got an idea. How about Heck and I join you in tracking for a few days? Maybe we can run down some information about Doolin, as well."

"No skin off my nose if you join us. We don't get paid any more or less for the heads we take in." His loud laughter caught on and filled the small saloon.

They were still laughing when he left with Chris and Heck, trailed by a few faithful civilian posse members.

In September, Tilghman ran across a peddler while out scouting ahead of the posse. The man allowed as how, for a greenback dollar, he'd tell him where an outlaw was hid. Said he'd heard the talk at a nearby post about a suspicious fellow begging at folk's doors in the area.

It would be worth looking in to. Members of the gang were desperate since it had been broke up. Might lead him to the elusive Doolin. He followed the peddler's directions and along with Madsen, Heck, and the posse, ran down Little Bill Raidler, cornering him in a nearby barn.

"You got nowhere to go, Raidler. Best you just throw your hands up and come on out." He done the hollering since the others didn't want to. They just wanted to shoot. He wanted to talk to the man, maybe find out about Doolin.

It didn't do no good. Gunfire was exchanged and things got pretty hot. While shooting concentrated out front of the barn, he worked his way to a side door till he had Raidler in the sights of his shotgun.

"Where is that no good Bill Doolin, you little maggot? You tell me, I won't blow your head off with this."

Raidler stared into the large shotgun barrel, pulled off a wild shot that missed Tilghman by a foot. "I ain't telling you nothing."

Shots broke out from the front where the other marshals were waiting. "You ain't coming out of there alive. Might as well tell me, or you're going through the gates of hell."

Raidler raised his pistol, aimed it at him. "Meet you there, you bastard."

Shaking his head, he squeezed off the trigger of the shotgun, hitting the outlaw full on.

He shouted at the others. "I got the sumbitch. You can stop the shooting. I got him."

To his surprise and dismay, the no good Raidler didn't die from his wounds. But he didn't talk neither. They packed him out, and he lived to hear Judge Parker sentence him to ten years. He never did rat on the gang leader.

And Tilghman still hadn't caught up with Bill Doolin. Sometimes he wondered if he ever would. Still, he couldn't stop trying. Besides, marshalling being his job, it probably didn't matter much who he was after. Any outlaw would do. Still the way he felt, it was Bill Doolin, the leader of the Wild Bunch, he needed to put down. So he bid Chris and Heck and the others goodbye and headed east where someone thought they'd seen him in Arkansas.

Eureka Springs, Arkansas
January 15, 1896

TILGHMAN RODE DOWN the busy street that curved and climbed through the large town scattered amidst the hills. Bath houses invited him in but first he wanted to get the lay of the land. The man he was looking for was here somewhere. He'd followed every lead along the trail across Arkansas. People paid attention, and they talked. He listened.

Fascinated by the houses clinging to steep inclines all over the city, he saw what attracted Doolin, plus there were so many people here it was a good place to hide.

But that was only true if you really hid. And Doolin wasn't hiding. He'd talked to several folks, who were anxious to brag how they'd talked to the famous gang leader. He probably thought he was far enough from Indian Territory and anyone who would think it was important where he was.

So, before he started his search in earnest Tilghman would take himself a bath. The morning after he arrived he strolled along the street until he came to a bath house that looked promising. He opened the door and stepped in. He went through everything, paid, and went into the bathing room where the spring was. When he looked up, his gaze lit square on Bill Doolin. In the flesh. Mostly just flesh. And the man hadn't spotted him yet. He didn't give him time. Slapping at his bare hip where his gun should be, he froze in surprise. How the hell could he have been so dumb?

Bill stared at him but one or two seconds, then at last realized who he was and launched himself.

In a few raucous moments it was all over. Tilghman proved to be the larger and the stronger of the two, and he overpowered Doolin easily. Later, he wondered what the other customers in the bath house must have thought of the two half-naked men wrestling around on the floor.

He hurried to see the outlaw and himself were dressed before going into the main room and out the front door. January was no time of the year to run around naked. Doolin in tow he went to the depot and wired Marshal Evett Dumas Nix in Guthrie, Oklahoma, that he had his man.

I have him. We will be there tomorrow. Tilghman.

When he rode in on the train with the famous outlaw in handcuffs, so many people jammed the railroad station in Guthrie he could scarcely fight his way through. They cheered and shoved each other to get a look at the famous outlaw. If only he'd shot the outlaw dead like he'd planned.

BEYOND THE BADGE

Bill Doolin escaped from jail on July 5, 1896, but Deputy U.S. Marshal Heck Thomas and his posse tracked him down and shot him to death on August 24, 1896.

Thomas was one of Oklahoma's famed "Three Guardsmen," alongside Deputy U.S. Marshals Bill Tilghman and Chris Madsen. Throughout the 1890s the trio relentlessly pursued the Wild Bunch—better known as the Doolin Gang— capturing those who surrendered and killing those who resisted. Thomas killed Doolin, Madsen led the posse that killed "Dynamite Dan" Clifton and Richard "Little Dick" West, and Tilghman was responsible for the death of William F. "Little Bill" Raidler. Together, the three men accounted for most of the gang's remaining members.

DIVIDED LOYALTIES: FRANK DALTON

1882

STANDING TALL FACING the flag of this United States Frank Dalton held up his hand and was sworn in before Marshal Thomas Boles. As he said the words his chest swelled with pride. Enforcing the law was important to him. He would walk into the middle of a gun fight to stop those who stole, raped, and killed. By God and country, he would.

Shaking hands with Marshal Boles, he smiled. "I hope you know how serious I'm taking this, Marshal."

"I hope you know how serious it is, Frank. You can get yourself killed out there, so be careful. Them danged bullets hurt too. Now, I've got your first warrant already. You know you can take a posse with you should you feel the need. Find some good, brave men and get busy. Congratulations." Boles handed Frank a silver badge. "Best if you don't wear this carelessly. Sometimes have it inside your vest when you're looking for someone. The word gets around, you know. But wear it with pride when getting your man. Now, good luck and come back with this bastard who shot four of his buddies in their sleep so he could make off with their goods. He was last spotted at his folks farm over in the Choctaw Nation. Someone there can direct you to the place. Careful, he's a mean killer."

Pinning the badge on his vest where everyone could see it, Frank hurried from the Fort Smith Court House. The whole danged town would soon know he was a Deputy U.S. Marshal. Maybe Marshal Boles was right about hiding it on occasion, but this wasn't one of them. He headed for The Mule Shoe to meet his friends who were waiting to lift a glass to his appointment. His brothers Bob and Grat would be there too, though they thought him abrupt for taking wearing the star so seriously.

He shoved his way through the double doors into the noisy, smoky saloon. The odor of cigars and beer washed over him, as did the loud greetings of his brothers.

"Well, did you sell yourself to the law?" Grat raised his glass.

"You bet, and I'm buying this round to celebrate too. It's a mighty fine feeling knowing I'm going out there to keep law and order."

"I think you've lost your mind, but I love you anyway." Bob slapped him on the back. "As long as you're buying, I'll take one of those too." He indicated the glass Grat drank from.

A few of his friends crowded around to congratulate him.

"Already have my first warrant to serve. A fellow shot his traveler friends and stole their goods. Shot them in their sleep. What some men will do. I can't figure shooting someone who wasn't facing me. Or someone who hadn't done anything to me. Can you?"

He eyed his brothers. "Marshal Boles suggested I take a posse after this one. Why don't you boys go along? Get a feel for this kind of lawing. There'll be five hundred dollars to split."

Bob turned up his glass and gulped down the sweet ale. "Hell, why not? I don't have anything else to do today, it seems. When do we leave? I'm ready to do me some legal killing myself. Good thing they finally let deputies share in the reward. Makes it worth the trip, anyways."

Laughter swelled from the group and several of them followed Frank outside. "Man I'm after has a family over in the Choctaw Nation, so I figure that'd be the first place to go. If he ain't there, we might coax one of them into telling us where he might be.

"Get your horses and some rations for a few days ride and meet me at the edge of town in an hour. We'll ride out and figure to get over there tonight sometime. We can surprise the sucker at dawn if he's around anywhere close."

Already living a wild life, his brother Bob was bad to think up mischief that walked too close to lawbreaking. Maybe he could settle him down by having him tag along on a posse to see just how exciting this way of life could be compared to the one he had a leaning for. Tough and hard riding, the Daltons would make good lawmen, if he could just get them going in the right direction. How proud the family would be, seeing all the Dalton boys, riding side by side, out chasing down outlaws. Imagine that.

The gun battle with the killer was brief. When they cornered him in the barn, he threw down his gun.

"Well, that was less than exciting." Bob looked disappointed.

Grat raised his six-shooter. "Might as well bring him down here, save hauling him back."

Frank grabbed his brother's weapon and tossed it to the ground. "We'll take him in proper. Let the judge decide what to do with him."

Reluctantly, Grat holstered his Colt. "Shit, you ain't no fun at all."

Would he ever settle that boy down? Though it looked like Bob might make a good deputy someday, he held little hope for the younger Grat who showed greater leanings toward stealing than riding for the law. One day he might have to arrest him, or God forbid shoot him down to keep him from killing.

Back home at their ranch, he approached Grat further about his actions. "I don't like having to put you down like that in front of the posse. You can't act like a real lawman out there, I'm gonna have to toss you off."

"Yeah, you and your high falutin ways. Like you're the boss or something. No one would of seen what went on except us and not one would've said a word if we'd shot him. He had a smoking gun in his hand. I would swear to that as would the rest of the posse. He was an outlaw with a price on his head."

Frank grabbed Grat by the shirt front. "Dead or alive, you blasted fool. He was worth as much alive as dead, so why shoot him unless we had to? You need to learn a bit more before I'll take you out again."

"Well, don't worry. I won't ask to go again, and don't you ask me. I got me some more important things coming up. Go right ahead with your foolhardy ways, and I'll go mine. But I'll take my cut from the reward if you don't mind."

"Oh, you'll get it, don't worry. I hope someday I don't see you in the sights of my Colt, that's all I can say."

"Hah, you'll never get the chance."

Frank stomped from the room. That was maybe a bit foolish of him, but dealing with that boy was tiring. Later, Grat apologized for his behavior and continued to ride occasionally on a posse with him and Bob, but Frank saw in his brother a real dislike for sticking to the law. He expected one day to see the younger Dalton ride off into the sunset with lawbreakers and wished he could stop him.

Good thing Bob had taken to the task so well. He rode posse with Frank often over the next five years, and they took down plenty of owl hoots.

In November 1887, Deputy James Cole, who had become a good friend,

John Franklin "Frank" Dalton (1859–1888) served as a Deputy U.S. Marshal and was the older brother of Bob and Grat Dalton, leaders of the infamous Dalton Gang.

asked Frank to accompany him to pick up Dave Smith, a horse thief, over in the Cherokee Nation. Bob asked to go along, so they took him with them.

"I'm thinking we'll have to do some tracking to catch up with him. He was last seen camping along the Arkansas with his brother-in-law, Lee Dixon, Dixon's wife, and a man named William Towerly, already a coldblooded killer. Might be a tough take-down, and I could use some help."

Thinking to himself that a horse thief like Smith would be easy to capture, Frank rode out a bit ahead of the other two deputies as they approached the camp. On spotting them, Smith went wild and without warning opened fire. Something hot slammed into Frank's chest and knocked him off his horse. It was like a fire exploded inside his body, one that wouldn't go out.

Helpless, he lay on the ground clutching at his chest and gazing at the blue sky while bullets like angry bees dived close enough to sting. Gun smoking in his hand, Bob appeared at his side.

"Lay still, now. Cole just killed the son of a bitch who shot you." Bob pivoted on one knee and fired several times into the fray.

Sucking air, he reached out for his brother. So much to say, unable to speak the words while the world went from gray to a shimmer of brightness. He could no longer see Bob's face. Was this the day he was killed? Never had he believed it would happen to him. After unending, constant, noisy gunfire, and a pain he could scarcely bear, all went silent. Maybe he had died. But no, Bob touched his forehead with the back of a hand.

Cole appeared. His voice wavered over Frank. "Is he dead? Looks dead. Hell, I'm sorry, but I gotta go for help. Smith is down, and I got both Dixons, but I'm hit. Didn't see where Towerly went. I'll make it. Be back soon with some men and a wagon."

Bob's voice came muted. "I'll stay with him. Hurry."

Frank struggled back to consciousness. Goddamn, he had to rise. Lifted his head. Bob stood nearby with his back turned watching Cole ride off. Yonder came Will Towerly on horseback, aiming his Colt. He pointed it at him. Mouth open, he couldn't make a sound. Couldn't move.

No, no, please don't. Was that his voice shouting the words? No, nothing came out. The man was going to shoot. Him? Or Bob? Or both? He could make no sound. He strained.

Shouted. But Bob.... Dammit, Bob wasn't looking. He'd be next. Didn't he know Frank was still alive?

Tell Towerly to stop. He'd already been shot. He didn't have to do it again.

Bob, good Christ, Bob. Didn't he know Towerly was a murderer? He'd kill them both.

Frozen, he stared into the muzzle of the Colt pointing his way. It fired, bucked. It was like being hit in the head with a hundred pound hammer. Brightness around him turned dim, then dimmer. The pain faded, then darkness covered him like a blanket.

AT THE SOUND of horse hooves, Grat looked up from helping Dad muck out the barn. Bob, riding in alone. What had happened to Frank? Maybe he—but no, he would've come in with his brother. Afraid he knew different, hoping he was wrong, he hurried to meet Bob. Dad dropped his gaze and went back to forking old hay out the wide door, like he didn't care.

Running to meet Bob, Grat captured the bridle. "What is it? You look terrible."

Clothes covered in dirt, Bob dismounted and led his horse into the barn in silence. Grat followed, asked no more. The worst had happened or Frank would've been with Bob. By then, Dad had put up the fork. He paused to watch the two boys, as if he didn't want to know what they were talking about. It was like Bob to be close lipped about stuff. The family was used to putting up with his silences. But this.

Coming out of the tack room, Bob touched Grat's shoulder. "Come on inside. I don't want to tell it twice." He turned to look at Dad. "You too, Dad."

"Where's your brother?" Dad's face washed to white, his eyes narrowed. "Where the hell is he?"

Bob's expression and silence told what words couldn't.

It was enough for Grat. Frank was dead. That's all it could be.

He followed Bob, pulling him back with a firm grasp. "Where's his body? What happened?"

"I left the body at the undertakers. No sense in carrying him all the way out here. Best if the folks don't see it."

Unsure if that was a good decision, Grat followed Bob into the house where some of the younger kids were playing. Dad waited inside the door, like he might run out at any moment. Frank was the oldest, and Dad hadn't really wanted him to go to work for the U.S. Marshals. He thought all the boys ought to help with the farm after the family moved into Oklahoma.

"How in hell can I explain what happened to Frank? I don't know where to begin."

"With what happened, son. Where's Frank?" The harsh question made the kids stop what they were doing. Their stares swung from their brothers to Dad who glanced over at Grat as if he'd had something to do with this. He shrugged. What could he say? He didn't yet know what his brother Bob would say. But Frank was dead for sure. He waited along with the rest of the family, drew in a deep breath that sounded like a sob. But men don't cry. How many times had he heard that within the walls of this house where all fifteen children had grown up?

Dad took Bob's shoulders. "Dammit, are you too ashamed to admit you might have let something happen to Frank?"

"Dad, I... he... dear God in Heaven, they killed him. Right in front of me. I couldn't do anything."

Great cries of denial broke out from Mama and the kids. "No," she screamed. The sound tore at his soul. The kids all took up bawling, even the older boys. So boys could cry after all. What a strange thing for him to think right now.

Dad stared down at Bob. "Hush, Mama. You just hush and let him tell it so we know." His aging voice broke, but he held it together.

"The bastard shot him in the head after he was dead. Once wasn't enough for him. I went down beside him to hold him. Deputy Cole shot the bastard what killed our Frank. All I could do was hold Frank and cry. I'm sorry, so sorry I couldn't do more."

"I told that boy the Marshal Service would be the end of him." The door slammed, and Dad was gone, escaped to the front porch where he often took refuge from the noise inside the small house. Even in winter, Grat would sometimes find him huddled out there while the chatter of children all but overpowered his attempt to discipline them.

Later in the barn, while they readied a wagon to pick up Frank's body and carry him up to Coffeyville for his funeral service and burying, Grat tried to comfort Bob. He was sure tore up over this. Reckon he would be too had he seen Frank die.

Once Bob told him how much he liked riding with the deputy marshals. "It's exciting, more than anything. I guess it's the danger of getting killed that makes it that way."

At the undertakers, as they loaded Frank's casket into the wagon, he couldn't help but wonder if Bob still felt that way. If he ever thought Frank would... get killed, that is. He was so strong and brave. He couldn't believe it, either, even gazing into his brother's still face with the bullet hole in his forehead.

"You gonna quit now?" Grat scuffed a boot in the dust.

"Hell, no, I ain't gonna quit. I'm gonna ride out and prove that us Dalton's ain't cowards. Why don't you join me? I'm telling you, Grat, it never felt so good as when I'm out there dodging bullets, shooting back, taking down the worst outlaws. It's dangerous as all get-out, and that's what I like about it. You would too. I myself don't plan on getting killed."

"Neither did Frank." He shouted the words. "Who shot Frank? If I was to join the marshals, I could go after him and shoot him down, couldn't I?"

"Not this one. Deputy Cole shot him after he killed Frank. Too bad he couldn't cut him down before he put that bullet in Frank's head, though. But you could ride and take down others in Frank's memory. He was a damned good deputy. One of the best, they say, for being brave and honest."

"And what did that get him? But I'll tell you what. Let's go in tomorrow, and I'll sign up." Grat was ready to prove he was as good as his brothers.

Bob shook his head. "After the funeral, Grat. Dad and Mom want him buried in Coffeyville. So after this is done. It's best if we lay him to rest first, pay our respects, then Mom and Dad will be proud of us for doing our duty."

"Reckon I could just take Frank's place?" Right then, Grat was in a mood to shoot every outlaw on the face of the earth. Pay them back for his brother Frank's death.

"I don't see why not, but that'll be up to Marshal Boles. It's him that gives us our jobs, or tells us who we go after with warrants or just cause they're wanted. You can ask to pursue a certain outlaw or gang, but he decides." Bob spit between his toes.

"You and me brother, we can shoot ever one that comes our way. We don't have to take them in long as they hold a gun in their hand." Anger muted Grat's grief.

He and Bob left Frank's funeral to ride back to the courthouse in Fort Smith. Sending the boys a dark glare, Dad helped Mom and the kids into the wagon and headed for the farm in Oklahoma. Back in Fort Smith, Bob took his brother's arm and led him inside to where Marshal Yoes stood smoking a cigar.

Yoes watched them approach, held out a hand to Bob, then acknowledged his introduction of his brother Grat.

"I'd like to take Frank's place, sir." Grat struggled to get the words out, but it was all he had to say.

"Well, son, if you're anything like your brother, there'll be no problem. He was a fine man, and I'm sorry as hell he was killed. He will be missed. Let's go in to the office, and we'll get things figured out."

The marshal sat behind a cherry-wood desk where he drew out a sheet of paper. "I wondered if your brother might be interested in taking Frank's place, but perhaps...?" He glanced at Bob, who waited in the doorway, then addressed Grat.

"Sit down, son. Do you read and write?"

"Yes, sir."

"Good, not that it's a requirement, I'd take your mark, but read this, then if you agree, sign it, and I'll swear you in. You do understand this is a dangerous job?"

"Yes, sir." By then, he was shaking like a leaf. This was really happening. Somehow he'd been doubtful, but they were signing him on as a marshal to take Frank's place.

"Put up your hand."

Grat obeyed.

"I hereby swear you in as a Deputy U.S. Marshal of the Western District. Now, son, you are a deputy, not a marshal, so you do remember that though some folks will call you Marshal. You will work out of the Fort Smith division as did Frank. You will report to me and take assignments from me." Yoes glanced toward Bob, turned to present Grat with a six-pointed silver star, told the boys to go on home and be with their family. "Come on back in next week, and we'll see what we have for you."

It was over like that. He now represented the law in the Western District of Arkansas, and he was ready to head out. Next week was too far away.

THE FOLLOWING YEAR while working as a Deputy Marshal for the Muskogee court he took a bullet in the left arm trying to serve an arrest warrant on a Native American outlaw, but it didn't slow him down long. He went back out on the trail in less than a month.

The next year he arrested a number of fugitives. He loved his job and went about it in a wild manner.

On an April morning in 1890, Grat sat beside Bob outside the court house. That's how they got caught to ride over into Oklahoma together. Marshal Yoes came outside to fetch them. Those who hung around got the jobs, and the Daltons hung around.

A large man with dark features, Yoes was known as Black Jake, but the deputies didn't call him that. Not to his face anyway. He handed a warrant to Bob. "This man shot and killed Deputy Marshal Cox over in Claremore, Oklahoma. Fair description on the flyer. Bring the sumbitch back. Five hundred dollar reward, but I'd like to see him hung, so I'd appreciate it if we could get him alive." He fastened a dark-eyed gaze on Grat. "Hear that?"

"Yes, sir. I'll do my best. Unless he shoots at us or runs away."

Yoes stared at him a minute, then turned and marched off, boot heels clacking on the stone floor of the courthouse until the door closed behind him.

"A long ride." Bob mounted his quarter horse. It danced and waited for Grat to climb on his mount, a larger red dun. "You heard what Yoes said, didn't you?"

"Why you always think I'll do something I shouldn't?" He let the nervous horse turn a circle in the street and took off, breaking the speed limit on the busy thoroughfare.

One of these days he'd ride out alone and bring back the worst outlaw out there, like Tom Cook or Cherokee Bill and show them he was the best deputy of all two hundred of them. Wouldn't that surprise everyone?

The ride to Claremore was quiet. They met a few folks, all minding their own business. All greeted them, and they helloed back. The day was warm. Someone's dog chased a squirrel across the road and up a tree.

"What's this feller's name shot Deputy Cox? Do we know of him?"

"Names Alex Cochran. Nah, we don't know him, but he's a big ole boy with long hair. Says on the flyer he sits a spotted horse."

A few hours later they topped a small rise to get a good look at the approach to Claremore. Riding big as you please down the middle of the road was a man on an Appaloosa. Big horse, made the man look a bit smaller than they'd expected.

Grat shot over his head. "Hold up there. U.S. Marshals. Want to talk—"

He didn't get a chance to finish, for the old boy whipped that big horse into a gallop, moving fast as he could away from them. Bob reined in, leaped from his horse, took his rifle to a nearby rock, rested it there, and shot both the rider, then his horse.

Mouth open, Grat rode toward the downed outlaw in case he was still alive. Good God. "What the hell, Bob?" It wasn't like him to shoot a man in the back.

More like me.

His brother was one hell of a shot. Must've been three-hundred yards or more between them and the horse and rider. He rode at a gallop the whole way, hauled up and jumped down into the dust, turned and looked behind him. Yep, at least three hundred yards. Bob was truly a great marksman.

He bent over the still man, pulled off a glove, and touched his throat. Nothing there. Marshal Yoes wouldn't be happy about this. But at least this was one who wouldn't be pardoned by any of those ignorant politicians back east who had no idea what was faced by lawmen here. They liked to overturn Judge Parker's findings.

Best thing was, he hadn't shot him. Bob would have to take the blame for that. There was $250 each reward minus their trip expenses. Not a bad day's pay.

Unfortunately, the body they carried back on his horse was that of Alex Cochran's son. After quite a stir, especially from the family, Bob was sent to work for a time under the Wichita court to escape their ire. Though he was still in the Osage Nation, he and Grat seldom met up after that.

In spite of the excitement of getting to shoot at and capture men escaping, it appeared to Grat that owl hoots went away with a lot more cash and goods than deputies. But he kept still, at least for then.

He missed riding with his brother. One night in a post in the Choctaw Nation, the owner approached Grat while he drank in a dark corner.

"I'm a lookin' to buy some whiskey. Hear tell you and your brother are selling it. Maybe you could steer me right."

Grat grabbed him by the collar. "What brother? What you talking about? I ain't got no brother that sells whiskey."

The man tilted his head. "Aw, come on. Bob and Emmett both cutting a wide swath selling whiskey in Indian Territory. You mean, cause you're a marshal they keeping you in the dark about their illegal commerce?" The man grinned, showing tobacco-stained teeth. "Figgered you was selling it too."

Grat cocked a fist and hit the ugly sumbitch on his jaw. One of his teeth popped out on the floor. He lay there a moment, massaging his chin. "Well, hell, don't get so blamed uppity."

Bob, selling whiskey?

It soon proved true. Grat ran across his brother in a saloon in Fort Smith a while after that. He was so happy to see him that he hugged him, patted him on the back. "I've missed you sorely, how you doing?"

Looking down, Bob rubbed a big thumb over the lip of his glass. "Reckon you ain't heard. I was busted from the service."

Grat frowned. "What in the tarnation for? Ah, shit. It's I heard you was selling whiskey."

"Ah, wasn't that. Me and Emmett got in a battle with a bunch of Injuns, like to tore up a village and reckon we made a lot of noise. I suppose we was drunk. Anyway, Commissioner Fitzpatrick got word of it, called me in and demanded my badge. Then he discharged me from the service." He downed the full glass of beer.

"Aw. I know how much the Marshaling service meant to you. Cain't you do anything about it?"

He twirled a fingertip in the wet bar. "Nah, don't reckon I'll try. Say, want to go home and get Emmett? He's got some hell-bent ideas for taking over Indian Territory. Thinks I learned so much about the lawmen while I served we can get away with anything we please. How about it, Grat? You ought to be about tired of keeping the law. There's more out there if we don't." He pounded his brother on the back.

He was enjoying his job a lot, so much so that he turned his brother down.

Not too long after that he spotted a young black boy grab an apple off a cart in Muskogee, grabbed the little ragamuffin by the arm and shook him.

"Boy, I want you to stand over here agin' that wall. Tall and straight now. Don't move." He placed the apple on top of the kid's head, nestled it into the thick mass of black hair.

Eyes wide, the boy stared up at him.

He shook a finger under his nose, took a few steps backward, raised his Colt and aimed at the apple tottering on the child's head. "This'll teach you to steal apples. Don't you move, now, you hear?"

The little coward screeched bloody murder when the bullet cut the apple in two, then ran off down the street. Everyone standing around laughed and so did Grat.

A couple days later Marshal Yoes caught him out on the street. "In my office, Deputy. Now."

Inside the old fool dismissed him from the service. Said he couldn't be a marshal anymore because of his little stunt. Grat ground his teeth, but held his tongue. From what he heard, Yoes wasn't beyond shooting him in the foot to see he didn't walk for a while. So, fuming, he stomped away and rode home. This would make Dad and Mom happy anyway. Maybe it was for the best. Now he could join up with Bob and see what he had in mind.

BEYOND THE BADGE

Indeed the Dalton boys found plenty to do. Gathering up a number of outlaws, Bob, Grat and Emmett robbed banks and trains throughout Oklahoma for the next eighteen months before their careers came to a screeching, deadly halt in Coffeyville, Kansas. In 1892, they attempted a double bank robbery. The two Daltons, among other outlaws, were killed in the shootout. Emmett survived, was wounded and served fourteen years in prison. So came the end of two men who had served bravely as Deputy Marshals, the only reason for their mention here.

FORTY-TWO YEARS ON THE JOB: JAMES WILKINSON, EARL OF KENT

SOMETIMES JAMES WENT as long as a month without thinking of his heritage and what it could mean to his job possibilities. He could very well do better than ride for a rough and downtrodden gathering of law enforcement officers known as Deputy U.S. Marshals. Without uniforms and wearing badges handmade out of coins from their pockets, the deputies were a scraggly bunch who worked for a marshal appointed by a president who had seldom, if ever, set foot as far west as the Mississippi River.

Often he looked around and wondered what he, an Earl by British rule, doing riding with them, chasing murderous lawbreakers across country settled by Colonists? He could be living comfortably in Gloucestershire. Perhaps not in a family castle, but at least in an abode that outdid this... this shack he and his deputy mate were about to settle in for the night.

This trip to gather prisoners for the court had gone with very little trouble. Almost peaceable enough to be disappointing, in fact. James had joined this scruffy group because he craved fun, needing more excitement than dances and royal parties offered. Why else ride to pursue what his mate Ayers called owl hoots? He had to write that one down in his diary of American sayings. The list was growing.

His time in the Colonist's Union Army had introduced him to a life he found thrilling, one he would never give up. That of putting oneself amidst the danger of death. Actually daring his God to offer him the protection he needed to ride between bullets. He now found that same thrill serving the U.S. Marshals. After two years of service, he could not give it up. It was his chosen way of life.

In pursuit of John Billee, Deputy Ayers regaled him of some of the man's brutal crimes, and so he was surprised to have had such an easy time capturing the so-called dangerous outlaw and his two henchmen. He never wanted to drag in prisoners who were thought innocent of their crimes. These outlaws, owl hoots if you will, were so well behaved as to be like children on a lark. Perhaps this was a joke played on him by some of the deputies who had fun mocking his word usage. Most of them didn't speak the English language. What they spoke was only a crudely close copy.

Now on the way back to Fort Smith with their prisoners, two posse members, hired in case there was trouble, kept a wary eye on the three prisoners while Deputy Ayers pitched in helping James gather wood for a fire. For days in pursuit of their prey, they had settled each night in the dark to keep from being spotted. A dry camp, the Colonists called it. Ayers called it damned inconvenient.

Now they had the men on their warrants in custody, and it was time to relax and enjoy coffee and a hot supper of ham and gravy served over what the Colonists called biscuits. They would sleep indoors in the leaning shack using their saddles for pillows. Ah, what comfort. A hole-filled roof overhead. If he moved his head just right, he could spot stars.

"Keep a wary eye on this one." James cocked a thumb toward the murderer who had come without protest, which in itself made him wary. Everyone was unquestionably worn out from the long dusty ride to fulfill the warrants on the three prisoners, and this could make them careless. Be good to settle down, build a nice fire, and stir up something to eat. But doing so would take their attention away from their duty. Relieved nothing untoward happened, he paused for a long moment to stare across the huge prairie land surrounding them. The setting sun painted the western sky in brilliant golds and reds. What unending beauty this land offered.

He pointed toward the distant rolling plains. "What's in that direction?" Though reluctant to show his lack of knowledge of a land that to an Englishman appeared far more tremendous than anywhere he'd ever been, he had to get to know this vast place he had chosen in which to carry out his work. The only way he could learn was to ask, and so he took a chance on being looked upon as ignorant. People here were prompt to judge lack of knowledge as ignorance.

"The Creek Agency is just past yonder hills." Ayers gestured off to the left. "We'll be in Fort Smith tomorrow evening and be rid of these yahoos." Again he pointed out the correct direction. "Be my guess that at least Billee will be sent up the gallows steps, though our current Judge Story can be bought off with a pint or two, Billee is painted red in the blood of his victims."

An affable man, Ayers made a decent riding companion on James's outing. "Must be a dreadful punishment, dying with a rope around ones neck. It would appear that such a painful treatment would stop so many committing such crimes when they know they shall hang."

Ayers struck a Sulphur match and held it to the shavings he'd carved with his jackknife. The odor tickled James's nose, and he snorted, rubbing the smell away.

With a chuckle, Ayers blew the flame to life. "You'd think so, wouldn't you? But it don't. This land is choke-full of the meanest sums'a'bitches on God's green earth."

Once the flames licked into the dried wood, Ayers settled back against his saddle and James memorized some more words he hadn't heard. "What brought you to this country anyways? All the way from England. Must've been strange crossing the big pond and coming to a new place like this. I'd find it scary, in a way. Nearly druther be caught in a gunfight in the middle of a cyclone."

James chuckled. "About was like that. Was years ago now I came, though. I was just a kid when I arrived more eager for a new life than anything else. I became caught up in your Civil War before I knew what was happening. Liked the fighting though. Got out and wandered about for a spell. Couldn't become involved in much of anything for long. I traveled for a spell and tried one thing, then another. When the fort was closed at Fort Smith and the federal court opened there, I discovered the U.S. Federal Court for the Western District of Arkansas, and I couldn't wait to join the Marshals service. And that took longer than I thought it might. I had to learn something about finding my way without getting lost. It wouldn't do for a deputy marshal to wander about with his prisoners and not know which direction to ride, now would it?"

Ayers got a big kick out of that and both had a good laugh. "But you are here, so you must've finally found your way around our huge district."

"When I'm not sure, I take a posse or another deputy with me. Like here. Now." He spread his arms. "I still manage to get myself turned around in this vast western country though, but it is breathtaking."

Ayers laughed. "Good to always have someone with you or you'll just run in circles. From what I hear you've already set quite a record of arrests and captures on your own. How long you been in the service?"

"Joined in seventy-two. I'm just getting started good. Have learned to follow marked trails fairly well. Just don't put me down in the middle of nowhere." He laughed and Ayers joined him.

Later James scrubbed out the iron skillet, set it on a hot rock beside the fire to dry, and made his bedroll. The biscuit had been palatable, though a bit dry. Gravy helped that, though. He glanced over at the possemen, relaxed with their heads on their saddles. "You check those prisoners to make sure their chains are good and tight?

One of the men, name of Jason, answered. "Yep, they won't get loose."

After relieving himself in the brush, James settled beside Jason. "You sure those chains are secure?"

"Yeah. Couldn't bust one with a ten pound hammer. Due you to stop your worrying. Your friend Ayers checked them."

He should still get up and check but an experienced deputy like Ayers should know how to secure prisoners, and he was worn out. He was still a bit nervous over how easily they had taken John Billee. Odd how he'd come along quietly when they picked him up on the warrant. He'd expected a fight or at least a flight. Their low conversation soon grew silent till there was no sound but occasional snoring.

A scrambling and shouting awoke James who came to his feet into a midnight black sky, gun in hand. Eyes not accustomed to the dark, he dodged gunfire. Returned shots in its general direction and was hit on the side above the hip bone.

Lord Jesus. Might as well been struck by a flaming cannonball. Scarcely able to move he fought to dodge the wild flying of bullets. All he could see was brief glances in the flashing of gunpowder, the bullet like a brand in his side.

He stumbled, fired blindly at the flame of gunfire in the darkness. "Ayers, where are you? You hit?"

"Here." A low growling voice out of the smoke. "Onc't. You?"

Immediately, he aimed away from the man's voice and squeezed the trigger. After he and Ayers emptied their Colts in the same direction all went silent. Had they hit their targets? Shot again, this time in the arm, the pain from both wounds kept him from rising. Using one leg he shoved himself along the ground toward the location of the gunfire to check everyone.

He soon came upon the body of a posseman, then the wounded and struggling Billee. He bent over him, checked the wound. "Don't you worry, we'll soon have that patched." He turned to shout. "I'm hit, Ayers. But we got Billee. You okay?"

"I'm alive. What the hell happened?"

"It would appear our prisoners escaped their bonds. Perhaps they were let loose by one of our trusted possemen. I don't know."

A groaned reply from the man across the smoldering fire. "I'm telling you. Bastards slipped their cuffs, got my gun."

That was doubtful, but he didn't say anything yet. Ayers built up the fire so they could see. After a while of settling and patching each other's wounds, James wadded his bandana into his side to stifle the bleeding.

Ayers helped him rip the bottom off his shirt and tie it around his waist, then he did the same for Ayers whose damage was less severe.

The deputy straightened his bandaged arm and winced. "Best if we ride on over to the Creek settlement where we can get these took care of. It could be a lot worse, I expect. We ain't dead. Yet."

"Yeah, I've seen worse. Glad I didn't kill this one." James doctored Billee's arm and leg. "I detest hanging as payment for what these men do, yet I hate worse to have to shoot one. There's a Man above who will judge him, not I." One thing James firmly believed in was a vengeful God. And he was content to leave man's suffering to Him.

WHEN HE LEFT England, he had no knowledge of a place called Arkansas and pronounced Arkinsaw. Nor would he have believed that a woman called Mary Jane Majors would steal his heart so completely. But that's precisely what happened while he was home in Fort Smith healing from the damage he'd taken during the Billee incident.

Early one Sunday morning, before the bells called parishioners to worship, James made his slow way toward the Episcopal Church. The wound in his side continued to give him trouble. He would find a good seat in the center of a pew where he could be comfortable and not have to stand to let folks in. His mind on getting back to his job, he paid little attention to the woman who slipped in beside him. Until he took a deep breath. She smelled like the sweet golden flowers that grew on the trellis outside his small abode. He couldn't help but turn to take in her lovely features.

Sitting tall in the wooden pew, she cast a glance his way from hazel eyes, then lowered her long lashes as if bowing. The corners of her finely drawn lips turned up in a half-smile, and he was startled when her eyes flashed as deep a green as a woodland pool.

Because of his Royal upbringing, he murmured, "ma'am?" in his most polite voice, and fought the urge to rise, click his heels, take her hand, and kiss it. And if he knew these American Western women, she would slap him silly should he try such a thing.

So, as if ensconced within a bubble, he sat still as a statue and heard little of what the priest had to say. Was it possible that at long last he had met the woman of his dreams? Trouble was, he had not met her, and had no notion how to do so. A battle raged within him. He had no business getting involved with a woman. She would not like him going out on horseback to exchange gunfire with outlaws. And she could not talk him out of it. Even if he was the man for her. But that might not be true. How did one know for sure? Yet the longer he sat beside her and breathed the same air as she, the more he knew for sure, he had to have her. And he was an absolute ninny for thinking she would have him for he would tell her the truth about his job and how he could not quit it.

So, when everyone stood to go, he jerked himself to life and rose. She came up like a flower growing beside him to stir the sweet fragrance. Of course, he should allow her to step in the aisle first. Instead, he moved out into the crowd, made her a space, and guided her into the moving parishioners. Her smile rocked him on his heels.

He felt like he had when he was fourteen and his third cousin pulled him into a dark corner, placed his hand on her breast, and kissed him with a busy tongue. Frightened and thrilled all at one time. Shaking all over and unable to stop.

Here he was. A man who had gone to war and aimed a rifle and killed with it and crawled away from enemy fire through blood soaked fields, and a beautiful woman frightened him. All he wanted was to ride out after some outlaw he could haul back to Fort Smith and turn over to the new Judge Parker. A young man recently appointed to see to the proper cleaning up of Indian Territory after horrible mismanagement over the past years.

So he hurried away and visited the newly appointed Marshal Fagan the following day. With a few warrants in hand, he rode out, trying to forget the beautiful young lady who had touched his heart with her smile and green eyes. How could a man ask such a beauty to consider spending her life with someone like him? Someone who shot and often killed for a living?

He returned in a few weeks with three lawbreakers chained together on their horses. Perhaps he had rid himself of his desire of the woman. At church that Sunday, he saw her talking to a young man. Heat surged within him. He had not rid himself of the desire to have her. He fought the need to walk right up to them and hit the young ass with a doubled-up fist to show him he could not have her. He didn't. It would not be dignified, and an Earl of Kent was always dignified to a fault.

So he ran down Marshal Fagan once more and carried some warrants away again. When he returned with a string of prisoners, Fagan took them all in, paid him his due, and fingered through some older wanted posters. Peering over his shoulder, James punched a finger on one of the tattered pictures.

"What about him? He looks like a good candidate."

"I thought you was courting that pretty Mistress Jones. Take some time off, put your personal life in order. What's wrong with you, anyways?"

"Aw, what kind of church-going pretty lady like her wants a man who deals with outlaws all the time?"

"Well, you don't have to do it, do you? It can't be you need the paltry sum of money."

"It isn't that I need. I want to see these men treated fairly, brought in, and tried. If I don't do it, who will?"

"They's plenty of men has to do it. The likes of you, a Lord or whatever, sure don't need it."

"Tell me about him." He pointed again at the gnarly looking face on the wanted poster, discounting Fagan's words. "You can't tell me a black man was treated fairly."

"Oh, you think the likes of you can straighten out our justice system? You're crazy as a loon. Men like these chops folks up in pieces, mistreats the women, shoots and burns, and does everything else evil to them under the sun. Nothin' to do with their skin color."

"So tell me what happened to him? Where is he now?"

"Free as a bird." Fagan made wings out of his hands and fluttered them away. "Couldn't get the witnesses to testify. He brutally murdered two companions, burned half their bodies to hide who they was, then lied his head off when he was arrested. Court couldn't get no proof... this was years back when our judge always had his thumb up his ass so he couldn't really judge a decent case. A cold-blooded killer, this one, and not cause he was black. It's cause he was the devil incarnate. If we could get the witnesses gathered back up and bring the case before Judge Parker, it'd be different. You talk to the daughter of the family he burned up in their own house, maybe you'd change your mind. There's proof in the records that he lied about the case and what he did. The posse proved he was the guilty man with some blood evidence where it shouldn't have been if he was telling the truth."

"Give me that one, then."

"I told you, witnesses are scattered, most have moved away. Even this Diggs has left the country. You'd never find them all, not even a portion of them."

"If I find them, can we bring them back here for a trial?"

"Hell, yes, but you won't."

"Get me the file. Is it handy?"

"Here at the courthouse, covered in dust and cobwebs. Why you doing this?"

"Cause I want to prove I'm a good lawman who believes in punishment. It's just that I don't like torture of prisoners and plenty of the deputies do."

Two hours later, he had the files for the Diggs case. Fagan gave him the use of a desk there in the courthouse, and he went to work reading and making notes.

THE FREED KILLER, name of Diggs, lived down in the holler out north of town where the hills began. Of course he'd lit out. James smiled at the thought. He liked to pick up some of the ideologies from the Ozarks and lit out was a favorite. He'd check real quick in case Diggs had returned, which a lot of outlaws did. There was a church for the black at the end of a rutted path and Sunday found him wearing his overalls and an old straw hat and waiting back in the trees behind the tumbling down shack where several black residents gathered to worship.

There was no blood in Diggs wagon where he said they attacked him. The only blood was around the men he killed so brutally. One nearby neighbor said he'd heard shots and shouts and watched Diggs after he'd dragged two of the family members from their wagon onto the ground and hacked at them with a double-bitted axe. There were never two men attacking Diggs according to witnesses going down the road. The money stole from the drover was found on Diggs. Deputies brought him to Fort Smith for trial. Parker wasn't judge yet then, and no witnesses appeared though there were some. Even with the good case against him he was released.

After giving the case a long, long reading, James reported to Marshal Fagan. "It looks to me like we might be able to run down these witnesses including the companion he shot if that's what it takes."

Marshal Fagan gestured a thumb's up. "Give it a try. Be best to find Diggs first and get him comfortable here in our jail. Then start in on the witnesses. They're all listed in the record books. Stay in touch in case I need you on something else."

"Give me a hand locating their whereabouts. I mean on a map. I'm not real familiar with your country except mainly where we fought the war."

Fagan nodded. "Wouldn't hurt to talk to some deputies who might hail from where these folks have gone once you know that. Some witnesses could be reached by wire and beckoned back if you can find out where they went. Usually neighbors or church folk or people in the local saloons know where a family has moved to."

James rose and grabbed his hat. "It shall give me a good chance to learn more about your fine country away from the Territory. I will get on it." He scooped up the maps and headed for the records office. He was almost out the door when Marshal Fagan hailed him. "When you find Diggs, don't turn your back on him. Remember, he is a cold blooded killer."

"Yes, I shall remember that."

Determined to close the case, yet with no experience running down people in an unfamiliar land, he went to work in earnest. The man who had survived the killings had moved to Michigan. James's friend, Herb Anderson, recommended he take a train to the small town outside Detroit where he could begin his search. Fagan guaranteed payment of the cost of return for him as well as the folks who had witnessed Diggs's flight away from the crime that morning. Their witnessing, along with objects found where the crime took place, would be enough to convict.

Diggs had hung around Fort Smith first so that's where James began. He walked down in the holler that Sunday and found the black church. He leaned up against the siding outside the front door. There were records kept of folks who bought land. All he needed was a clue, and he could find where they went to church, where they were baptized.

Storekeepers, saloon keepers, and church pastors all know their attendees. In the small Michigan town, he found his target victim, the survivor of Diggs spree, in the second church he visited and spoke to the pastor. Seems he was happy to have survived and joined the church first thing when he moved there.

On top of that, one of the witnesses of Diggs's flight was a close friend of the witness who moved away. James promised the two of them a share of the reward still being posted for Diggs if both would return to Fort Smith and testify against the outlaw in Judge Parker's court.

Feeling confident, he returned to Fort Smith where he looked into the other witnesses' church membership and learned where he'd moved to. He wired the station there, requested the man return his wire and a few days later received a short message. One more to go but after a few weeks he lost hope for this one. Dismayed he went to visit Marshal Fagan.

"If I can't find this gentleman, do I have enough to go to the judge and see Diggs convicted?"

Fagan went over all the records about the Diggs killing and the statements. He turned the information over to the prosecuting attorney, then hunted James down.

"Looks like we've got a case here, Deputy. Good job. Very few deputies would've been content riding all over this country to drag back folks for an old case long since forgotten."

"I have never enjoyed anything so much as searching your countryside. Not only did I help solve this killing, I became acquainted with the fine people who live and work in your country. Makes me happy to have taken this job of protecting the likes of them from the likes of men such as Diggs."

STILL, THE ONLY other thing that would make him happy was having the beautiful woman who attended the Episcopalian church in Fort Smith. Why shouldn't a man be content in both his work and his enjoyment? So, the following Sunday he made his third trip to the church and managed to sit next to the woman who smelled so sweet and had such a beautiful smile. She turned to him and used that very weapon.

On a beautiful spring afternoon in 1877, when he was home from "running the frontier" as she called it, she married her Earl of Kent in the church where they had met.

They had six children. She died in 1892. He never remarried, as it turned out she had been the love of his life, only next to his work riding the Territory which he continued to do.

BEYOND THE BADGE

When the United States District Court for the Indian Territory was established in 1895, Wilkinson moved to Vinita, in the northeastern part of the territory. He served variously as field deputy and jailer there until 1913 when he retired due to illness. By this time, at age seventy-one, he had served forty-two years as a Deputy U.S. Marshal, the longest recorded tenure in the history of the service. During his eventful career he had made nearly 1,000 criminal arrests and precarious transports of prisoners in deadly and dangerous Indian Territory. In the line of duty, he had been shot and wounded thirteen times and carried the mark of an arrow on his ankle. He died in 1916 and was buried in Vinita, Oklahoma. His death was mourned by the entire town who had all learned to love their imported Earl of Kent.

THE GOING SNAKE MASSACRE: A BLACK DAY FOR THE MARSHALS

YEARS OF RAIN had long ago washed clean the bloody grounds around Whitmire School. Yet as I supported him, Grandfather took shaky steps as if avoiding the pools.

Arm tucked in mine, he gestured with the other hand, his rheumy eyes steely in the afternoon sunlight. "Not far from here fell the marshals, caught unawares. It was a day of serenity until all ripped apart the silence."

I glanced at the front door of the Tahlequah Land Office. As we approached, Grandfather had traveled elsewhere in his mind, as often was his habit. What if he did not recognize Zeke Proctor? Would it really matter after all this time? It would, indeed it would, for there would be no more chance to make peace. Peace between two old warhorses, both of whom knew they were right, oh so very right.

For their actions brought about the terrible battle that saw a possible eleven Marshals sprawled dead among the bodies scattered around Whitmire School on that awful day.

But Grandfather lifted a single finger, quickly spotting his old enemy. Zeke sat square and straight on the bench just outside the office, wearing a broad brimmed black hat. Long black hair hung beyond his shoulders. His ebony eyes fastened on us until the men's gazes met and held. The drums of many years vibrated the air around us. The Cherokee blood in my veins matched the rhythm, and I went back to the day when it all started. Long before I was no more than the lingering spark in my father's eyes.

The Cherokee Going Snake district was divided into the Keetoowah Society. The Proctors believed in keeping to the Cherokee ways and denying any white dealings. The remainder of the district, largely made up of Becks including Grandfather, called White Sut, wished to mix as quickly as possible into the so-called civilized society.

I will never forget Grandfather sitting within a circle of us children. His eyes dark and frightening as he began his tale.

"That evil Zeke Proctor had a look about him that put the fear of the wild bear in everyone. Some of us refused to stand down from our own beliefs, though. On a cold November day, he came to the mill called Hildebrand by Aunt Polly and Jim Kesterson, thought to be her husband after the one called Steve, who owned the mill, was killed in the war."

He paused to wave a hand around. "No one knows what was on Zeke's mind, but the gunfight that broke out caused him to shoot your Aunt Polly, who lay dead on the ground outside the mill. It did not take long for us Becks, true Cherokee, to gather up sides and go in search of this bad man. The member of one family is not allowed to take the life of one from another family. Zeke was an evil man who did not obey that tradition."

Grandfather, being the storyteller he was, turned his head slowly from one child to another. We who sat on the floor, mouths agape, eyes wide, held our breaths till he went on.

"You see, we all lived in the Going Snake District, a place named for a great chief who came here along the Trail of Tears. He was called Eenah-tah-tah-oo, or Snake That Crawls Along."

He pounded on his bare thighs. "Going Snake district was separated by two strong, huge families who each believed they ran things. And here they were, the Becks and the Proctors, divided by the forbidden killing of an innocent woman. Over the years the sky and air became like a summer storm with winds and rains that come and go and never end their ferocious attacks. We could not get along at all. Shootings, men causing terrible things to happen to anyone they could corner, chase, or cut down with arrow or gun.

It continues to this day, the Becks taking vengeance on the Proctors and them fighting back at every turn in the trail. It has been very bad for a long while. Those with Cherokee blood, those adopted through marriage, those part white and part Cherokee, each tribe members claiming sides at every turn. But always the Proctors, who followed the Keetoowah Society on one side, on the other the Becks, who preferred the white man's ways."

Zeke Procter, catalyst of the 1872 Going Snake Massacre, in which 12 members of the posse—including two Deputy U.S. Marshals from Fort Smith—were killed or wounded.

Slapping his hands together to call back our attention, he shook his finger around the circle. "And as was bound to happen, after years of hiding and killing of his own, Zeke Proctor was finally called up to pay for his sins. There would be a trial. So much excitement. Everyone claiming their side and waiting for the results when the white men had their say. Some set on Zeke being hanged, others sure he must go free.

"Oh, children, it was terrible times. Often I rode across the prairie, never sure I would arrive home without being cut down. Everyone became fearful for their lives. Taking sides, all planned on going to the Whitmire School where the trial would be held, guns at the ready to fight if the decision went wrong." He held his palm on his chest. "And I one of them. Those were dark days indeed, but the worst was yet to come."

Grandfather coughed and Mama brought him water to drink before he could go on. Inside me something tried to crawl up out of my belly. A sour, hot creature that scared me to the bottom of my heart. I was a mere half-grown child when I heard this story, and it put the fear of all the gods in me. For I had grown up on the stories told by mamas to their misbehaving children to get them to mind. I shuddered inside.

When Grandfather went on, he shouted the first words. We all jumped. "Ponies carrying men who carried weapons. Men afoot bearing arms. The white deputies and Lighthorsemen and the worst of both families, all arriving at once. Gathering with them those who had stood about to see what might happen. It was soon as bad as could be." His finger covered his lips, and he whispered, which was even more frightening. "Shooting each other all around the school till dead bodies lay everywhere. Bloody ones, moaning ones, crying ones. Ah, it was awful to see."

He fell forward over his crossed legs, and we all let out a dreadful cry, thinking the worst. That his story had frightened him to death. But then he sat up as if struggling and hugged his belly. "I myself shot but not dead. Uncle Black Sut not so fortunate. We would bury him later."

"I broke into the court and aimed at Zeke with my shotgun. His brother Johnson grabbed my weapon and my finger squeezed, shooting him full in the chest. Badly hurt he grabbed my shotgun and the innocent in the trial, by the name of Mose, I believe. He sat at the judge's desk. He fell and died on the floor. I would not have stopped till all were cut down had Sam Beck not stepped in front of me. Though he was shot, I was right after that. Men fell on all sides, weapons roared inside… outside… everywhere. At last, we knew we could not win. I was dragged away, and we fled. Too many guns, too many still standing on the Proctor side. After the sky grew dim with evening the roaring stopped, the shouting faded, the sound of horses fleeing carrying those who had ridden their ponies. Men running, women crying, children screaming for Mamas and Papas. It was truly a massacre of both Cherokee and Whites."

Grandfather lowered his head as if in prayer, and we children shuffled around thinking him finished with his story. But then he raised to stare at each of us in turn. "Those killed were laid side by side on the Whitmire front porch to wait for their kin to claim them. Later we heard that U.S. Marshals were killed and thought we might all pay for that in the worst way."

He shrugged. "It was a long time before I recovered, and when I did, it was all over. Zeke had fled and gone into hiding. It was declared too dangerous to go in search of him. All we could tell of this awful battle was the ground around the school still red with blood."

Standing there with my Grandfather, White Sut, I still recalled his story from my childhood. I learned that the U.S. District Court had sent two Deputy U.S. Marshals and a sworn posse of eight others to arrest Zeke Proctor if the Cherokee court released him. As I grew up, I learned that when everything was finally settled between the Whites and the Indians, Grandfather and some of his friends were indicted for the murder of Johnson Proctor. Zeke Proctor was indicted for murder of some twenty of those killed that day. Grandfather and Zeke Proctor remained mortal enemies, though all indictments were eventually lifted. In February 1874, the Cherokee National Council passed a general amnesty.

Perhaps on this day in Tahlequah they would meet and at last end the feud. I never knew who arranged it, but I hoped they would make peace at long last.

My heart pounded with the memories of the stories told over the years. Maybe this was a mistake. This man who faced us was a killer. Proctor took a step forward, gaze holding Grandfather's. Here they were, two old men with one final chance to stop the years' long feud.

Yet all I could think was grab him, run with him, take him away from this place, from this killer.

At last Grandfather spoke, his tone soothing my fears. "We are too old to fight. But I am game, and I know you are too. I will walk away if you will."

I held my breath. Would these two old men, White Sut Beck and Zeke Proctor, at last end the years' long hostility or would another wild battle break out between them and the warfare continue to split the Cherokee Going Snake political subdivision forever?

Zeke nodded in agreement and touched Grandfather's chest with a flat palm.

Without more, the two tough, proud old men turned and left the land office by different ways. The feud was over, without formality, without fanfare, without speeches. Nobody had backed down. Nobody had won. Nobody had lost.

Which was how it should have ended.

BEYOND THE BADGE

Even if we could travel back in time, we would still miss much of the truth hidden in history. No witness sees everything, and no two people remember the same event in quite the same way. As a storyteller, I can only attempt to relate this important episode as faithfully as the surviving accounts allow.

Few events loom larger in the history of the United States Marshals Service in the Western District of Arkansas than the Going Snake Massacre. Historical accounts differ, but between eight and eleven members of the federal posse were killed—at the time the greatest single loss of life suffered by the Marshals Service in one incident.

The story that follows is told through the voice of the granddaughter of White Sut Beck, one of the men wounded in the fight. Her real name has been lost to history, so I have given her one for the purposes of this tale.

Zeke Proctor, who survived the battle, continued to play a prominent role in Indian Territory. In 1877 he was elected Cherokee senator from the Going Snake District and was regarded by many of his people as a hero. Ironically, in 1891 he was later appointed a Deputy U.S. Marshal, a position he held until around the turn of the twentieth century.

Among those killed in the posse were Deputy U.S. Marshal Jacob G. Owens and posse members William Hicks, George Selvidge, Jim Ward, Riley Woods, and three of the five Beck brothers—Black Sut Beck, Sam Beck, and William Beck. Wounded in the fighting were Deputy U.S. Marshal Joseph G. Peevey, posse members Paul Jones and George McLaughlin, and White Sut Beck.

LEDBETTER'S RUN: FRANKLIN "BUD" LEDBETTER

1894

LEDBETTER'S BREATH BLEW misty in the railroad car as it rattled its way west. Being the lone guard on this run of the Katy suited him. No doubt he could handle anything that might happen, including an attempted robbery, which he would welcome just to break the boredom. Piled along the end of the car, green bags held the payroll for the gang at work laying rails for the American Express Company. Stretching, he fisted his Colt and ran gloved fingers over the Winchester lying beside him. Ready for anything that might happen.

Damn Cook gang liked hitting these runs, and they'd been at it now for months without being stopped. He volunteered to stop them. Just let 'em come. He rose, eyed the prairie flashing past between cracks in the boxcar. Hiding the payroll in a plain old boxcar behind the company's usual car was his idea. Putting him in here alone, his too. Bastards. Thought they were smart, but he'd outsmart them this time.

Buildings in the distance to the south meant they were passing by Muskogee.

Above the noisy rattle of the wheels, shots blasted the thin winter air. Stripping off his right glove, he swept a look alongside to see upward of half-a-dozen men on horseback coming up fast. Headed for the payroll car. He'd put a stop to that. Get their attention real quick. Taking aim through a hole he cut one down, then another and another. Surprised the remainder fell back, but they wouldn't stop at that. Now they'd come after him, then the money. Just what he wanted. Noises on the outside and the door opened. Two men leaped in, firing blind as they rolled to the floor. Colt in hand he shot twice. Hollering they rolled out the door. Thumping on wood told him there were more still coming.

Quick as a cat he went down on his stomach, Colt back at the ready. A bullet cut the floor at his feet. They were shooting through the cracks from behind. A volley from several. He flipped onto his back, fired through the siding at the one behind who yelped.

The door clanked open, three jumped in hoping he was down. He wasn't, by God, and he turned the car into a shooting gallery. With shouts and howls, they were gone. Pawing for the Winchester, he clambered over top of the money bags. Opened fire at the open door. The bouncing car saved their hides. At least six of them running around catching horses or climbing on double with their pals.

Hell's fire, he'd baited the Cook gang. Only wounded some. All were getting away. Look at 'em run like hell, though. A few more shots from the Winchester cut leather on two. They vanished into the distance, while the train pulled him away. For a moment he considered leaping out, catching one of the horses left behind, and taking off after them. But they had too much fire power and too much of a lead. He'd never catch them. Yet he had kept them from robbing the American Railway Express, known as the Katy. He'd done his job and sent them away, plenty of them carrying his lead.

I'll be blast. The Cook Gang. One day he'd lay hands on some of them, and they'd have hell to pay. But this time he had to let them go and stay with what he had been hired to guard

The railroad and everyone else called him a hero. It got around all over town he'd fought off the entire gang single-handed. He'd just as soon they let it go, but he smiled and let them shake his hand. Hell, he'd only managed to run them off. It wasn't like he broke up the gang or anything. Sure, plenty of 'em trailed blood, and he probably succeeded in embarrassing them just a bit.

1895

LEDBETTER SHUFFLED THROUGH pages of supplies unloaded off the express wagon. Assured he had everything included in the delivery to the mercantile, he turned to speak to the owner, Horace Ogle. Out on the road a man waving a gun leaped in front of the second wagon loaded for delivery to the Creek

Disbursement Center. Without warning, he stopped in the path of the big dray horse and shot him.

Like he had himself been shot, Ledbetter stopped dead in his tracks. What the hell? Who did something like that?

The dray, fondly known as Ollie in his stable, took two faltering steps and went down. Long legs folded in among the halters and chains holding him to the double wheeled wagon. Blast it all. He'd faithfully pulled the heavy load of supplies all the way here from Fort Smith.

Kicking and whinnying, Ollie struggled to untangle and rise. Scrambling over top of the stack of boxes on the boardwalk, Ledbetter tackled the man as he turned to move out of the road toward him. Elbow across his neck, he ground down hard, then drove his knee deep between his legs. Despite the horrible screaming he held him like that till he stopped writhing around in the dirt.

Sprawled across the heaving barrel chest, Ledbetter hollered at a bystander. "Go fetch Marshal Rutherford. Someone bring me my rifle from the other wagon. Now, goddamn it."

His driver, name of Sammy, raced up with his rifle "Take care of Ollie, would you? Go shoot the poor horse. Now."

"But, sir, it's Ollie."

"Now. Go. And if someone don't arrive with the marshal, I'm gonna blow this fella's brains out so I don't have to hold him down any longer."

He stuck the barrel of his Colt in the struggling fella's ear. "See this, mister? I'm fixin' to put a bullet through your head if you don't settle down. Ought to anyway. You bastard, you killed my horse."

A hand gripped his shoulder from behind. "I'm here, James, let me have the bugger. You can let him go now. I've got him."

Marshal Rutherford jerked him to his feet. "What set him off?"

"Danged if I know. I had two wagons coming in and had stopped here with the first one. The second is for the Creek Center, and I had waved him around and come back to supervise the unloading of this one. This sumbitch ran into the center of the road and shot my dray horse. Danged if I know why, and he ain't talking."

"Oh, he will. If you take that gun outta his ear. Give him a chance. I'll get some men to come down and handle your horse. What a blamed tragedy."

Ledbetter glared at the marshal's prisoner, hauled off and swung a fist into his gut. The man doubled over and wretched. "That's for killing my horse, you son of a bitch." He turned to Rutherford. "Find out why he did that, would you,

James Franklin "Bud" Ledbetter (1852–1937) was a Deputy U.S. Marshal hired by U.S. Marshal Samuel Morton Rutherford.

Marshal? Put him away deep, or I might change my mind about letting him live. That dray was the best one I had for pulling heavy loads. Never balked a time. Damned shame."

Bud stalked off to finish deliveries and see to the mess in the middle of the road. It was late in the day when he finished and sent the wagons back to Fort Smith loaded with cotton bales from nearby farms. They would be loaded on flatboats for shipment down the river to a port in Louisiana. Weary from several long days on the road plus supervising the unloading, then dealing with a gunslinger killing Ollie, his favorite horse, James retired to the Pale Moon Saloon. He was well into his fourth drink when Marshal Rutherford floated into his foggy vision.

"Join you, Bud?"

Unable to move his tongue, he nodded and gestured toward the empty chair with one hand. "I shall... shall I order us another drink?"

"Us does not appear to need one, but I'll have one if you don't mind. Your friend over in the jail said you could come over anytime, and he'd kick your ass for you."

"He say why he shot my horse? It's me ought to be kicking his ass stead of the other way around."

"You took him down pretty hard. Big as he is and all."

"He shot my horse."

"Not being intolerant or anything. Don't blame you one bit. Seems the man didn't like you helping the Creeks. You ever consider going to work for me? We could sure use some more Deputy Marshals around here. Someone who deals with the Cook gang like you did a while back would make a heck of a good marshal.

"We're trying to corral over a thousand bad 'uns to clean up this territory as well as the future state of Oklahoma. Want to make it safe for settlers."

"So that's what that was about? My hauling to the Creeks. I'll still kick his ass. But I might consider your offer. Could be more enjoyable than working for an express company. Marshal pay ain't great, but satisfaction of sending outlaws over to the judge for punishing might make it worthwhile."

"Does that mean yes?"

"Means I'll think about it. Soon's I finish off this man's whiskey."

Right then he'd like nothing better than to wade into a crowd of no-goods and lay 'em all out. Man killing his horse right in the middle of the street and thinking it okay. Territory was filled with no good sons of bitches, all trying to take what weren't theirs and killing for it too.

Best wait till he was sober, though, to decide. Never could do anything right proper with his noodle crazed with whiskey. He was smart enough to know that.

The marshal left sometime after that, but he kept right on sipping until he finally went into some shadowy place. He awoke to dark, empty silence. After a while, he figured out where he was, rose to his feet, and stumbled between tables in the empty Pale Moon Saloon. Someone keyed the door open from the outside and let him out.

A young deputy marshal shook his hand. "Feeling any better, Bud?"

"You been out here all night?"

The deputy stepped from under the boardwalk cover and peered up into the starlit sky. "Almost all night. Marshal wanted me to make sure you got out with a key. Said you might take off the door."

Ledbetter laughed, then held his head. "Oh, Lord, tell me why a man does something like drink hisself stupid. And yeah, I might've took off the blamed door, hadn't you been here. I reckon he might be right. Not a bad place to grab a night's sleep."

"Said to send you on up to the jail if you woke up early. You could sleep in one of the cells providing you withheld killing his only prisoner till morning when he's sending him over to Fort Smith. Is it true he killed Ollie?"

"'Fraid so. How'd you know?"

"I helped clean up the wreck, and we carried him out to bury him. You gonna join the U.S. Marshals?"

"My if you ain't filled with questions. What's your name, Deputy?"

"Junior Speckman." The kid fell in beside Bud, who walked down the center of the street, swinging his head from left to right.

"Well, I'm leaning that way. You like it?"

The kid stuck out his chest. "Hell yeah, nothing like herding an outlaw to jail. Gives a feller a feeling of having done something good."

"Well, here we are at the jail. You coming in?"

"Nah, I been on all night. Sun's coming up. Reckon I'll head on home. We're riding out in a few hours. There's word the Buck Gang's busy with their usual badness. Maybe we can round up some more of them. Wild how Indian Territory attracts the worst, ain't it?"

"The Buck gang, huh? Maybe I'll see you later, then. Say, thanks for taking care of Ollie. I appreciate it." The young man strode down the road, proud as could be. Good to meet some fine youngsters. Be enjoyable to ride with some too.

Mind made up, Bud Ledbetter went inside the sheriff's office where U.S. Marshal Rutherford was leaned back in a chair, snoring softly.

A FEW WEEKS later, delivery business finished, Bud rode into Muskogee intent on joining the U.S. Marshals. Instead, he was in time to hear gunfire. Always on the lookout for trouble, he nudged Rafe into a gallop. The town was fairly peaceful compared to some in the Creek Nation. It surprised him to see a gang of Creek surging down the street. Waving guns and other weapons, they surrounded the jail about the time he arrived. Inside the marshal was barricaded firing at the men but doing little damage.

Bud spurred the dancing horse into the center of the fracas and leaped to the ground.

The marshal halted fire.

"Okay, boys. Let's settle down. Give the marshal his say. What's up?"

Kicking his way through the crowd and slamming a few heads together, Bud pivoted to block the door. One of the attackers swung a long board at him. He twisted it away and swatted the man across the butt, lifting him right off the ground. "Come on now, what's up?"

"Hang them. Hang them." Most of the gang could speak very little English, but they knew those words and shouted them over and over.

"Hey, okay, let me get inside. Hold your fire and your tongues."

He slipped through a crack in the door. "Who you got in here they want hung, Marshal?"

"Aw, hell. Me and two deputies are trying to guard five members of the Buck Gang. Brought 'em in yesterday. They killed Deputy Speckman and attacked some settlers and Creeks. I've got 'em to send on over to Fort Smith."

"Killed that young kid? A real shame. Let's make sure they get over to Fort Smith. Let the judge hang 'em."

Furious, Bud slipped back out the door, shoving some of the bigger ones aside who were trying to get through. He took a board away from one and swatted two off their feet, turned to block the door and face some more, ready to fight.

Creek leader Pleasant Porter leaped onto the boardwalk and held both hands high in the air. "See who is guarding the jail, men? Look who it is. You rush the door some of you will get killed. That is Bud Ledbetter. He will take you down you try to get through him. Who is ready to die today? Those men in there are going to Fort Smith to be hung for what they did. No use in any of you dying for it."

Ledbetter took another swing just to prove what Porter said was true. Bopped an ole boy across the back knocking him flat on his face. Plenty of the crowd had seen him put down bullies in the saloon or out in the street two and three at a time. He wouldn't lie, he liked a good brawl.

The crowd obviously considered the truth of their leader's words and Ledbetter's reputation. They began to mumble and broke up into smaller groups before leaving.

Marshal Rutherford came out and shook Porter's hand, thanked him, then did the same with Bud. "I hope you came over to join up. You'll be a fine addition to our Deputy U.S. Marshals. I expect you'll earn your ten cents per mile and two dollars per diem."

Ledbetter joined the marshal in a good laugh. He had his own plans where money was concerned. Now that deputies could earn the rewards offered for outlaws, he was going to run down and capture some of the most wanted of them. There was plenty of money and satisfaction in that.

MIDDLE OF THE night and Bud darted swiftly from one building to another through the red light district of Muskogee. All the whiskey joints were empty but wouldn't be for long. Way before the sun came up there'd be wagons circled around them as if the Indians were set to attack. It was pretty much the opposite. Once in a while, White owl hoots came to load their share of rotgut and lightning delivered from stills surrounding town. No one had so far been able to put an end to the trade that sent so much whiskey into Indian Territory.

Intent on doing some damage to the trade, Bud had joined up with a few other deputies under Rutherford. Since locating the stills was well-nigh impossible, it was time to hit the distribution efforts. It was a touchy situation. Whiskey was only illegal in sales to Indians in the Territory, Muskogee being in the Creek Nation.

Set to butt some heads together, he joined with the other deputies on the lookout at the known major joints. Their aim, to destroy as much product as possible. Any gunfire would mean they were free to fire back. That's the part he liked best.

Deputies scattered everywhere in the darkness where they could hide. Once crates of whiskey, lightning, rotgut, anything it was called, were loaded to haul off into the Territory, the fun began. As the men finished stacking the final precious load into the wagons, weaponry of all types cut loose from the concealed deputies. When bullets slammed through them from all sides, jars and bottles popped and rattled, glass flew everywhere. The rank smell of liquor sprayed into the night air.

Teams danced in their traces, some breaking free and racing down the street, leaking a trail through the dirt. Return gunfire broke out. The surprised whiskey runners, not sure what to shoot at, blasted away in all directions. Windows of nearby joints and more distant shops shattered. Outbreaks of gunfire lit up the dark night. Wagonloads of lightning exploded, sending a team racing crazily toward downtown, leaving its fiery trail behind. Another left town, the ball of eerie burning whiskey lighting up the trees alongside the road and reflecting in the river.

All but ignoring the danger, Bud moved to the center of the road, sending bullets in every direction as fast as he could shoot and reload his Winchester. It was as if he felt invincible to harm. Wagons not on fire, and still with a driver, left town as fast as they could. Men ran in all directions, some cut down by one of the deputies firing into the melee. Before the riotous outbreak died away, dawn outlined the church steeples that sliced into the sky. Only the groans of men, mules, and horses remained when the bells sounded for church gatherings that Sunday. People made their way around the mess, more determined than ever to worship their God.

Marshal Rutherford kicked back his chair, rose, and slammed a fist on the desk. "Be damned if I ordered you to destroy half the joints in this town. Looks like the road was hit by a Union attack. What were you thinking?" He glared from one deputy to another, who stood in his office, heads hanging.

None made a reply. Bud had a few but wisely kept quiet. Even he knew when to keep his mouth shut. And take whatever punishment was coming. It would be worse to talk back.

"Well, I don't suppose any of you have a logical explanation. Like someone tripped and fired a gun that set off the... the whatever the hell we can call that."

Bud stepped forward. This might be the time to speak up. "Sir, I'm afraid I was aiming my Winchester, had it cocked and everything when—"

"When it went off? I seriously doubt it, but coming from you it's a plausible if stupid excuse. What I'm looking for here is a reason to tell the city council so they won't call for us to be run out of town. This town does have a Federal Courthouse, therefore it expects U.S. Marshals to keep the peace. Is that what you call keeping the peace?"

Bud raised a finger. "Tell them they shot first? We were just defending their town?"

"Oh, yes. That will work. I'll try it." He pointed at the door. "Out of here, all of you. Now."

"One more thing, Marshal." Bud wasn't ready to give up yet. "Assure them that the whiskey trade through Muskogee has been destroyed, and they don't have to worry about it causing any more trouble."

"Now there's an idea. Tell you what. I'm going to let you appear at the next meeting and explain things, you do it so well."

Bud nodded. He'd enjoy doing that, but the marshal wouldn't like what all he had to say to the fine politicians of this town.

"I'd collect your badges, but I need every blasted one of you. Do me a favor and think before your burn down any more of this town, would you?"

1897

BUD WAS RIDING a new horse, the finest Silver Bay he'd ever laid eyes on. Trouble was he was a mite touchy. Took a groan or a laugh for a giddy up. Rutherford told him that the horse was a mite like its new rider and liked to stir up trouble just for the hell of it. He'd named the stallion Shiner. He didn't have the Bay's normal regulation seven black points, but rather had a black streaked silver mane and tail with four black legs and ear points that counted for seven. He was big, at least sixteen hands, and shone silver in the moonlight, a bit darker in daylight. Heck Thomas said he should've named him Ghost instead.

When he got the chance, he rode with Heck, Chris Madsen, and Bill Tilghman. The men known as the Three Guardsmen because of all the cases they solved and outlaws they took down. Was pleased to hear himself ranked right up there with them. Like him they enjoyed raising hell and breaking heads when it was called for. And they decided when that was. Because of them and marshals like them, Indian Territory was fast getting cleaned up. Their behavior was what it took to do so.

The Jennings gang erupted like fury the last few months in October when they robbed a passenger train near Chickasha and a few days later took down a Santa Fe passenger train near Edmond, Oklahoma. To Bud's relief, Marshal Rutherford agreed when he offered to go out and put a stop to their antics. The man had to know what to expect from Bud Ledbetter.

A posse was called for, but everyone was involved in the harvest or driving cattle into winter pasture, so Ledbetter said he'd go on his own.

"I don't doubt it, but is it wise? They're four pretty tough *hombres.*"

He laughed. "I'm tough enough, myself. I'll be back with them within a week or two. Besides, I could use that railroad reward that's being offered. One of these days I might buy me a ranch."

"I don't doubt that a bit, Bud. But you be careful and don't get too brave. I'd hate to have to bury you."

"Do me a favor, Marshal. If you have to, just put my still body on that Silver Bay out there and face him west. That'll do."

The next morning just as the sun sent a path down the street, the silver bay followed the early daylight out of town. Far as Ledbetter was concerned, this was what he was meant for. Hunting down outlaws. And being alone didn't bother him one bit. At the site where the gang had robbed the Edmond train, he picked up their escape tracks and headed across the prairie.

The first night out he settled down right near where the Jenningses had spent the night, maybe only a couple of days earlier.

Most gang members aren't real bright. They tend to hole up in their favorite haunts, spend time drinking in their old hangouts, and they take it for granted they'll never be caught. But he could catch them. And once he did, no way could they shoot their way out.

Bud picked up a stick and lit it in the fire, then held the glowing end to his cigar. Itching to catch these latest lawbreakers and put their tails in a twist.

The third day of hard tracking, deep in the Creek Nation, just as darkness blanketed the rough prairie land, he was still riding along, eyes taking in the scene in every direction. Under a spread of trees along a creek bank he spotted the glimmer of a night fire.

He dismounted, crouched, and tied Shiner to a sapling. He'd walk the rest of the way. Get a closer look. Before he could move away a dark shadow with wide wings plunged out of the sky, clawed feet scraping over his head.

All he could do to keep from yelling in surprise. Fearful he'd made some noise he pulled his Colt and dropped onto the ground so as not to throw his own shadow.

He crept toward the flickering fire and sound of low conversation. This wasn't a big gang, not like the Cooks, but they could do some dangerous shooting. Four old country boys, could shoot squirrels out of a tree from a hundred yards away with a twenty-two. Did better with a .44, when they didn't mind blowing their quarry to hell and back. He wouldn't take any chances. But he'd won a gunfight with this bunch once before, and they'd lit out. This time that wouldn't happen. Ay God he was better than that.

He peered through the low brush, got a good look at a face or two in the firelight. It was the Jenningses all right. One moved away, gathered his horse's reins, and crept into a patch of moonlight. Way too close to Bud.

"Hey, someone's out there." He'd been spotted.

The gang scurried around, doing their best to gather spooked horses and get away. With the Winchester in his saddle, he raised the Colt. Confident he could at least get a couple of them, he aimed at the moving figure nearest and squeezed off a shot, swung toward another and squeezed again. Both hollered, only one went down.

Forced to turn their panicking horses loose they scurried into nearby brush, firing wildly. Bark chipped off trees, zinged off rocks.

"Give it up, we've got you surrounded." His voice echoed back at him.

He shot fast into the shivering bushes. Stupid idjits thought brush would stop bullets. Running low, he dropped behind a tree and reloaded the Colt, emptied it into the clearing.

"Deputy U.S. Marshal Ledbetter. You know how good I am with this Colt. Might as well give up."

Two men hollered and emerged, hands throwed up in the air. The other two lay on the ground flailing around. Not dead. Yet. They knew they would be under his word.

The two who weren't hurt got tied to a tree while he settled their horses. Under the aim of his Colt he put them to work helping their two wounded friends till all were mounted. This was when they could take a chance and run. But they didn't. If he'd been anyone else, they would've, but these old boys knew him. They ran, he wouldn't hesitate to shoot them in the back. So they were done.

The railroad company offered a good sized reward for these four. He'd be happy to have it and the Marshal would be happy to have them in jail.

Ledbetter provided security for Creek allotment transfers, quieted some race riots, busted up gambling dens and whiskey joints, arrested infamous criminals, and kept a tense peace as statehood approached. After many years as a federal deputy marshal he became sheriff of Muskogee County. Respected by the citizens for his professionalism and honesty, he retired from law enforcement in 1928.

ACKNOWLEDGEMENTS

FIRST AND FOREMOST, my sincere thanks to Roan & Weatherford President & CEO Casey Cowan. He is not only my publisher, but a trusted friend who has supported my writing for nearly a decade and designed more perfect covers than I can count. An offhand comment from him sparked the idea for this project, and he encouraged it every step of the way.

I am also grateful for the thoughtful work of Don Money, Jerry Hogan, Amy Cowan, Dennis Doty, and the late Bob Giel, each of whom helped edit this book, along with the many other hardworking editors who have kept me on track over the years.

Last but never least, my deepest love and respect go to the members of the Northwest Arkansas Writers' Workshop. Your encouragement and fellowship have meant more than I can say.

ADDITIONAL READING

Barnhill, Brenda, *M. Charles Barnhill, Deputy U.S. Marshal.* Self-published.

Brodhead, Michael J., *Isaac C. Parker: Federal Justice on the Frontier.* Norman: University of Oklahoma Press, 2003.

Burton, Art T., *Black Gun, Silver Star: The Life and Legend of Frontier Marshal Bass Reeves.* Lincoln: University of Nebraska Press, 2006.

Enss, Chris, and Kazanjian, Howard. *Tilghman: The Legendary Lawman and the Woman Who Inspired Him.* TwoDot, 2024.

Goldstein, Norm, *Marshal: The Story of the U.S. Marshals Service.* Washington, DC: Brassey's, 1991.

Harman, S. W., *Hell on the Border: He Hanged Eighty-Eight Men.* Fort Smith: Phoenix Publishing Company, 1898.

Harrington, Fred Harvey, *Hanging Judge.* Norman: University of Oklahoma Press, 1957.

Lumpkin, Montie, *Path of the Buffalo: The Story of a United States Deputy Marshal in the Indian Territory.* Self-published.

Samuels, Nancy B., *It Took Brave Men: Deputy U.S. Marshals of Fort Smith.* Fort Smith: Fort Smith Historical Society, 1999.

Shirley, Glenn, *Law West of Fort Smith: A History of Frontier Justice in the Indian Territory, 1834–1896.* Lincoln: University of Nebraska Press, 1957.

Walker, Gary C., *Indians, Outlaws, Marshals, and the "Hangin' Judge": A True Story of Justice in the Old West.* Little Rock: Butler Center Books, 2007.

www.ingramcontent.com/pod-product-compliance
Lightning Source LLC
LaVergne TN
LVHW090319160826
845684LV00011B/70/J

* 9 7 9 8 8 9 2 9 9 1 3 0 8 *